VULNERABILITY AND FLOURISHING

VULNERABILITY AND FLOURISHING

Cristina Lledo Gomez
John N. Sheveland
Editors

**THE ANNUAL PUBLICATION
OF THE COLLEGE THEOLOGY SOCIETY
2024
VOLUME 70**

Maryknoll, New York 10545

Founded in 1970, Orbis Books endeavors to publish works that enlighten the mind, nourish the spirit, and challenge the conscience. The publishing arm of the Maryknoll Fathers and Brothers, Orbis seeks to explore the global dimensions of the Christian faith and mission, to invite dialogue with diverse cultures and religious traditions, and to serve the cause of reconciliation and peace. The books published reflect the views of their authors and do not represent the official position of the Maryknoll Society. To learn more about Maryknoll and Orbis Books, please visit our website at www.orbisbooks.com

Copyright © 2025 by the College Theology Society

Published by Orbis Books, Box 302, Maryknoll, NY 10545-0302.

All rights reserved.

All Vatican documents are available at Vatican.va.

No part of this publication may be reproduced or transmitted in any form or by any means, electronic or mechanical, including photocopying, recording, or any information storage or retrieval system, without prior permission in writing from the publisher.

Queries regarding rights and permissions should be addressed to: Orbis Books, P.O. Box 302, Maryknoll, NY 10545-0302.

Manufactured in the United States of America

Library of Congress Cataloging-in-Publication Data

Names: Gomez, Cristina Lledo, editor. | Sheveland, John N., 1973- editor.
Title: Vulnerability and flourishing / Cristina Lledo Gomez, John N. Sheveland, editors.
Description: Maryknoll, NY : Orbis Books, [2025] | Series: Annual publication of the College Theology Society ; volume 70 | Includes bibliographical references. | Summary: "Contributors address theological themes of vulnerability, abuse, suffering, healing, flourishing, and thriving"—Provided by publisher.
Identifiers: LCCN 2024056212 (print) | LCCN 2024056213 (ebook) | ISBN 9781626986107 (trade paperback) | ISBN 9798888660652 (epub)
Subjects: LCSH: Vulnerability (Personality trait) | Pastoral psychology. | Psychology—Religious aspects—Catholic Church. | Christian ethics.
Classification: LCC BF698.35.V85 V855 2025 (print) | LCC BF698.35.V85 (ebook) | DDC 253.5/2—dc23/eng/20250113
LC record available at https://lccn.loc.gov/2024056212
LC ebook record available at https://lccn.loc.gov/2024056213

Contents

Introduction   ix
Cristina Lledo Gomez and John N. Sheveland

Vulnerable Harmony: A Vision of Ministry
with LGBTQ Christians in Singapore   1
Alfred Kah Meng Pang

Trans Catholic Vulnerability and Flourishing in the Church   17
Jason Steidl Jack

Beyond the Closet, Toward the Horizon:
Contemplative Practice as Queer Flourishing   28
Barbara Anne Kozee

"Unknowing" God and Intellectual Disability:
Retrieving a Fourteenth-Century Perspective   39
Susan McElcheran

The Two-Fold Virtue Reconsidered: Humility, Magnanimity,
and the Technocratic Paradigm   50
Katherine Tarrant

Technocratic Eschatologies: Hope and Flourishing
amid an Artificially Intelligent Future   62
Stephen Okey

A Franciscanized Ecology of Technology   73
Cristofer Fernández

v

CONTENTS

Gun Violence, Vulnerability, and Flourishing   84
  Tobias Winright

There Is a Balm: Vulnerability, Challenge, and Hope   101
  C. Vanessa White

Not Enough Time to Flourish: Vocation, Work,
and Leisure in Catholic Higher Education   118
  Christopher Welch

The Vulnerability and Flourishing of Girls   130
  Cynthia L. Cameron

Gloria Dei, Vivens Homo: Vulnerability and Flourishing
in Post-*Dobbs* "Hard Cases"   141
  James T. Bretzke

Women, Synodality, and Social Poetry   153
  Callie Tabor

The Annunciation: A Biblical Handmaid's Tale   164
  Alaina Keller

Weakness as the Conduit for the Mechanics of Grace:
Paul's Paradoxical Spirituality of 2 Corinthians 12:5–10   175
  Brett McLaughlin

Relearning Vulnerability: Sifting Through Jean Vanier's
Legacy of Care and Abuse   185
  Elise Abshire

Attunement and Safeguarding in the Parishes: Perspectives
of a Diocesan Priest   197
  Anthony V. Coloma

La Fiesta de La Virgen de la Puerta: Vulnerability
and Flourishing Concretely Exemplified 208
Caitlin Cipolla-McCulloch

Paradoxical Flourishing: Theology as Embraced Vulnerability 218
Richard Lennan

Contributors 233

Introduction

Cristina Lledo Gomez and John N. Sheveland

In the wake of various sexual abuse crises and patterns of abuse and cover-up in churches, other youth-serving organizations, and society at large, which deny voice and agency to many, attuning to the various and evolving ways vulnerability can be experienced is an important work of a posttraumatic church and society. How might we begin to understand vulnerability today, deconstruct and analyze its various manifestations, and build up a way of life that cares for and protects the vulnerable, as a society and church? When can vulnerability be considered a good, and when is it subject to manipulation and harm? When might vulnerability even pave a way for the flourishing of all? How might the church reimagine itself if its teaching on the preferential option for the poor were to be expressed more intentionally as a preferential option for the vulnerable? Moreover, how might flourishing be understood within Pope Francis's expansive vision for integral human development, integral ecological conversion, and synodality, which provides some of the necessary conditions for an ethic of flourishing for church and society rather than persistent vulnerability to abuse, harm, or retraumatization?

The 2024 annual convention of the College Theology Society explored these questions and more through the theme *Vulnerability and Flourishing.* As coeditors of this year's volume, we ourselves understand vulnerability not only as the possibility of being harmed or violated but also as the condition of being alive, embodied, and created to be in relationship with others and God; a precondition of entering into relationship and remaining in relationships of love and authenticity

ix

necessitates a level of vulnerability. While vulnerability is often defined as a weakness in various circumstances, St. Paul the Apostle has taught us, in that classic text from his letter to the Corinthians, that, paradoxically, we might find strength in our weakness (2 Cor 8:10). But we also understand such poignant descriptions of Christian spiritual reality and its complex and windy road can be and have been utilized for harm. We particularly understand vulnerability in connection to the German discourse on "Vulneranz" as "the power to inflict harm."[1] It is "the special readiness to use violence, even explosive violence, in connection with vulnerabilities."[2] In the case of church abuse and coverup when the church leadership saw itself as being vulnerable, it justified further harm of victims in order not to face the consequences of the initial abuses. As Hildegund Keul explains, "The desire to protect one's own institution contains a potential for violence: one wounds the other to protect oneself from being wounded."[3]

Vulnerability and abuse, though, could not be explored without also exploring protection, healing, agency, and resilient living while managing, for example, ongoing illness or contradiction—even the possibility of flourishing in various religious, cultural, and political contexts. Flourishing is about more than simply existing or surviving. It is about the possibility of living in healthy relationships with self, others, the whole of creation, and God. While this does not mean the absence of or absolute protection from harm, it does mean having enough resources—internal and external—to heal or recover from, or to live resiliently with, ongoing frailties or vulnerabilities.

We are inspired by the understanding of flourishing as *buen vivir*, "good living," the idea of "life in abundance" as defined by the Amazonian Indigenous peoples and referred to by Pope Francis in his *Final Document* on the Amazon Synod. In this document, Pope Francis explains *buen vivir* as something "fully realized in the Beatitudes" (Mt 5:1–12). Further, he writes,

> It is a matter of living in harmony with oneself, with nature, with human beings and with the Supreme Being, since there is inter-

---

[1] Hildegund Keul, "Vulnerability, Vulnerance and Resilience—Spiritual Abuse and Sexual Violence in New Spiritual Communities," *Religions* 13, no. 5 (2022): 2. Cristina thanks Tracy McEwan for pointing out this German discourse on *vulneranz*.

[2] Keul, "Vulnerability, Vulnerance and Resilience," 2.

[3] Keul, "Vulnerability, Vulnerance and Resilience," 2.

INTRODUCTION　　　　*xi*

communication throughout the cosmos; here there are neither exclusions nor those who exclude, and here a full life for all can be projected. Such an understanding of life is characterized by the interconnection and harmony of relationships between water, territory and nature, community life and culture, God and various spiritual forces. For them [the Amazon peoples], "good living" means understanding the centrality of the transcendent relational character of human beings and of creation, and implies "good acting." This integral approach is expressed in their own way of organizing that starts from the family and the community, and embraces a responsible use of all the goods of creation.[4]

We thus understand flourishing as a right for all of God's creation, even though many, if not most, do not experience this ideal, and some experience it less so than others. Flourishing can only work if it involves the flourishing of all and not only some. This means taking seriously our interconnection with each other and all of creation but also changing our behavior so that we become facilitators of flourishing communities rather than facilitators of communities of harm and retraumatizations. As Pope Francis himself says in *Fratelli Tutti,*

At a time when everything seems to disintegrate and lose consistency, it is good for us to appeal to the "solidity" born of the consciousness that we are responsible for the fragility of others as we strive to build a common future. Solidarity finds concrete expression in service, which can take a variety of forms in an effort to care for others. And service in great part means "caring for vulnerability, for the vulnerable members of our families, our society, our people." In offering such service, individuals learn to "set aside their own wishes and desires, their pursuit of power, before the concrete gaze of those who are most vulnerable... Service always looks to their faces, touches their flesh, senses their closeness and even, in some cases, "suffers" that closeness and tries to help them. Service is never ideological, for we do not serve ideas, we serve people.[5]

---

[4] Pope Francis, *Final Document. The Amazon: New Paths for the Church and for an Integral Ecology* (2019), no. 9.

[5] Pope Francis, *Fratelli Tutti: On Fraternity and Social Friendship* (2020), no. 115.

The chapters in this volume attest to the different ways the church, in its various manifestations, can be and has been of service to others, helping to bring about the flourishing of all. At the same time, the chapters also show how the church has participated in the diminishment and destruction of others, including the earth. They seek to explore what "good living" can even look like in an environment of a history of abuse and current and ongoing harms in the church and in the world. Such hurts go even deeper when the source of harm comes from the church itself.

This is what we see in the opening chapters of this volume beginning with Alfred Pang's "Vulnerable Harmony: A Vision of Ministry with LGBTQ Christians in Singapore." Rather than fight current church teachings, Pang considers what pastoral ministry in the Catholic church with LGBTQ Christians looks like in Singapore, which is sensitive to the polarizing forces around issues of sexual diversity. He navigates this difficult space by calling for "generous spaciousness" that holds the vulnerability of LBGTQ Christians as burden and gift in their faith journeys, allowing them to build their sense of self as completely loved and accepted by God in community.

Jason Steidl Jack similarly speaks of ministry to LGBTQ communities and what they entail, in "Trans Catholic Vulnerability and Flourishing in the Church." The aim of his chapter is to display a dual history of the church both centering at times and other times marginalizing this community who are vulnerable to harm. As a community that has been marginalized by church teaching and practice, Jack seeks to give voice to their suffering so that the church might rethink what and how it teaches on gender and sexuality. As a community who has also received care and engaged themselves in care for each other as church, Jack hopes to show valuing, and respecting LGBTQ communities is not a new ask; it is part of church history. In "Beyond the Closet, Toward the Horizon: Contemplative Practice as Queer Flourishing," Barbara Anne Kozee proposes that the theoretical and anthropological underpinnings of queer theory on gender and sexuality are resonant with Karl Rahner's theological anthropology and understanding of divine mystery. She helps the reader to see that "attending to the concerns of queer epistemology and Rahnerian anthropology" at the same time "shows how cultivating contemplative awareness to divine mystery and love can be an ethical practice for queer flourishing."

INTRODUCTION

What happens when cognitive ability and therefore the capacity to understand and give assent to propositions of faith is in question? This is what Susan McElcheran explores in " 'Unknowing' God and Intellectual Disability: Retrieving a Fourteenth-Century Perspective," where she challenges knowledge of God as reliant on rational thought rather than the whole body and the affect. She uses *The Cloud of Unknowing* as an example of this way of knowing God beyond the intellect.

In "The Two-Fold Virtue Reconsidered: Humility, Magnanimity, and the Technocratic Paradigm," Katherine Tarrant also delves into our rich Christian tradition to provide age-old answers to new questions. In this case, the "new" question is the "threat of anthropogenic climate change" in this technocratic age. While denial and dissonance, on the one hand, or ecomodernism, on the other, have been two opposing responses to our ecological crisis, Tarrant proposes a third response: turning to the virtues of humility and magnanimity, age-old values to face this "tide of crisis."

Stephen Okey also seeks to address the current issue of the technocratic paradigm and how it applies to our thoughts about artificial intelligence (AI), in "Technocratic Eschatologies: Hope and Flourishing amid an Artificially Intelligent Future." Like Tarrant, he sets out the narratives on AI, which are on opposite ends but are linked in many ways, including the existential risk they seek to address. In the end Okey helps us imagine a third discourse by moving from technocratic eschatologies to an integral eschatology.

Cristofer Fernandez's chapter, "A Franciscanized Ecology of Technology?," ends this small section on alternative responses to our ecological crisis and the technocratic paradigm, using Christian tradition. Fernandez proposes we view the crisis through the lenses of lady poverty and the planet, concepts considered in the Franciscan intellectual and spiritual tradition, to "assess the growing case of artificial intelligence," to name "technocratic vulnerabilities," and to reimagine "eco-social flourishing."

In Tobias Winright's chapter, "Gun Violence, Vulnerability, and Flourishing," we see a different technology, the gun, bring up questions about our vulnerability as a society and how, as Winright states, school shootings violate the "purpose of human life," which is to flourish. Motivated as an ethicist by his personal experience of gun violence, Winright examines the College Theology Society statement against gun violence, exploring how moral discourse on the topic remains naive, unnuanced, and even dangerous, which in turn has implications for its persuasiveness and reception. He proposes a focus on victims rather than guns to help the cause against gun violence.

Like Winright, Vanessa White also turns to her own experience to shed light on experiencing vulnerability and flourishing, but in the academy. In "There Is a Balm: Vulnerability, Challenge, and Hope," White shows us the vulnerabilities the academic can experience, especially as a woman, a person of color, and an early scholar. Through her Womanist storytelling methodology, we learn how it is possible to flourish in academia, "to maintain and sustain a healthy, wholistic, and joyful life as a theological educator, minister, and academic." But they are won on various battlegrounds and with much heartache.

Chris Welch also speaks about the battleground in the academic space but, this time, from the perspective of students. In "Not Enough Time to Flourish: Vocation, Work, and Leisure in Catholic Higher Education," Welch uses his empirical study on students' work and leisure experiences while studying to provide insight into how students are vulnerable and what universities and staff might need to provide to facilitate their flourishing.

In "The Vulnerability and Flourishing of Girls," we narrow our focus on student experience to the experience of White, middle-class, and cisgendered adolescent girls. In this chapter, Cynthia Cameron argues that "academic theology tends to be written and read by middle-aged adults." Thus, she says when we engage in theology, "the default human being" for consideration is often the middle-aged adult. Cameron seeks to rectify this problem by taking one portion of the population, the adolescent White middle-class girl, and viewing vulnerability and flourishing through their lenses.

A particular point of vulnerability for both girls and women is the contested area of their bodies and the other lives they hold in them. In "*Gloria Dei, Vivens Homo*: Vulnerability and Flourishing in Post-*Dobbs* 'Hard Cases'," James Bretzke navigates this difficult space by turning to "traditional Catholic bioethics, feminist perspectives and legal analyses," to "yield greater insights into both vulnerability and flourishing in this highly controversial area."

Callie Tabor's chapter, "Women, Synodality, and Social Poetry," helps us to shift the deadlock on the place of women in the church by invit-

INTRODUCTION

ing us into a different ecclesial imaginary. That is, rather than debating about a theology of womanhood or rejecting such theologizing, Tabor shifts the discourse using Pope Francis's own language on social poetry, inviting the church to imagine instead women as social poets. In Francis's own words, social poets "create hope where there appears to be only waste and exclusion." Tabor argues that by applying this idea to women, it unlocks them from gender essentialist constructions, which result in both sides of the debate at an impasse.

The typical medium for conceptualized womanhood in the Catholic Church is Mary, the Mother of God—and partnered with this picture of ideal womanhood is ideal female behavior, particularly slavehood masked as servanthood (to men, children, and the whole of society). This cause has especially been promoted by a certain interpretation of Mary's "yes" at the annunciation and self-identification as "the handmaid of the Lord." Alaina Keller's "The Annunciation: A Biblical Handmaid's Tale" helps women in the church to reclaim the word "handmaid" by showing it not as "women's passive fiat to authority" but a share in Jesus's own ministry in his claim to being God's own handmaid.

Brett McLaughlin also helps us in our reclamation of a concept typically viewed negatively in the world, weakness, and shows how St. Paul saw it as "the conduit" for God's grace, and therefore an enduring strength for us in "Weakness as the Conduit for the Mechanics of Grace: Paul's Paradoxical Spirituality of 2 Corinthians 12:5–10."

But as already mentioned above, such paradoxes in the spiritual life can be misused to abuse vulnerable persons in the church. This is what we find in Elise Abshire's "Relearning Vulnerability: Sifting Through Jean Vanier's Legacy of Care and Abuse." She delves into the tough question of "holding in tension the beautiful and the harmful."

Similarly, in "Attunement and Safeguarding in Parishes: Perspectives of a Diocesan Priest," Anthony Coloma grapples with the church as a space of abuse and harm rather than the expected place of hope and safety. As a diocesan priest, he takes the first necessary step of listening to the victim-survivors, as much as it pains, and he asks—where do we go from here as a whole parish to commit ourselves to an ethic of safety and reparations?

Caitlin Cipolla-McCulloch's "La Fiesta de La Virgen de la Puerta: Vulnerability and Flourishing Concretely Exemplified" contrasts this vision of the church as vulnerable and continually causing harm, seeking a way to operate differently. As the title suggests, Cipolla-McCulloch presents a vision of flourishing of the baptized not inside a church and not led by a liturgical leader. Rather, the vision entails an event held in the streets and with the coequal participation of the town's people, themselves motivated by their devotion to La Virgen de la Puerta. There are eucharistic resonances to their gathering. But as an outside observer, Cipolla-McCulloch hesitates to make such theological reflections as they must ultimately be the theological reflections of the people of the town themselves.

Last but certainly not least, we conclude the volume with Richard Lennan's compelling chapter on "Paradoxical Flourishing: Theology as Embraced Vulnerability." Lennan helps us to see that the call of theologians to creatively respond to the times must ultimately be viewed within the context of a long history of theologizing. Our theologizing must not fall into the trap of "cosmetic adjustments to prevailing methods for expounding and communicating faith." Rather than siloing ourselves into theological "camps" or viewing our own theologies as definitive (even answering tomorrow's questions), he calls us to ground ourselves in the understanding that our theologies will always be provisional and always entail a communal dimension. By embracing this vulnerability in theologizing, we allow for the flourishing of the discipline, ourselves, the church, and the world.

We end this introduction with the acknowledgment that the 2024 annual convention of our College Theology Society was held on land in which violence against its Indigenous peoples, the Cheyenne and Arapaho peoples, occurred in 1864, resulting in the deaths of over six hundred Indigenous children, women, and men. This event was so horrific it would be renowned in history as the Sand Creek Massacre and 2024 would mark its 160th anniversary. We also acknowledge that Denver is the site of the Columbine High School massacre, where two senior students killed twelve classmates and one teacher and injured twenty-four other students. It would come to be known as the deadliest mass shooting in a K–12 school in the history of the US until the Sandy Hook elementary school shooting in 2012 and the Uvalde school shooting in 2022. The year 2024 would also mark a significant year for the Columbine school shooting as it would be its twenty-fifth anniversary. It was thus timely and appropriate for the theologians of

INTRODUCTION　　　　　　　　　　　　　　　*xvii*

the College Theology Society to explore the theme of *Vulnerability and Flourishing* in 2024 at Regis University, Denver, CO. We, the editors of this volume, hoped that, by exploring this theme, the College Theology Society might lend its strengths to focus not only on the violence and vulnerabilities of the past and present, but to articulate how and what flourishing is possible into the future.

We thank the presenters of the conference for being willing to explore this theme with us, and we thank all who submitted their papers for blind peer review, particularly the contributors to this volume. As editors, we are grateful to members of the College Theology Society and beyond who accepted our invitations to serve as peer reviewers. We are grateful for the partnership that the College Theology Society enjoys with Orbis Books and especially Acquisitions Editor Tom Hermans-Webster, with whom this volume's editors have now worked on two books together and are the better for it. This volume being a collaborative work of the College Theology Society gives us pause to recall in gratitude all members of the College Theology Society who preceded us and on whose shoulders this work and our gifts, such as they are, depend. This volume is dedicated to all members of our Society—past, present, and future—with gratitude for all that has been shared and received in friendship.

Vulnerable Harmony

A Vision of Ministry
with LGBTQ Christians in Singapore

Alfred Kah Meng Pang

LGBTQ issues continue to be contentious, emotionally charged, and deeply polarizing in our churches and society.[1] While LGBTQ people have become more visible and vocal in Singapore, the city-state that prides itself for being multiracial and multireligious is at large culturally conservative. Section 377A of the Penal Code—a law inherited from the British, which criminalizes sex between men—was finally repealed in November 2022. At the same time, the Parliament passed a bill to amend the Constitution to protect the heterosexual definition of marriage from legal challenge by the law courts. Mr. Lee Hsien Loong, then prime minister from the ruling People's Action Party (PAP), said, "Taken together, these are balanced, wise steps forward."[2] This is an accommodation reached after the government's extensive consultation with various segments in Singaporean society, including religious leaders and representatives from the LGBTQ community. Even then, the

---

[1] I wish to thank the pastor of the LGBTQ ministry for his comments on an earlier draft of this chapter. I am especially grateful for members who have given me permission to reproduce their responses on vulnerability. My utmost gratitude to God for the friendship and faith shared in this community, which has been the subject and inspiration for this work. All views in this chapter are, however, my own.

[2] Channel News Asia, "Repeal of Section 377A and Constitutional Amendment to Protect Marriage Definition 'Major Milestone' for Singapore: PM Lee," November 30, 2022, https://www.channelnewsasia.com/singapore/pm-lee-hsien-loong-section-377a-repeal-constitution-marriage-definition-major-milestone-3111161.

lead-up to the repeal was met with opposition from a group of people who called themselves the Protect Singapore Townhall. Their fear is that the repeal would open the floodgate for LGBTQ activism to further push for changes to the traditional definition of marriage and family, which would in turn affect children negatively.[3]

Nevertheless, this repeal has shifted the state of relations between LGBTQ people and Singaporean society. In an opinion piece published by *The Straits Times*, columnist Mui Hoong Chua writes, "the gay community is no longer a criminalized sub-group to be made invisible, but a legitimate minority group that deserves dignity and a voice. Singaporeans will thus have to update their mental frame to think of the gay community as a legitimate minority group and treat them with respect."[4] Churches are now challenged to engage more openly with issues of sexual diversity. For the Catholic Church in Singapore, Pope Francis's call for synodality since 2021 has also enabled LGBTQ Catholics to speak their experiences of hurt and hope, paving the way for a more listening and discerning church rooted in Christ's merciful embrace of all. What might pastoral ministry with LGBTQ Christians look like in the local Catholic Church called to be synodal, in the context of a post-377A Singapore that is sensitive to the polarizing forces around issues of sexual diversity?

I address this question as a practical theologian and as a cisgender gay Catholic engaged in a diocesan Catholic ministry with LGBTQ persons in Singapore. This ministry was set up upon the initiative of the Archbishop, Cardinal William Goh in 2017. As a practical theologian, I begin with the lived faith of Christians in concrete communities with a focus on how practices of discipleship are cultivated in ministry.[5]

---

[3] Wei Kiat Ng, "Townhall Urges Against Repealing Section 377A Without Safeguards for Marriage, Families," *The Straits Times*, August 18, 2022, https://www.straitstimes.com/singapore/politics/town-hall-urges-against-repealing-section-377a-without-safeguards-for-marriage-families.

[4] Mui Hoong Chua, "Section 377A: Repeal Was Respectful but Is Talking About Sexual Orientation Still Taboo?," *The Straits Times*, February 21, 2023, https://www.straitstimes.com/opinion/section-377a-repeal-was-respectful-but-is-talking-about-sexual-orientation-still-taboo.

[5] Kathleen A. Cahalan and James R. Nieman, "Mapping the Field of Practical Theology," in *For Life Abundant: Practical Theology, Theological Education, and Christian Ministry*, ed. Dorothy C. Bass and Craig Dykstra (Eerdmans Publishing, 2008). As they highlight, "Practical theology engages Christian ways of life and therefore takes as its basic tasks the promotion of faithful discipleship" (Cahalan

VULNERABLE HARMONY

Drawing on my experiences in the ministry, as well as responses about vulnerability from members in the community, I distill a pastoral approach that nurtures what Wendy VanderWal-Gritter calls God's "generous spaciousness."[6] Emerging from this ministry is an approach to pastoral accompaniment that forms LGBTQ Christians in vulnerability as a practice of discipleship. Our communal witness as vulnerable agents in Christ calls the church to walk together vulnerably as God's people toward harmony. I propose a vision of ministry with LGBTQ Christians in a mode of vulnerable harmony that moves the church toward becoming more spacious in God's generous love, beyond the suffocating polarization over issues of sexual diversity.

Vulnerability as Burden and Gift

For this chapter, I invited members from the community to share the ways in which they have experienced vulnerability as an LGBTQ Christian in Singapore in general, and within the ministry in particular. Their responses reveal how vulnerability is paradoxically experienced as burden and gift.

Vulnerability is a burden in view of LGBTQ Christians *being at risk of* social stigmatization, prejudice, and discrimination in a cisheteronormative culture. As reflected in the following responses,

> For LGBTQ Christians such as myself, vulnerability often arises from the tension between our sexual orientation or gender identity and faith. It can be challenging to reconcile our authentic selves with the teachings and beliefs of our religious community. This struggle can lead to feelings of isolation, fear, and a sense of not fully belonging.

> Being vulnerable has been daunting in churches that do not accept me, and I have also faced rejection in ministries due to my sexuality. This has made me realize that being vulnerable is a risk because conservative churches and Asian values in Singapore do not accept my struggles.

---

and Nieman, "Mapping the Field of Practical Theology," 66).

[6] Wendy VanderWal-Gritter, *Generous Spaciousness: Responding to Gay Christians in the Church* (Brazos Press, 2014), 6.

4 *ALFRED KAH MENG PANG*

Underscored is a vulnerability due to what critical theorist Judith Butler conceives as precarity, "a politically induced condition in which certain populations suffer from failing social and economic networks of support and become differentially exposed to injury, violence, and death."[7] Precarity "points to an order of relations in which the livability of some is structurally rendered more *socially* vulnerable to being injured and expunged through a complex engendering of social, cultural, political and economic norms that is imbued with power."[8] The precarity of LGBTQ Christians stems from how their lives fall outside the dominant frame of cis-heteronormativity. The ecclesial discourse on sexuality and gender identity in the Roman Catholic Church reproduces this cis-heteronormative culture, which renders LGBTQ persons marginalized and *socially* vulnerable to being misrecognized; misunderstood; unseen; unheard; and, in some cases, hurt, harmed, and killed.[9]

Yet, as moral theologian James Keenan points out, Butler's writings also draw out vulnerability as foundational to our capacity to respond responsibly toward one another. He cites Butler, who argues, "Ethical obligation not only depends upon our vulnerability to the claims of others but establishes us as creatures who are fundamentally defined by that relation."[10] Vulnerability as such "should not be reduced to being precarious."[11] Rather, it is more primordially "the human condition that allows me to hear, encounter, receive, or recognize the other even to the point of being injured."[12]

Vulnerability is, in other words, a relational posture of openness toward the irreducibility of the other, holding out the possibility of being mutually transformed through recognizing our interrelatedness as a common humanity marked by diversity in creation. As Keenan

---

[7] Judith Butler, "Performativity, Precarity and Sexual Politics," *AIBR, Revista de Antropologia Iberoamericana* 4, no. 3 (2009): ii.

[8] Alfred K. M. Pang, "The Precarity of LGBTQ Catholic (Religious) Educators: A Theological Provocation to Teaching as a Call," *Religious Education* 116, no. 5 (2021): 457, https://doi.org/10.1080/00344087.2021.1985757.

[9] For a further discussion on how the Roman Catholic Church's discourse on sexuality and gender identity contributes to the non/mis-recognition of LGBTQ Christians as persons that is intertwined with their precarity, see Pang, "The Precarity of LGBTQ Catholic (Religious) Educators," 455–59.

[10] James F. Keenan, SJ, *The Moral Life: Eight Lectures* (Georgetown University Press, 2023), 26.

[11] Keenan, *The Moral Life*, 25.

[12] Keenan, *The Moral Life*, 24.

highlights, "When we recognize that the word vulnerable does not mean being or having been wounded, but rather means being able to be wounded, then it means being exposed to the other."[13]

Vulnerability does not preclude our woundable-ness. Our woundable-ness discloses vulnerability more deeply as a dimension intrinsic to our desire for communion and integral to our capacity to connect with one another. Vulnerability is thus constitutive of a relational ontology that grounds our moral responsiveness toward one another as created in God's image and likeness. It is "what allows us to be connected and therefore to love."[14]

This more expansive understanding of vulnerability allows it to be experienced as gift. In its shift "from being something to avoid to being something to express,"[15] vulnerability is not only experienced by LGBTQ persons as a precarious state of *being at risk of*. It is also enacted in the risk that we as LGBTQ persons freely and audaciously *choose to* take as an act of Christian witness in faith, as echoed in these responses:

> Vulnerability comes from courage and grace that I gain from having faith in God's will. It comes when I am able to have confidence to come out to strangers around me, and even to priests. I am willing to be vulnerable for Catholics, especially conservative Christians, so that they are able to see me as a person, instead of a label.

> They say when we are vulnerable we expose ourselves to many negative aspects. But vulnerability has helped me see the goodness of God, not only in my life but in the lives of others in my community. It made me realize that a person who can be vulnerable in front of many possesses the spirit of God because it allows them to feel for another the pain brought about by judgment and rejection from others. Such vulnerability also holds a space open for the joy and hope that God will bring.

---

[13] James F. Keenan, SJ, "The World at Risk: Vulnerability, Precarity, and Connectedness," *Theological Studies* 81, no. 1 (2020): 138, https://doi.org/10.1177/0040563920907633.

[14] Keenan, *The Moral Life*, 31.

[15] Keenan, *The Moral Life*, 30.

Such risk is a "queer virtue," as Elizabeth Edman puts it: "queer people take enormous risks simply by being ourselves in the world."[16] "This kind of risk," she continues, "is the verb form of faith. It is the lived iteration of trust in something bigger than your immediate security, bigger than whatever threat exists to your security."[17] It is neither "thrill seeking" nor "recklessness."[18] To come out to oneself and others as LGBTQ *and* Christian is a risk propelled by a desire for honesty and authenticity, grounded on a trust in God who riskily creates us for love, and whose love renders God-self powerfully vulnerable in being *with* and *for* us through the mystery of the Incarnation. "God takes risks in all that God does because God is vulnerable and God's vulnerability informs our own."[19] To risk being vulnerable to ourselves and with others as LGBTQ people of faith becomes a gift when it is a free response to God's vulnerability that forms and transforms us to love with bold compassion as Christ does. "And so we risk," Edman writes, "knowing that we are part of a life, a love, a truth that cannot die."[20]

Emerging from the community is a pastoral approach that recognizes and allows for the complex and paradoxical ways in which LGBTQ Christians navigate relations of vulnerability as burden and gift. Pastoral accompaniment serves our flourishing as LGBTQ Christians when it creates a trusted space for God's vulnerability to be encountered through each of us and as we are in community. As a community member puts it,

> Receiving others who have been vulnerable with me in revealing who they are has allowed me to see that it is possible to be both Catholic and gay. Because of the vulnerability of others, I am able to recognize myself (through people like me, the precious broken ones in need of a Savior) in the People of God.

He continues by saying, "when I meet someone and they show me their wounds—that I am human too and doing the best I can—there is a lived experience of faith." The language of wounds is striking as it

---

[16] Elizabeth M. Edman, *Queer Virtue: What LGBTQ People Know About Life and Love and How It Can Revitalize Christianity* (Beacon Press, 2016), 47.

[17] Edman, *Queer Virtue*, 56.

[18] Edman, *Queer Virtue*, 56.

[19] Keenan, *The Moral Life*, 27.

[20] Edman, *Queer Virtue*, 58.

recalls the intimate moment in which the resurrected Christ showed Thomas the wounds on his hands and side (cf. Jn 20:24–29). In displaying his wounds, Christ "give[s] us the courage to remove our armor, our masks, and our makeup and look not only at the wounds and scars that we conceal beneath them from others and often from ourselves but also at the wounds we have inflicted on others."[21]

At the heart of our pastoral approach, then, is taking the risk to allow the mystery of Christ's love to touch us in and through our shared experiences of isolation, rejection, grief, and violence as LGBTQ persons because these are also the wounds suffered and borne by his crucified body resurrected. In recognizing Christ's vulnerability through his marginality with us as community, we find courage and strength, hope, and healing as God's beloved. The community is in turn called to incarnate this gift of God's vulnerability as disciples, to live our beloved-ness from within and out with others as church from the margins.

There is the question if and whether there are limits to this more capacious understanding of vulnerability. As Keenan highlights, "Is everyone as able to be vulnerable to the other, and should everyone be as vulnerable to the other?"[22] These are critical concerns, especially for marginalized communities who are burdened yet again with risking vulnerability. Here is where it is crucial to recognize that vulnerability is not opposed but integral to our agency as whole persons. Ethicist John Wall writes, "All human beings from birth to death must negotiate a lifelong dynamics of agency and vulnerability in relation to one another. Being-in-the-world is from the beginning both passively constructed by others and societies and actively constructed by a self."[23] Hille Haker echoes Wall in her conception of an "ethics of vulnerable agency [that] embraces autonomy, but it understands it and reinterprets it, in part, as the capacity to open up to the other, in part as the capability to respond to the other, including in the right to say no to the other's demands and desires."[24] Drawing on Hille Haker, Keenan argues, "Vulnerability is still prior to all, but we need agency to decide whether and how we should recognize and respond."[25]

---

[21] Tomáš Halík, *Touch the Wounds: On Suffering, Trust and Transformation*, trans. Gerald Turner (University of Notre Dame Press, 2023), 62.

[22] Keenan, *The Moral Life*, 31.

[23] John Wall, *Ethics of Light of Childhood* (Georgetown University Press, 2010), 40.

[24] Hille Haker, cited in Keenan, *The Moral Life*, 33.

[25] Keenan, *The Moral Life*, 33.

8 ALFRED KAH MENG PANG

What this means for the pastoral accompaniment of LGBTQ Christians is that it dignifies when our capacity for vulnerability is reclaimed as a dimension of being fully human in our interrelatedness, wherein God's life is graciously experienced in the experience of our sexuality and gender identity. Our human flourishing lies in the way we can still choose as agents when and how to respond to our vulnerability. In a context where the burden of social oppression still exists, pastoral ministry with LGBTQ Christians ought to support us to discern spiritually when and how to express our vulnerability as gift so that it may not be manipulated and exploited within the wider ethical task of discipleship formation. This is cultivated within the community by a pastoral approach that incarnates what Wendy VanderWal-Gritter calls "generous spaciousness."[26] Generous spaciousness awakens us to hope in Christ's faithful presence at the periphery, transforming the burden of our precarity into an edge for prophetic witness as agents in a vulnerable relation of belonging to one another in God. Generous spaciousness forms us in vulnerability as a practice of discipleship.

Vulnerability in "Generous Spaciousness"

Writing as a Canadian practitioner engaged in pastoral care for LGBTQ Christians in conservative evangelical churches, VanderWal-Gritter argues against approaches that take as their starting point and goal the defense and promotion of a uniform theology on sexuality and gender identity. Such approaches are often preoccupied with policing sexual morality and boundary maintenance that entrenches the hostility between conservatives and liberals in their stance toward same-sex relationships and marriage. They fuel polarization that obscures the nuance and complexity in how LGBTQ Christians actually navigate their everyday lives of faith, beyond concerns about sex and marriage:

> The affirmative voices call for the unimpeded opportunity for LGBTQ people to experience self-fulfillment through sexual intimacy, relationship, marriage, equal status, and so on. The traditional voices point to a path of self-denial and suffering as the way we live out God's standards. For a gay Christian, when hap-

---

[26] VanderWal-Gritter, *Generous Spaciousness*, 26.

VULNERABLE HARMONY **9**

piness and suffering are pitted against one another, this dilemma can disintegrate into a no-win situation and a source of shame.[27]

What often goes unheard is a range of voices from LGBTQ Christians in the middle, especially those who long for a spacious community to share their stories of struggles and hopes, explore their questions about faith and sexuality together as church without fear, judgment, or condemnation.

Instead, she argues for a pastoral approach that nurtures "generous spaciousness" that values as its starting point "the spiritual formation inherent in the experience of exploring intimate relationship with God and with each other as we wrestle through these difficult questions and challenges [around LGBTQ inclusion] and face the inevitable differences that result. Its posture seeks to be one of openness that is inquisitive, personal, relational, and dependent on the Spirit."[28] It honors and attends to the unique realities of LGBTQ Christians in flesh and blood, not as ideological objects but as human persons desiring to live faith relationally in an authentic and committed way as church.

Generous spaciousness does not require us to discard the different theological positions we have about sexuality and gender identity. It calls us to hold them open in a posture of curiosity, suspending the urge to win people over to any one side in a tug-of-war. "Rather than fleeing the discomfort of disagreement," writes VanderWal-Gritter, "I believe we are called to submit ourselves to the Spirit's work of increasing our humility, graciousness, and generosity. To sequester ourselves in a community of uniformity stunts our growth in learning to love those with whom we disagree."[29] Decentering a fixation on sexual morality, generous spaciousness is about discerning how the Spirit is forming and transforming churches in the way of fruitful mature discipleship through the difficult path of dialogue with the LGBTQ community in the diverse ways that faith and sexuality are being negotiated in and as the Body of Christ. At stake is the credibility of the church's witness to God's reconciling love that has been deeply fractured by polarization.

VanderWal-Gritter's work has been constructive in my thinking about LGBTQ ministry since my return to Singapore after my doctoral

---

[27] VanderWal-Gritter, *Generous Spaciousness*, 103.

[28] VanderWal-Gritter, *Generous Spaciousness*, 26.

[29] VanderWal-Gritter, *Generous Spaciousness*, 174.

studies in Boston. My theological education at Boston College has led me to be critical of the magisterium's moral teaching on homosexuality. While the teaching asserts the dignity of homosexuals as human persons who "must be accepted with respect, compassion, and sensitivity,"[30] its anthropology is arguably limited by an understanding of sexuality divorced from human relational experiences and advancements in the natural and social sciences.[31] The ministry that I am in, however, upholds the official teaching. As you can imagine, I wrestled with this clash.

Yet, I have also been struck by a pastoral approach that prioritizes being a community that nurtures relational belonging and friendship in Christ. The pastoral approach seeks to create a formative space that invites LGBTQ Christians to dialogue truthfully, wrestle courageously, and discern prayerfully as a community not only where God is present in our individual journeys integrating faith and sexuality but also the mission that God is calling us to as church. While open and receptive to my critical questioning, the community has also challenged me to see how even the most LGBTQ-affirming theologies can lock me in and out of the diverse and hidden ways that God as gracious mystery works in their lives. My experience of ministry with this community has taught me that what I regard to be liberating in pastoral approaches informed by LGBTQ-affirming theologies may not necessarily be desired or seen as meeting individual needs at their specific point in life.

There is thus a generous spaciousness that we extend to one another within the ministry as an LGBTQ community of faith. As our pastor frequently says, we are a "motley crew" gathered by a generous God. Generous spaciousness also forms us in a discipleship of vulnerability open to ambiguity as the creative ground of the Spirit. Leaning vulnerably into ambiguity holds open the possibility of God encountering LGBTQ persons in multiple and surprising ways as protagonists in our unique journeys of faith. Even with the tensions arising from these differences, "space is given to allow the other to live according to one's conscience, where judgment is withheld, where instead of a spirit

---

[30] *Catechism of the Catholic Church*, no. 2358.

[31] For instances of such critique, see Todd A. Salzman and Michael G. Lawler, *The Sexual Person: Toward a Renewed Sexual Anthropology* (Georgetown University Press, 2008); Margaret A. Farley, *Just Love: A Framework for Christian Sexual Ethics* (Continuum, 2006). See also Pang, "The Precarity of LGBTQ Catholic (Religious) Educators."

of contempt there is a spirit of humility, listening and caring for one another."[32] It is important to highlight that giving one another this space does not mean casting aside or disregarding the magisterium's teaching on sexuality. Rather, it calls one to discern more seriously and make sense more deeply the significance of the teaching for their own lives.

More than providing a safe space, the ministry is at a point discerning how generous spaciousness may be extended to engage the wider Catholic Church in Singapore on issues of sexual diversity and inclusion. To be clear, this vulnerability to ambiguity in gracious spaciousness should not imply that anything goes. The reality is that dialogue with LGBTQ people in churches is happening at an uneven table, given the cis-heteronormative ecclesial discourse on sexuality. As a community member puts it,

> Vulnerability is also letting go of power or the need to be seen as having all the answers and instead recognizing that often there are no easy answers. I wish the church could be as vulnerable, following the example of Jesus who became a human baby, and start acknowledging the difficult questions, and that it is possible that the church has caused pain, even if unintended.

Herein lies the prophetic call from the community to the church to be vulnerable: to recognize with humility how we as the people of God have not loved as Christ did. Generous spaciousness is a practice of kenotic love that ought to provoke all as church to examine and empty ourselves of assumptions that keep us from seeing one another in our complex dignity as human beings created in God's image and likeness. These assumptions are locked in accumulated layers of prejudice, fears, mistrust, hurt, and hostility. For the cis-heterosexual majority, in particular, it is an openness and willingness to lay down their structural privilege, and to truly listen with an awareness of how the table of dialogue with LGBTQ Christians has been uneven in the first place.

Gracious generosity is not a posture contented with agreeing to disagree, especially when such a position continues to dehumanize LGBTQ persons. As VanderWal-Gritter asserts, "Nothing about this is wishy-washy or weak. This isn't relativism. This is learning to live graciously with one another despite disagreements, while focusing

---

[32] VanderWal-Gritter, *Generous Spaciousness*, 185.

12   *ALFRED KAH MENG PANG*

on Christ to grow in you the fruit of his Spirit. Nurturing generous spaciousness demands courageous humility."[33] Courageous humility is only possible with vulnerability. My hope for the LGBTQ ministry is to foster a more authentic inclusion by walking the way together as a vulnerable church toward harmony.

Walking as a Vulnerable Church Toward Harmony

Harmony is lifted as a goal and process of accompanying LGBTQ Christians as church in Singapore because of its cultural resonance generally for those of us in Asia. Notably, the Federation of Asian Bishops' Conferences (FABC)—of which Singapore is a member—and its offices have developed a theology of harmony as pivotal to being a dialogical church at the service of God as life in the context of pluralism in Asia.[34] In an important paper entitled *Asian Christian Perspectives on Harmony*, the Theological Advisory Commission (TAC) speaks of harmony as "an Asian understanding of reality that is profoundly organic, i.e., a world-view wherein the whole, the unity, is the sum-total of the web of relationships, and interaction of the various parts with each other. [...] The parts are understood in terms of their mutual dependence."[35] It reinterprets the Christian tradition through a vision of harmony drawn from Asian religious, cultural, and philosophical traditions. In doing so, harmony serves as an overarching framework for the FABC to make sense of the distinctive ways in which God is calling the churches in Asia to build God's Reign of peace and justice in the context of pluralism.

There is much about harmony to unpack theologically in the FABC documents that is beyond the scope of this chapter.[36] However, I wish

---

[33] VanderWal-Gritter, *Generous Spaciousness*, 188.

[34] As noted by the Bishops' Institute for Interreligious Affairs (BIRA), "Harmony seems to constitute in a certain sense the intellectual and affective, religious and artistic, personal and societal soul of both persons and institutions in Asia." BIRA, cited in Jukka Helle, *Towards a Truly Catholic and a Truly Asian Church: The Asian Wayfaring Theology of the Federation of Asian Bishops' Conferences (FABC) 1970–2020* (Brill, 2022), 51.

[35] Theology Advisory Commission, *FABC Paper 75: Asian Christian Perspectives on Harmony* (March 1996), no. 3.4, fabc.org. Hereafter cited as *FABC Paper 75* followed by paragraph number in the text.

[36] For a recent analysis of Asian harmony and the FABC, Helle, *Towards a Truly Catholic and a Truly Asian Church*, 51–69.

to lift here its potential as an ecclesiological foundation for the pastoral accompaniment of LGBTQ persons in Singapore. Significantly, the TAC proposes "the Church as communion is the sacrament of harmony of the humankind."[37] Harmony as the goal of God's mission is brought forth in Jesus Christ and through the Spirit as process calling the church to become an "instrument of dynamic harmony."[38] Recalling St. Paul's conception of reconciliation and recapitulation in Christ,[39] Christ is the "bringer of harmony" by "breaking down social barriers encrusted in customs and traditions and entrenched in social structures":

> He breaks down barriers set up by greed, pride, discrimination, lopsided social norms, and even religious distortions. Outcasts become sisters and brothers. Sinners are worthy of compassion. The hungry, the thirsty, the prisoners, the naked bear the divine presence. And God is our Father. In the freedom and communion that Jesus offers, a new creation dawns. The human community is reborn. Indeed the time of fulfillment has come. Life in abundance is in our midst. The Kingdom is here.[40]

Christ is as such the "sacrament of new harmony" of which the Church is "servant-sacrament" that incarnates with humility the values of the Reign of God: "love, mercy, forgiveness, justice, compassion, unity, peace, as proclaimed by Jesus Christ—are the seeds of the new harmony inaugurated by him."[41] The Asian church is called to walk the way of harmony through "a triple dialogue" with people interculturally and interreligiously, and with a preferential option for the poor, as "fellow wayfarers to God's Reign" in life.[42] "Dialogue is the primary mode for the Church in Asia in the promotion of harmony. But like our Master, we will be able to foster harmony only by taking the path of a love of preference for the poor."[43]

It is this liberative–prophetic dimension in FABC's ecclesiology of harmony that I wish to lift up as a frame for envisioning the pastoral

---

[37] *FABC Paper 75*, no. 3.3.3.1.

[38] *FABC Paper 75*, no. 3.3.3.4.

[39] Helle, *Towards a Truly Catholic and a Truly Asian Church*, 57.

[40] *FABC Paper 75*, no. 4.6.

[41] *FABC Paper 75*, no. 5.2.6.

[42] *FABC Paper 75*, no. 4.11.6.

[43] *FABC Paper 75*, no. 4.10.

accompaniment of LGBTQ persons in the churches in Asia, generally, and in Singapore, particularly. FABC's theology of harmony has so far been developed with interreligious dialogue as its main focus. I contend there is a need to extend it as a contribution of the Asian churches to ecclesial engagement on sexual diversity issues. This is especially needed considering the recent *Bangkok Document* from the FABC General Conference on the occasion of their fiftieth anniversary. It identified "LGBTQ+ people [as] highly marginalized and face varied forms of stigma and discrimination based on their distinct sexual orientations, gender identities and expressions."[44] It is worth noting that the accent is not on sexual morality but on the need for "great sensitivity, discernment and care" on gender issues.[45] Dialogue that makes a preferential option for the poor must now be extended to those of us who are marginalized by our sexuality and gender identity, and at the intersection of different cultures and religious traditions in Asia.

It is crucial to highlight that the idea of harmony is not at the expense of social justice. True harmony calls for justice and complements it:

> Harmony is promoted neither by a blanket-acceptance of the unjust status quo, nor by compromising with evil, nor by an involuntary tolerance of the other, but by a courageous condemnation of evil in its various forms, and an active tolerance, if not a charitable acceptance, of the other in his or her otherness […] Harmony is neither a compromising with conflictual realities, nor a complacency about the existing order. Harmony demands a transformative attitude and action, to bring about a change in contemporary society.[46]

Inherent in FABC's conception of harmony is not simply an accommodation of differences, but an active allowance for differences to emerge that interrupts the status quo, drawing attention to the plight of those who are socially marginalized. This counters the common association of harmony with uniformity and conformity.

For future consideration, I have found contemporary scholarship

---

[44] FABC General Conference, *Bangkok Document: Journeying Together as Peoples of Asia* (March 15, 2023), no. 43.

[45] FABC General Conference, *Bangkok Document*, no. 44.

[46] *FABC Paper 75*, no. 5.4.1.

on Confucian thought to be generative in deepening this liberative–prophetic dimension of harmony. Philosopher Chenyang Li retrieves Confucian harmony as "a dynamic, generative process, which seeks to balance and reconcile differences and conflicts through creativity and mutual transformation."[47] As a verb rather than a noun, Confucian harmony is sustained by an inherent dynamic of manifesting and holding differences in "creative tension."[48]

Building on Li's work, educational theorists Li-Ching Ho and Keith Barton develop the notion of "critical harmony" to complement the Eurocentric emphasis on justice in terms of rights and equality in civic education.[49] "In many societies around the world," they contend, "a central social and political goal has long been not only justice but also harmony … about something more relational: living together in ways that recognize the value and necessity of connections with other people, as well as with the environment."[50] Criticality is crucial, especially given how harmony "can be [and has been] used as a justification for conformity, dominance, and authoritarianism."[51] Critical harmony, they propose, "requires an embrace of conflict and tension, a valuing of difference and even deviance, and judicious balance among diverse perspectives and areas of expertise."[52] The balance it strives for is dynamic; it "does not require equal attention to all perspectives" but considers "which views deserve to be heard, and at what moments,"[53] particularly those at the margins. Balance is as such "a corrective on power and a way of protecting the vulnerable, in pursuit of greater societal harmony, not an excuse for legitimizing abuses of power."[54]

These sources deepen the FABC's conception of harmony, which, I suggest, moves us toward that generous spaciousness in LGBTQ ministry. Enfolded in harmony is a vulnerability to embrace divergent voices

---

[47] Chenyang Li, *The Confucian Philosophy of Harmony* (Routledge, 2014), 1.

[48] Chenyang Li, *The Confucian Philosophy of Harmony*; Chenyang Li, "The Confucian Ideal of Harmony," *Philosophy East & West* 56, no. 4 (October 2006): 592.

[49] Li-Ching Ho and Keith C. Barton, "Critical Harmony: A Goal for Deliberative Civic Education," *Journal of Moral Education* 51, no. 2 (2022), 276, https://doi.org/10.1080/03057240.2020.1847053.

[50] Ho and Barton, "Critical Harmony," 276.

[51] Ho and Barton, "Critical Harmony," 280.

[52] Ho and Barton, "Critical Harmony," 280.

[53] Ho and Barton, "Critical Harmony," 283.

[54] Ho and Barton, "Critical Harmony," 283.

on faith and sexuality with curiosity and humility. This is a vulnerability that summons each of us to make room for the mystery of God's Spirit to mature us as disciples as we continue to dialogue and walk the path of LGBTQ inclusion together as church. This is a vulnerability that calls the church to lean into the discomfort of diversity that could be confronting without being confrontational, to stand in-between the spaces of our differences with the Spirit as the harmonizer and composer of oneness in the many.

Going Home to the Vulnerable Heart of Jesus

Emerging from my experience of ministry with LGBTQ Christians is ultimately a pastoral approach that is relational and communal, forming us in the art of Christ's vulnerability so that we can love ourselves and others as Christ does—boldly, justly, humbly, and authentically. The life of the community suggests how the pastoral accompaniment of LGBTQ Christians is inseparable from the task of discipleship as church. As a gay Catholic in this ministry and community, I am not at the margins with my LGBTQ siblings-in-Christ that the church reaches out to. Rather, we are at the margins who call God's people to be a more spacious church rooted in God's generosity who knows no bounds and crosses boundaries. As Timothy Radcliffe writes, "It is in the spaciousness of God that we will be completely at home because everyone will be."[55]

My hope is that this ministry with LGBTQ Christians grows in its mode of vulnerable harmony that goes beyond the forces of polarization to be a church that embodies God's reconciling love. It is perhaps by no coincidence that our community gathers weekly at the Church of the Sacred Heart. The Sacred Heart of Jesus reminds the ministry of God's vulnerable heart of love that not only stands in solidarity with the marginalized but is also broken open for harmony. It is in this Sacred Heart that our community finds a home. And it is from the Sacred Heart that we learn to be vulnerable. This vulnerability that dares us to risk for life's flourishing is the courage to receive deeply and respond fully to God who says, I choose you as Beloved. Now, go forth!

---

[55] Timothy Radcliffe, OP, *What Is the Point of Being a Christian?* (Burns and Oates, 2005), 131.

Trans Catholic Vulnerability and Flourishing in the Church

Jason Steidl Jack

Transgender-affirming discourse often includes two perspectives on trans experience in the Roman Catholic Church. The first highlights trans vulnerability within a faith community that can be prone to excluding, misunderstanding, and harming trans people. These rely on stories of trans suffering at the hands of church leaders to call for changes to magisterial teaching and pastoral practice.[1] The second emphasizes trans flourishing in the church, offering stories of redemption and hope at the individual and communal level.[2] How might we reconcile these two perspectives?

This chapter will examine histories of trans and allied Catholic advocacy as spaces where trans vulnerability and flourishing go hand in hand. Rather than seeing trans vulnerability and flourishing as mutually exclusive realities, we might see them in an agonistic relationship that creates possibilities for personal and ecclesial transformation.

Theoretical Background

In a recent article, Martina Vuk argues that vulnerability and flourishing are "co-existing, interdependent, and contingent aspects

---

[1] See, for example, Rebecca Bratten Weiss, "The Catholic Church's Gender Ideology Is Complementarian and Binary. That's Not How Nature Works," *National Catholic Reporter*, April 24, 2023, ncronline.org.

[2] See, for example, Maxwell Kuzma, "Holy Scars and Divine Welcome: A Transgender Catholic Flourishes at Outreach 2024," *National Catholic Reporter*, August 9, 2024, ncronline.org.

of human existence."[3] Vuk describes vulnerability as "a natural condition that is specific to living beings and an individual circumstance to be at risk of harm or exposure, but also a possibility towards change and growth in life's circumstances."[4] Flourishing, on the other hand, "is seen as an inclination to live a true, good and fulfilled life and as the ability to act rightly towards one self and others."[5] Although Vuk admits that vulnerability does not necessarily lead to flourishing, flourishing sometimes requires acknowledging vulnerability as a step toward becoming more "authentic, honest, and self-aware."[6] Living a healthy, integrated life may call us to "let go of our rigid agenda of control and allow ourselves to be open to embrace our human limitations, not-knowing, and uncertainty."[7]

While reckoning with vulnerability can contribute to an individual's growth, it also impacts the world around them. This is especially true for those whose lives are at risk due to systemic injustice and violence. Vuk explains that recognizing one's vulnerabilities "can result . . . in a person's motivation to fight against injustices, increase a person's potential for survival capacities, or contribute to the development of resistance and resilience."[8] When those most imperiled by forces such as racism, sexism, and ableism face the dangers and limitations they encounter, they may discover within themselves a powerful drive for changing the world.

As sexual and/or gender minorities, LGBTQ persons are vulnerable due to pervasive queerphobia, but the dangers inherent to queer life also provide a springboard for their flourishing.[9] Theologian and leadership coach Dominic Longo explains,

> Because of specific types of adverse experiences, in order to survive or thrive, LGBTQ+ people have to adapt, even when we do not wish to do so. Yet, while our differences exact a price,

---

[3] Martina Vuk, "Theological and Ethical Perspectives on Rethinking the Co-Existence of Flourishing and Vulnerability," *De Ethica* 8, no. 1 (2024): 25.

[4] Vuk, "Theological and Ethical Perspectives," 27.

[5] Vuk, "Theological and Ethical Perspectives."

[6] Vuk, "Theological and Ethical Perspectives."

[7] Vuk, "Theological and Ethical Perspectives."

[8] Vuk, "Theological and Ethical Perspectives," 31.

[9] For more information on anti-LGBTQ violence and systemic injustices, see Human Rights Campaign, "Reports," thehrcfoundation.org/reports.

queerness also catalyzes many kinds of creativity. Facing specific obstacles within the world and dilemmas within ourselves, we adapt creatively... Queer flourishing brings alive more of ourselves, including previously deadened parts and new parts waiting to emerge.[10]

LGBTQ Catholics and their allies are not unfamiliar with the dyad of vulnerability and flourishing in their experiences of the Roman Catholic Church, wherein teaching that harms LGBTQ people, institutionalized exclusion, and ignorance regarding LGBTQ lives are widespread.[11] The risks that LGBTQ Catholics take to practice their faith, however, can also be transformative for themselves and the church. As I write in my reflection on LGBTQ ministry, "The Church's mistreatment of queer Catholics is heartbreaking. Nevertheless, a painful history opens up to hope for the future. LGBTQ Catholics and their allies are tenacious. Decades of ministry provide a vision for what is possible in communities committed to justice and mercy."[12] By claiming their place in the church in spite of—and sometimes because of—opposition, LGBTQ Catholics and their allies conceive of fresh ways to advocate for themselves and thrive. This dynamic becomes clear in the histories of trans and trans-allied Catholics, whose interactions with the church reveal triumphs born out of hardship.

Trans and Allied Catholic Groundbreakers

Many US Catholics first learned about trans people in 1980, when publications, such as the *Los Angeles Times*, reported on Nancy Ledins, a former priest who had transitioned the year before.[13] Ledins was born in Cleveland, Ohio, and assigned male at birth. Ordained with the Missionaries of the Precious Blood in 1959, Ledins worked as a

---

[10] Dominic Longo, *Queer Flourishing* (Publish Your Purpose, 2024), queer-flourishing.com.

[11] See Jason Jack, *LGBTQ Catholic Ministry: Past and Present* (Paulist Press, 2023), and Gerard Loughlin, "Catholic Homophobia," *Theology* 121, no. 3 (May/June 2023): 188–96.

[12] Jack, *LGBTQ Catholic Ministry*, 3-4.

[13] John Dart, "Former Father William Now a Woman," *Los Angeles Times*, July 18, 1980.

history teacher, athletic director, and military chaplain, in addition to pastoring in Michigan and Colorado. Her story took a new direction in 1969, when, like many priests of the era, she left the priesthood life to marry a woman. Ledins's personal vulnerabilities grew over the next decade as she navigated gender dysphoria. In 1978, she divorced her wife, a precondition imposed by psychologists and medical doctors at that time for her gender transition. Accepting her identity as a woman meant coming to terms with life outside of priesthood and marriage, but she found the process liberating. After her gender transition, Ledins wrote to her parents, "For the first time in my life, I am running into and not from . . . What a healthy feeling! I am now very, very glad to be alive. . . . My buckets of tears (and there were many) are over. The sunshine is real."[14] On Holy Thursday 1979, Ledins underwent gender-confirming surgery.[15]

After her transition, Ledins found a new vocation as a pioneering electrologist. She moved to North Carolina in 1996 and joined an affirming Baptist community where she led worship and prayer, ministered the sacraments, and was beloved by fellow congregants until her death at eighty-four. In a 2015 prayer that marked the fifty-fifth anniversary of her ordination, she prayed, "Lord Father, my special thanks for the gift of ordination and ministry over the years . . . and thank you for letting me be here. Amen and Amen. Alleluia."[16]

After marrying in 1969, Ledins never again served as a Catholic priest. But her vocational work during and after ordination raises an important question: Is male identity necessary for ordained ministry? Ledins's experience suggests that it is not. In a Catholic hierarchy set against women's ordination, Ledins's transgender identity was and continues to be a potent critique of patriarchal beliefs and structures.

More recently, the story of Rev. Kori Pacyniak, a theologian who is completing their dissertation at the University of California, also illustrates the connection between trans vulnerability and flourishing. Pacyniak, raised in a Chicago Polish Catholic enclave, expressed their desire to become a priest at age eight. When their grandmother

---

[14] "Rev. Dr. Nancy S. Ledins," *LGBTQ Religious Archives Network*, February 2019, lgbtqreligiousarchives.org.

[15] "Rev. Dr. Nancy S. Ledins," *LGBTQ Religious Archives Network*.

[16] Tim Funk, "Church to Celebrate Life of Catholic Priest Who Found Peace as a Transgender Woman," *Charlotte Observer*, July 22, 2017, charlotteobserver.com.

TRANS CATHOLIC VULNERABILITY AND FLOURISHING

broke the news that only boys could become priests, Pacyniak retorted, "When I grow up, I want to be a boy."[17] From the start, their gendered self-understanding was tied to a deep sense of personal and vocational calling. This put them at risk within a deeply cisgender, patriarchal religious tradition that misidentified them as a girl.[18]

Pacyniak attended Smith College and was president of the local Newman Association. They stood out for their advocacy in the church. Pacyniak later remarked, "Other people wanted to become president. I wanted to overthrow the Vatican."[19] When studying at Harvard Divinity School for their master's degree, Pacyniak began to publicly identify as a trans male, but found traditional notions of masculinity too restricting and came out as trans nonbinary.

After a time at Boston University's School of Theology, Pacyniak moved to San Diego where, in 2017, they began serving as pastor of the Mary Magdelene Apostle Catholic Community, an independent Catholic Church. Their dream of becoming a priest was realized in 2020, when the Roman Catholic Women Priests ordained Pacyniak as the first known trans, nonbinary priest.[20] It was a learning moment for the group. Pacyniak explained, "The Roman Catholic Women Priests movement is made up of a majority of cisgender women—and there have been a lot of conversations, some difficult, in my time with them."[21] Their colleagues learned to use they/them pronouns, and their parish changed its liturgical language to be more inclusive of nonbinary people.[22] Pacyniak's persistence opened new spaces for trans people in the progressive Catholic community.

Since then, Pacyniak's vocation has grown among "those Catholics who feel there is no room for them within the Catholic Church. Jesus calls us to the margins, and my work on the margins of the institutional

---

[17] Rich Barlow, "Kori Pacyniak and the Women Priests Push for Changes in the Church," *Bostonia*, January 28, 2022, bu.edu.

[18] See Diane Dougherty, "Patriarchal Power in the Catholic Church," in *Hating Girls* (Brill, 2021), 177–201.

[19] Peter Rowe, "Transgender, Nonbinary, and Now a Catholic Priest," *San Diego Union-Tribune*, February 16, 2020, sandiegouniontribune.com.

[20] Rowe, "Transgender, Nonbinary, and Now a Catholic Priest."

[21] Barlow, "Kori Pacyniak and the Women Priests Push for Changes in the Church."

[22] Barlow, "Kori Pacyniak and the Women Priests Push for Changes in the Church."

JASON STEIDL JACK

church doesn't require a blessing from Rome."[23] Here, Pacyniak's existence outside the hierarchy benefits their ministry among outsiders. Although they are technically excommunicated due to their ordination, Pacyniak's priesthood embodies the pastoral priorities of Pope Francis's pontificate, which seeks to go to the margins of the church and dialogue with those excluded and hurt by the same church.[24]

Recently, Pacyniak has been completing their PhD at the University of California Riverside. Their dissertation, *Sacred Bodies, Sacred Lives: Trans Catholic Joy, Resistance, and Liberation*, offers an ethnography of trans Catholics.[25] The work explicitly challenges traditional Catholic teaching on gender, which relies on archaic Aristotelean and Thomistic frameworks.[26] Reflecting on trans experience, Pacyniak writes, "Our diverse bodies, genders, sexualities are a reflection of God's infinite and amazing diversity. To live our lives authentically, being true to ourselves and God who made us in God's own image is our purpose. What better way to preach God's love than to live into who God created us to be?[27] For Pacyniak, the gospel is good news for queer folks, whose ostracized lives embody the divine and whose stories reveal God's gracious work.

A third figure in the movement for transgender ministry is Sr. Luisa Derouen, a cisgender woman religious who has ministered to trans folks since 1999. She entered the Eucharistic Missionaries of St. Dominic in 1961 and spent most of her life serving in parish ministry, spiritual direction, and retreat work. In 1998, a year before Sr. Jeannine Gramick, the well-known cofounder of New Ways Ministry, was formally silenced by the Vatican, Derouen requested permission from her superiors to minister to gay, lesbian, and bisexual people.[28] She received a positive response, but, given the sensitive nature of the work, was asked to

---

[23] Barlow, "Kori Pacyniak and the Women Priests Push for Changes in the Church."

[24] For more on Pope Francis, see Andrea Riccardi, *To the Margins* (Orbis Books, 2018).

[25] Kori Pacyniak, "Transgender Catholics Research Study," https://www.trans gendercatholics.com.

[26] Craig Ford, "Our New Galileo Affair," *Horizons* 50, no. 2 (December 2023): 255–92.

[27] Kori Pacyniak, "God Doesn't Want You to Be Miserable," *New Ways Ministry*, February 4, 2024, newwaysministry.org.

[28] See Congregation for the Doctrine of the Faith, Notification Regarding Sister Jeannine Gramick, SSND, and Father Robert Nugent, SDS, May 31, 1999, vatican.va.

TRANS CATHOLIC VULNERABILITY AND FLOURISHING   **23**

remain discrete.[29] LGBTQ ministry would make her and her religious order vulnerable within an institutional church not ready to receive it.

Derouen needed resources to work with LGBTQ people, so she attended a gathering of Parents, Families, and Friends of Lesbians and Gays in Louisiana, where she lived at the time. At her first meeting she listened to a trans woman named Courtney, who told her, "You get this! We really need people like you. For many of us this is a profoundly spiritual journey but we don't have spiritual people who understand us and are willing to walk with us."[30] Derouen realized that her work would not be with gays and lesbians, but with trans folks.

Over the next couple of decades, Derouen companioned more than 250 trans persons. Derouen related, "Most transgender persons with any affiliation to organized religion have been told that to proceed with transition would be a serious sin. My primary message to them has been that when we are moving toward truth in our lives, God is with us and not against us. Truth never leads us away from God."[31] In addition to spiritual companioning and direction, she helped trans people through difficult relationships with their families and sponsored "Trans Awareness Evenings" to foster dialogue.[32]

In 2014, Derouen went public with her story in an *Al Jazeera* profile piece, taking the pseudonym "Sister Monica" to protect herself and her congregation.[33] She only fully came out in 2018, at which time she noted, "Transgender people are increasingly becoming visible in every arena of life. . . . Now is the time for me to stand with them publicly and give witness to their dignity and worth as human beings and precious children of God."[34] Publicly claiming her role as an advocate for trans people was risky, but it also brought worldwide attention to the trans community's spiritual needs. Now in her early eighties, Derouen is the most visible matriarch of the Catholic movement for trans affirmation.

---

[29] Sister Monica, "God's Hidden People," 2014, lgbtqreligiousarchives.org.

[30] Luisa Derouen, "Luisa Derouen Biography," *LGBTQ Religious Archives Network*, November 2023, lgbtqreligiousarchives.org.

[31] Derouen, "Luisa Derouen Biography."

[32] Derouen, "Luisa Derouen Biography."

[33] Nathan Schneider, "A Nun's Secret Ministry to the Transgender Community," *Al Jazeera*, March 2, 2014, america.aljazeera.com.

[34] "Derouen, "Luisa Derouen Biography."

Pushing the Boundaries of LGBTQ Catholic Ministries

In addition to individual advocacy, national LGBTQ Catholic organizations have expanded to include trans concerns in recent years. DignityUSA added the "T" to lesbian, gay, and bi ministry in the 1990s, when many LGBTQ groups began to include trans people in the movement's growing acronym. Just because DignityUSA claimed to include trans folks, however, did not make it so. Even within a national LGBTQ Catholic group, trans folks were often invisible. In the early 2000s, DignityUSA's organizing was far more focused on the struggle for marriage equality than the plight of trans people.[35]

That started to change when trans members organized a caucus to represent their needs at DignityUSA conventions. Fredrikka Joy Maxwell, a black trans Catholic from Nashville, recalled, "There was a realization that if we wanted any kinds of trans programming, we would need to do something ourselves."[36] In the late 2000s, Maxwell and other trans folks began sharing their experiences with the DignityUSA community to build awareness around the challenges trans people face. A 2009 DignityUSA newsletter was dedicated to the stories of trans Catholics and included an article on the origins of Trans Day of Remembrance, along with practical suggestions for local chapters to mark the somber day.[37] Liturgies marking the violence against trans persons served as a rallying cry for DignityUSA to do something about it.

A new wave of awareness crested in 2014, a time when many Americans were learning about trans people such as Laverne Cox and Caitlyn Jenner. That fall, DignityUSA's *Quarterly Voice* covered trans spirituality. The publication's editors acknowledged trans experience as "a topic that challenges the boundaries of traditional Catholic thinking" but also "one that speaks to the very core of DignityUSA's mission."[38] Though controversial to many gay and lesbian Catholics, the community's embrace of trans concerns brought new life to the organization. Soon, the

---

[35] "Recalling Our Roots," notes from DignityUSA Trans Caucus call, November 1, 2017, dignityusa.org.

[36] "Recalling Our Roots," notes from DignityUSA Trans Caucus call.

[37] Fredrikka Joy Maxwell, "DignityUSA's Transgender Day of Remembrance," *Dateline* 18, no. 10 (November 2009), dignityusa.org.

[38] DignityUSA, *Quarterly Voice* 12, no. 1 (Fall 2014), dignityusa.org.

group's board of directors underwent training to better support trans members. The movement was so successful that, following a national meeting in Boston, one participant beamed, "Trans activism is taking afoot in Dignity, and their voices want to be heard in Catholic dioceses across the country that will eventually inform and impact the Vatican."[39]

In recent years, DignityUSA has remained a vocal critic of transphobia in the institutional church, issuing condemnations of ecclesial rhetoric and theologies that dehumanize trans people.[40] In 2022, the ministry expanded its reach by spearheading a public campaign called *Beloved by God: A Declaration of a Catholic Commitment to Trans-Affirmation*, which was endorsed by several women's religious communities, progressive Catholic groups, and leading LGBTQ theologians and allies.[41]

Other LGBTQ ministries have also evolved to include trans concerns. One of the most prominent is Fortunate Families, a ministry in Lexington, Kentucky, that supports LGBTQ Catholics and their families through education and dialogue in dioceses, schools, and other Catholic institutions. What makes Fortunate Families remarkable is that, unlike other national LGBTQ Catholic ministries, it does not dissent from church teaching, allowing it to build strategic partnerships with church leaders who may not otherwise be open to LGBTQ concerns.[42] In developing its ministry to trans people, Fortunate Families risked alienating nonaffirming Catholics to address the pressing needs of trans Catholics and their families.

When Fortunate Families began in 2004, its primary mission was to support the parents of gays and lesbians who had a hard time integrating their Catholic faith with their children's sexuality. By 2017, when JR Zerkowski became the group's executive director, society had changed. Marriage equality was a constitutional right. Same-sex couples could live relatively normal lives without fear of persecution and violence. Instead of parents trying to reconcile their Catholic faith with their children's sexuality, families now reached out for help understanding

---

[39] Irene Monroe, "DignityUSA Moving Toward Radical Inclusion," *Windy City Times*, July 26, 2017, windycitytimes.com.

[40] See, for example, DignityUSA, "A Letter to Catholics About the Vatican's *Dignitas Infinita* (On Human Dignity: We Are with You)," April 8, 2024, dignityusa.org.

[41] DignityUSA, *Beloved by God*, belovedbygod.faith.

[42] Jack, *LGBTQ Catholic Ministry*, 72–77.

their trans family members.[43] To address the lack of resources for family members of trans people, Zerkowski welcomed Christine Zuba, a transgender woman and eucharistic minister from New Jersey, onto the board of directors in 2019.[44] In 2024, Br. Christian Mattson, a theologian who lives in the Diocese of Lexington, Kentucky, and is thought to be the first openly trans hermit, also joined.[45]

In addition to welcoming trans board members, Fortunate Families partnered with Sr. Luisa Derouen to create a pastoral formation program for accompanying trans people. She gathered resources from decades of ministry and designed a fifteen-unit online program with readings, videos, and testimonials to equip others for the work.[46] In its first year, nearly fifty parents, family members, and teachers of trans individuals completed the formation program, renewing Fortunate Family's commitment to supporting the families and allies of LGBTQ Catholics.

Conclusion

The stories of trans Catholics and their allies reveal the vulnerabilities and limitations they faced to grow personally, vocationally, and in communities of advocacy. Rev. Dr. Nancy Ledins left the certainties of priesthood and marriage to pursue her gender transition and new forms of vocational leadership. Kori Pacyniak risked the ire of a cisgender-biased, patriarchal church and lack of understanding within the women priests movement to pursue their priestly vocation. Sr. Luisa Derouen walked through the danger of publicly identifying as a woman religious who ministers to trans people. Trans members of DignityUSA claimed their belonging and fought for recognition in the LGBTQ Catholic community when it was dominated by cisgender concerns. Fortunate Families embraced vulnerability in the institutional church by including transgender people on its board of directors.

---

[43] Jack, *LGBTQ Catholic Ministry*, 77.

[44] Christine Zuba, "I Am a Transgender Catholic Woman," *Outreach*, June 5, 2022, outreach.faith.

[45] Jack Jenkins, "Catholic Diocesan Hermit Approved by Kentucky Bishop Comes Out as Transgender," *Religion News Service*, May 19, 2024, religionnews.com.

[46] Fortunate Families, "Transgender Ministry of Accompaniment," fortunate-families.com.

Facing potential and real adversity was transformative for these individuals and organizations, but it also rippled out to the broader church. Ledins's life raised questions about women's flourishing in the Catholic hierarchy. Pacyniak helped the women priests movement include trans and nonbinary people. Derouen made it possible for other ministers to follow in her steps. DignityUSA became an outspoken critic of transphobia in the institutional church, and Fortunate Family created a ministry formation program to change the church from within.

In their vulnerability and risk-taking, trans and allied Catholics moved the church toward justice and compassion. As the institutional church grapples with questions related to trans people and their flourishing, it might learn from the examples I've outlined above and, by grappling with its own vulnerabilities, insecurities, and unknowing, recognize that its relationship with trans people may ultimately depend on its embrace of humility and honesty.

Beyond the Closet,
Toward the Horizon

Contemplative Practice
as Queer Flourishing

Barbara Anne Kozee

In 1995, *Newsweek* magazine released a cover featuring three people behind the large words "Bisexuality: Not Gay, Not Straight, a New Sexual Identity Emerges."[1] While this cover does not align with our contemporary understandings of gender and sexuality, it shows the rapidity with which social consciousness of sexual orientation has evolved. The increased visibility of bisexual identity posed a problem to the idea that sexuality consisted of binary attractions, a problematization that would continue with the increased visibility of nonbinary gender identity in the coming decades. "Coming out" is no longer easily defined by stepping outside of a clearly defined closet into a universally intelligible idea of "homosexuality."

In this chapter, I consider the ways that queer theory of gender and sexuality has contested terms in the public sphere regarding "coming out" and "the closet" for the ways that they have created consequential binaries such as safety/vulnerability, public/private, queer/not queer. Instead, for queer theorists, creation as related to sexual identity remains in a constant state of renegotiation—there is something about

---

[1] "Bisexuality," *Newsweek*, July 16, 1995, https://www.newsweek.com/bisexuality-184830.

queerness that is always on the horizon, beyond our reach, and certainly beyond the language of the closet.

I argue that these theoretical and anthropological underpinnings of the field can be viewed as resonant with the theological anthropology of Karl Rahner, who stresses God as mystery, the incomprehensible ground of our being. Rahner's anthropology leads him to emphasize human flourishing as encountering the divine in freedom. Writing contemplatively in works such as *Encounters with Silence* allowed Rahner to implicitly develop an ethical component to his own anthropology: attentiveness to love.

Attending to the concerns of queer epistemology and Rahnerian anthropology shows how cultivating contemplative awareness to divine mystery and love can be an ethical practice for queer flourishing. Queer people view their lives not on a linear binarism of coming out of the closet and into a publicly intelligible queer category, but rather in line with the intersecting horizons of queer studies and Rahner's theology. Flourishing is a sexually integrated and distinctly spiritual journey toward love of God, self, and others—a constant state of discovery and becoming.

"The Closet" and Queer Theory of Identity

The modern gay liberation movement in the US dates itself to the 1969 riots at Stonewall Inn in New York. These riots abruptly brought the private sphere of queer and trans life into the public arena in a political way, demanding a right to exist without fear of policing or violence. Accompanying this irruption of marginal sexuality onto the public sphere was the rhetoric of "coming out." Eve Kosofsky Sedgwick's *Epistemology of the Closet* takes a critical look at the construction of language and the social function of terms like homo/heterosexuality. Sedgwick writes, "[E]ven the phrase 'the closet' as a publicly intelligible signifier for gay-related epistemological issues is made available . . . only by the difference made by the post-Stonewall gay politics oriented around coming *out* of the closet."[2] National Coming Out Day was founded in 1988 to celebrate living freely as gay or lesbian, an example

---

[2] Eve Kosofsky Sedgwick, *Epistemology of the Closet* (University of California Press, 2008), 14.

30   *BARBARA ANNE KOZEE*

of the solidification of the closet into national discourse. Sedgwick's argument is that the idea of the closet and of "homosexual" identity represented a new form of world mapping into binary categories. In this section, I detail the contestations that queer theories of identity have posed to the larger narrative of "coming out" and their anthropological implications.

The idea of queer visibility to which coming out of the closet harkens has been a source of distinct joy for the queer community. Around the world, Pride marches announce the presence of a wide range of sexualities and gender identities, celebrating pride in one's identity over the shame that can accompany the experience of being closeted. There are distinct ways that the celebration of visibility, being "out," has served to protect queer people in the legal sphere and in the workplace. In contemporary politics, this protection gains a renewed sense of relevancy when considering the introduction of the "Don't Say Gay" bill signed in March 2022 in Florida[3] and the history of "Don't Ask, Don't Tell" politics in the US military.[4]

Sedgwick does not deny the concrete social impacts that the possibility of being outside the closet has had for queer people. However, she writes that "[t]here are risks in making salient the continuity and centrality of the closet, in a historical narrative that does not have as a fulcrum a saving vision—whether located in past or future—of its apocalyptic rupture. A meditation that lacks that particular utopian organization will risk glamorizing the closet itself, if only by default; will risk presenting as inevitable or somehow valuable its exactions, its deformations, its disempowerment and sheer pain."[5] Sedgwick is concerned about the ways that working within an epistemology of the closet limits our imaginations of what is possible for queer flourishing. There is a way that the closet imaginary depends on the idea of certain vulnerable queer bodies, disempowerment, sheer pain.

As exemplified by the opening image of the *Newsweek* cover and public policy, there is a way that the closet contains a certain degree of

---

[3] Anthony Izaguirre, "'Don't Say Gay' Bill Signed by Florida Gov. Ron DeSantis," *AP News*, March 28, 2022, https://apnews.com/article/florida-dont-say-gay-law-signed-56aee61f075a12663f25990c7b31624d.

[4] "Repeal of 'Don't Ask, Don't Tell,'" *Human Rights Campaign*, https://www.hrc.org/our-work/stories/repeal-of-dont-ask-dont-tell.

[5] Sedgwick, *Epistemology of the Closet*, 68.

BEYOND THE CLOSET, TOWARD THE HORIZON   **31**

violence in its ordering of gender and sexuality into neatly packaged narratives that often operate in simplistic binaries. For Sedgwick, this is due to an approach to knowledge as stable and sexual categories as, therefore, easily identifiable. Queer affirmation, on the other hand, privileges unknowing. The hermeneutic that Sedgwick proposes in this foundational text for the field of queer theory is described by Gila Ashtor as "the will-not-to-know."[6] If the closet represents a clearly defined and knowable past and a neatly intelligible queer identity of the present and future, queer epistemology resists the idea that there is a completely "knowable" queer self. Queerness resists anticipating what is and is not queer. This insight from Sedgwick becomes a defining characteristic of the field of queer theory. The term *queer* exists as a noun, adjective, and verb. It is distinctive for its embrace of dislodgement and resistance to any real categorical definition. In this way, the category, at least in theory, aims to be in a constant state of self-critique and becoming.[7]

Against the stable knowing of the closet and a postcloset binary, the embrace of unknowing by queer theorists has produced an imagistic theory on temporality, futurity, and an understanding of queer identity that always exists in a state of longing for the unattainable realm of queer liberation. José Esteban Muñoz centers his book on queer survival around the image of a horizon: "Queerness is not yet here. Queerness is an ideality. Put another way, we are not yet queer. We may never touch queerness, but we can feel it as the warm illumination of a horizon imbued with potentiality."[8] Muñoz calls for queer people to strive "to think and feel a *then and there*."[9] This is not a dualistic or an other-worldly framework, but rather a call for attentiveness to queer practices and aesthetics that represent "a doing for and toward the future"[10] that Muñoz elaborates throughout his book.

Alison Kafer also theorizes about queer/feminist/crip temporality

---

[6] Gila Ashtor, *Homo Psyche: On Queer Theory and Erotophobia* (Fordham University Press, 2021), 40.

[7] Barbara Anne Kozee, "Gila Ashtor's 'Homo Psyche' a Bold Field Intervention Relevant for Liberation Theology," *National Catholic Reporter*, June 11, 2022, https://www.ncronline.org/news/opinion/gila-ashtors-homo-psyche-bold-field-intervention-relevant-liberation-theology.

[8] José Esteban Muñoz, *Cruising Utopia: The Then and There of Queer Futurity* (New York University Press, 2009), 1.

[9] Muñoz, *Cruising Utopia*.

[10] Muñoz, *Cruising Utopia*.

32 BARBARA ANNE KOZEE

in her foundational text for the field of disability theory. Kafer understands temporality as "flex time not just expanded but exploded; it requires reimagining our notions of what can and should happen in time, or recognizing how expectations of 'how long things take' are based on very particular minds and bodies."[11] Like Muñoz, Kafer aims to "explode" our understanding of temporality and to make contested what often goes unthought due to our assumptions about normative bodies. She suggests that the expansive imaginary around sex, gender, and disability that she proposes "can never be fully or finally achieved, but serves as a kind of hopeful horizon."[12]

It is striking how theological queer theorists can sound when attempting to understand the vulnerability of queer bodies and the violence rendered by certain rhetorical devices such as the closet. Sedgwick's opening chapter quote for her *Epistemology of the Closet* is from Marcel Proust's *The Captive*, where he writes of social "lies" or narrative myths that one overcomes: "that lie is one of the few things in the world that can open windows for us on to what is new and unknown, that can awaken in us sleeping senses for the contemplation of universes that otherwise we should never have known."[13] True to Sedgwick's argument, the Proust quote illuminates the beauty of unknowing and its possibility for awakening us, via contemplation, to a form of imagination or mystical knowing that would previously have gone unattained.

A turn to Rahner's theology and anthropology, connected to his contemplative writings in explicit ways, can help to illuminate a theological and contemplative dimension to how queer theorists define flourishing. Contemplative practice and regular encounters with the paschal process of knowing, unknowing, and knowing afresh pushes against the closet logic of gender and sexuality and cultivates a view on the self as always in the process of becoming.

Rahner's Anthropology and Contemplative Practice

Rahner appropriates the notion of horizon from the philosophy of Martin Heidegger, but the horizon he has in mind also has much

---

[11] Alison Kafer, *Feminist, Queer, Crip* (Indiana University Press, 2013), 27.
[12] Kafer, *Feminist, Queer, Crip*, 16.
[13] Marcel Proust, *The Captive*, cited in Sedgwick, *Epistemology of the Closet*, 67.

BEYOND THE CLOSET, TOWARD THE HORIZON   **33**

in common with that of queer theorists, such as Muñoz and Kafer. Rahner's interpreter, William V. Dych, emphasizes Rahner's approach to knowledge—which is often invoked, in part, by the image of the horizon—as moving "not from without, but from within existence"[14] such that theology is able to dialogue with modern anthropological concerns. In this section, I explore Rahner's understanding of God as mystery in the life of the believer and the ways that his invocation of the horizon becomes an explicit claim to knowledge and knowing similar to that of queer theorists. Rahner adds the theological stakes involved in queer flourishing.

In *Grace in Freedom*, Rahner meditates on "the little word 'God' "[15] and provides some musings on the topic. For Rahner, the word *God* simultaneously evokes the concept of higher being and recognizes the way that the term is always fundamentally limited, a failure to describe the full image of that to which it refers. This is the dynamic that leads Rahner to describe God as mystery. God, for Rahner, is both beyond our comprehension and the conditioning ground for how we experience ourselves, our interiority, and the world around us, our exteriority. We can become attentive to this dynamic, to the mystery of God.[16] God infuses the created world in an active form of presence. It is not we who confront the ground, but the ground of all that silently confronts us. Our situation of response to our creator is inescapable; it is the most natural thing that we could do. And when we do those hard or joyful activities of embracing death and life, we are fundamentally involved with something incomprehensible. In a sense, we are suddenly made aware of the divine creaturely dynamic. Moments of spiritual encounter reveal to us the infinite horizon of God and the long, eternal process of becoming.

This contemplative understanding of God illuminates the concepts of freedom, mystery, and transcendence that define Rahner's theology of relationship between God and creation. For Rahner, transcendental experience is how we enter in freedom into God's mystery. It is not merely an experience of knowledge, but also of the will and of free-

---

[14] William V. Dych, "Theology in a New Key," in *A World of Grace: An Introduction to the Themes and Foundations of Karl Rahner's Theology*, ed. Leo J. O'Donovan (Georgetown University Press, 1995), 4.

[15] Karl Rahner, *Grace in Freedom* (Herder and Herder, 1969), 183.

[16] Karl Rahner, *Encounters with Silence*, trans. James M. Demske (Newman Press, 1966), 193.

dom. Humanity's consciousness of God is that which is beyond the strictly definable, the God that exists prior to the human limitations of language. Rahner's theology begins with the person, the hearer of God's message. We experience uncreated grace in the mystery of our daily lives and the questions that it brings are the foremost ways in which we can understand God. The methodological choice to begin with the person and our questions makes human flourishing central to Rahner's anthropology, as we can choose to move in freedom closer in proximity or further from the horizon of God's mystery. It is this notion of our transcendental freedom to move toward a radically present yet eternally mysterious God, who we can know more fully through greater response to God's self-communication in our own beings, that is most compellingly concretized by the contemplative tradition and by Rahner's own contemplative writings. These are tools from within the tradition that aid all faithful in confronting deeply felt experiences, but it is rarely permissible to think them available to the queer person in the process of becoming.

In his book *Into the Silent Land* on the practice of contemplation, Martin Laird writes often of the role of attentiveness and stillness, accompanied by silence, in becoming attuned to God. "Discovering" God in contemplative practice is often about becoming aware of that which is already present, the ways that we already commune with God. This type of concentration that asks us to be still, to be silent, requires cultivation and practice. It is not easy to enter our deepest selves in a world of pain, suffering, and brokenness. Contemplation may seem like an activity set apart from our daily lives, but this could not be further from the truth; contemplation helps us to engage our lives more deeply. Contemplation requires that we look squarely at our feelings, including the most feared and negative emotions, and sit below them, on a deeper and forever deepening ground. By engaging contemplative practice, we learn "how *to be* in this wound. When we discover the silent core of this wound, we discover a place of noncondemnation, of silent, loving communion with God and of compassion for all."[17]

Bringing spiritual insights to bear on Rahner's anthropology suggests that cultivating a contemplative life can help one to live out their understanding of our free choice to move transcendentally along the

---

[17] Rahner, *Encounters with Silence*, 121.

BEYOND THE CLOSET, TOWARD THE HORIZON **35**

infinitely distant horizon of knowing God. Contemplation allows us to encounter God as mystery in our daily lives and to feel ourselves in relation to a creator. We can embrace the unknown and become more ourselves.

Encounters with Silence

Rahner's own contemplative writings in *Encounters with Silence* make explicit the ethical practices that can accompany and thus allow us to "live out" his anthropology. Rahner's engagement with contemplation is a manner of *being in the wound*. Throughout the ten prayers of the book, positioned as communication between Rahner and the various ways he chooses to name God in relation to himself, there is a sense of the dependence of Rahner on the creator. Rahner's prayers more explicitly draw out an ultimate understanding of love. There is a way that this felt form of love is best experienced and articulated contemplatively in prayer and guides our relationships to God, ourselves, and others. For queer people, practicing self-love and love of God and others in contemplation can become a horizon of discovery and a regular ethical practice and way of living that privileges the mysteries we are to ourselves and diminishes the relevance of the closet binary.

Love is a central concept in *Encounters with Silence*. In "God of My Life," Rahner emphasizes the incomprehensible mystery that is God in ways that harken to his academic insights. This reflection on God culminates in an understanding of God as love. "Only in love can I find You, my God. In love the gates of my soul spring open, allowing me to breathe a new air of freedom and forget my own petty self. In love my whole being streams forth out of the rigid confines of narrowness and anxious self-assertion."[18] By entering into love, Rahner experiences the freedom that he writes of, transcending the narrow elements of his cognition and unifying with that which is mystery. There is, indeed, a felt experience of joy in this prayerful unity: "In this state of joy my mind no longer tries to bring You forcibly down to its level, in order to wrest You from Your eternal secret, but rather love seizes me and carries me up to Your level, into You."[19] Rather than the seeking of the

---

[18] Rahner, *Encounters with Silence*, 8–9.
[19] Rahner, *Encounters with Silence*, 9.

36 BARBARA ANNE KOZEE

human mind, entering joy allows Rahner to be found and seized by the love of the divine.

Love experienced in the world is present in Rahner's prayers "God of Knowledge" and "God of My Daily Routine." In the former, Rahner emphasizes the limits of traditional understandings of knowledge, saying, "[I]t seems to me that knowing touches only the surface of things, that it fails to penetrate to the heart, to the depths of my being where I am most truly 'I.' "[20] While knowledge is limited, love is transcendent. Rahner asks, "How can we approach the heart of all things, the true heart of reality? Not by knowledge alone, but by the full flower of knowledge, love." Rahner is limited in his own knowledge of his experiences of the world and of suffering. He relies not on his own ability to understand, but rather on loving a God who enlightens on an incomprehensible horizon. Both love and the response to love allow Rahner to contemplate the core theological categories of his academic anthropology. This love, for Rahner, is infused throughout all things and represents a horizon, a constant state of (be)coming. In "God of My Daily Routine," Rahner writes practically from a sense of cultivating awareness to divine mystery among the mundane activities of daily life. Worldly contemplation can lead us to encounters with the divine, even in the most mundane moments.[21] Cultivating contemplative awareness allows us to experience and discover love *in the world* in a very distinct way.

Rahner ends *Encounters with Silence* with an Advent prayer, a contemplation on the God who is to come. He muses on the annual liturgy of entering into a state of patience and waiting for the coming of a God who has, in a sense, already come. But is it so that God has really already come? "Are You the eternal Advent? Are You He who is always still to come, but never arrives in such a way as to fulfill our expectations?"[22] In this way, what does it mean to be a people in waiting? Rahner evokes his image of the horizon: "Are You only the distant horizon surrounding the world of our deeds and sufferings, the horizon which, no matter where we roam, is always just as far away?"[23] Rahner prays with the tension between the desire and longing for the coming of God's nearness and

---

[20] Rahner, *Encounters with Silence*, 29.

[21] Rahner, *Encounters with Silence*, 52.

[22] Rahner, *Encounters with Silence*, 80.

[23] Rahner, *Encounters with Silence*, 80.

yet the incomprehensibility that always puts God at a distance, on the horizon. Rahner's anthropology in this Advent prayer creates a situation of existential agony, perhaps. He ends the prayer with an insight about God's perpetual coming: "Slowly a light is beginning to dawn. I'm beginning to understand something I have known for a long time: You are still in the process of Your coming. Your appearance in the form of a slave was only the beginning of Your coming . . . Actually You haven't come—You're still coming . . . Behold, You come. And Your coming is neither past nor future, but the present, which has only to reach its fulfillment. Now it is still the one single hour of Your Advent[.]"[24] The agony becomes peace, as Rahner considers incarnation in perpetuity, a process that comes to bear on the present, the radical now, as much as the historical event that we celebrate in Advent liturgy. Christ, the ultimate microcosm for Christian anthropology, exists in a constant process of discovery and (be)coming. In this way, Christ becomes near to humanity, and especially to the queer person.

Scholars of sex and religion such as Donna Freitas have shown how the existential ability to integrate spirituality and sexuality threatens queer existence.[25] The Trevor Project's annual survey of LGBTQ youth details perpetually high rates of youth suicide,[26] and data show the negative impact of organized religion in the lives of queer people.[27] In the wake of this violent closet epistemology rendered onto vulnerable queer bodies, it is important to see the embrace of sexuality as contemplative journey within the confines of queer flourishing. Just as queer theorists celebrate the aspects of queerness that are on the horizon or "not yet here" as countercultural acts of self-love, Rahner's contemplative writings show a love of self, God, and others that goes beyond resisting or repressing fear of the unknown toward grounding spirituality and prayer in that very mystery and the perpetual process of incarnational becoming. While the intersections between Rahner

---

[24] Rahner, *Encounters with Silence*, 85–87.

[25] Donna Freitas, *Sex and the Soul: Juggling Sexuality, Spirituality, Romance, and Religion on America's College Campuses* (Oxford University Press, 2008), 187–99.

[26] "2022 National Survey on LGBTQ Youth Mental Health," *The Trevor Project*, https://www.thetrevorproject.org/survey-2022/#intro.

[27] Bec Roldan, "Many LGBTQ+ Women Face Discrimination and Violence, but Find Support in Friendships," *National Public Radio*, July 1, 2023, https://www.npr.org/sections/health-shots/2023/07/01/1185536324/many-lgbtq-women-face-discrimination-and-violence-but-find-support-in-friendship.

and queer studies may have limits for Christian ethicists, especially for attempting to construct a normative sexual ethic, this mutual acknowledgment of the horizon of becoming is profound.

Conclusion

The horizon is a theoretical line, created by the apparent meeting of the sky with the earth. It depends entirely on one's perspective and standpoint. The view of the horizon for one person may look different than that for another standing just twenty feet away. The closer one moves toward the horizon, the farther it moves away. It is in these ways that the horizon of queer studies and Rahnerian anthropology asks a certain humility of humanity. The closet and the idea of coming out of the closet as a fully realized and intelligible queer person depends on a certain approach to knowledge of gender and sexuality as fixed and uncontested. There is both lived and existential violence that is perpetuated onto vulnerable queer bodies as a result of the closet. Queer flourishing according to this queer and Rahnerian horizon of freedom, transcendence, and the mysterious relationship between God and creation is in some sense achieved through the practice of contemplation. Attentiveness to God as the ground of our beings allows love to become the center of the Christian life, a consequential revelation for young queer people who often struggle to see themselves as capable of being loved. Rather than rigid and finite forms of knowing, our experiences of sexuality and gender become an integrated part of a lifelong spiritual journey, a place to encounter the divine. "We can master life with scientific formulae insofar as one has to make one's way among various events, and this may be frequently successful. But man himself is grounded in an abyss which no formula can measure. We must have sufficient courage to experience this abyss as the holy mystery of love—then it may be called God."[28]

---

[28] Rahner, *Grace in Freedom*, 195.

"Unknowing" God and Intellectual Disability

Retrieving a Fourteenth-Century Perspective

Susan McElcheran

People with intellectual disabilities are particularly vulnerable to exclusion from the sacraments and other aspects of the life of the church. I knew a young man named Liam who was preparing to receive his First Communion and who was refused as a candidate for the sacrament on the grounds that he was completely nonverbal and "wouldn't understand." Erinn Staley tells a similar story about the baptism of a girl with Down Syndrome whom I will call Rosie. A woman attending the baptism remarked how sad it was that Rosie would never be able to receive the Eucharist because of her lack of cognitive ability to understand it.[1] Embedded in such stories is the implicit theological claim that the ability to understand and accept logical propositions of faith is the only way by which God is known. Even though advances in cognitive neuroscience show that cognition is not exclusively brain centered, and that bodily, social, and affective processes contribute to knowledge-making,[2] a model in which propositional logic is central

---

[1] Erinn Staley, "Intellectual Disability and Mystical Unknowing: Contemporary Insights from Medieval Sources," *Modern Theology* 28, no. 3 (July 2012): 385.

[2] Shaun Gallagher, "Embodied Rationality," in *The Mystery of Rationality: Mind, Beliefs and the Social Sciences*, ed. G. Bronner and F. Di Iorio (Springer, 2018); Enrico Petracca, "Embodying Bounded Rationality: From Embodied Bounded Rationality to Embodied Rationality," *Frontiers in Psychology* 12 (September 2021), https://doi.org/10.3389/fpsyg.2021.710607.

40   SUSAN McELCHERAN

persists.[3] However, there are streams of thought within Christian tradition in which God is known more through affect than through reason. In this chapter I challenge the tendency to frame knowledge of God primarily in terms of the capacity for rational thought, and I use *The Cloud of Unknowing* as an example of affective and embodied knowledge of God.[4]

The term *affect* has a broader and more inclusive meaning than the narrower term *emotion*. Affect has historically included such concepts as passions, appetites, desires, emotions, impulses, and movements of the will.[5] Especially in medieval writers, affect has been seen as a channel of knowledge, as evidenced by Thomas Gallus who saw the principle of affection as a cognitive power, "the supreme cognitive power possessed by man, whereby the soul obtain[s] knowledge-in-love,"[6] and *The Cloud of Unknowing*, which asserts that God may be fully known by love but not by thought.[7] These strands of Christian thought assert not only that affective knowledge of God is valid but that it enables a closer approach to God than purely intellectual knowledge. I do not advocate an abandonment of rationality. Instead, I argue in company with many disability theorists and feminist scholars that we have inherited, largely from the Enlightenment, an impoverished and narrowed view of rationality, and that our understanding of reason needs to be expanded. My argument begins with a brief survey of some historical roots of this narrowed view of rationality and how it

---

[3] This in spite of Catholic teaching, as in Vatican II's *Dei Verbum*, in which God's revelation is first a matter of self-communication, and secondarily a propositional communication: Pope Paul VI, *Dei Verbum* (1965); see also Gerald O'Collins on *Dei Verbum*'s primary sense of revelation as "intimate communion" in addition to the secondary, propositional sense: Gerald O'Collins, "Vatican II's Theology of Revelation," in *The Oxford Handbook of Vatican II*, ed. Catherine E. Clifford and Massimo Faggioli (Oxford Academic, 2023), 201–16.

[4] This discussion is part of a larger project that uses mimetic theory as a bridge between intellectual disability studies and the Christian mystical tradition. See Susan McElcheran, "Masks, Morons, and Monsters: Stigma Theory and Intellectual Disability Studies in Conversation with Mimetic Theory," in *Contagion: Journal of Violence, Mimesis, and Culture* 32 (forthcoming).

[5] For a survey of the interrelation of affect, emotions, agency, and identity in Western thought, see Barbara J. McClure, *Emotions: Problems and Promise for Human Flourishing* (Baylor University Press, 2019).

[6] Thomas Gallus, *Glossa* (PL 122.272B, 274C, 279B, 282A).

[7] Phyllis Hodgson, ed., *The Cloud of Unknowing and the Book of Privy Counselling*, Original Series 218 (Early English Text Society, 1944), 26, lines 3–5.

"UNKNOWING" GOD AND INTELLECTUAL DISABILITY **41**

limits and distorts our perception of the human knowledge of God, and then proceeds to retrieve a pre-Enlightenment perspective in the anonymous fourteenth-century treatise on prayer *The Cloud of Unknowing*. I use this text because it focuses on movements of desire in the will as a way of knowing God and so is a clear example of strains of thought within the Christian tradition that support affective and embodied ways of knowing.

Rational Autonomy
and the Denial of Interdependence

The vision of reason that took hold powerfully in Western thought in the eighteenth-century Enlightenment[8] linked rationality with independence, freedom, and equality. For instance, Immanuel Kant and other eighteenth-century thinkers defined a person as a free agent endowed with rational autonomy. Liberal political philosophy proposed a society arranged by independent individuals organizing for mutual benefit. The "social contract" envisioned by thinkers such as Thomas Hobbes and John Locke assumed free, equal, and autonomous agents able to negotiate with others according to rational self-interest.

Disability thinkers have pointed out how this vision of rational autonomy limits the value accorded to kinds of knowledge that are not individualistic but are based more in human interdependence. Theologian Thomas Reynolds points out that the ideal of rational autonomy is based on a vision of individuals as self-creating and self-defining through their independent decisions. This view excludes interdependency and care for those with disabilities, since it bases equality on ideals of normalcy that stress individual autonomous agency.[9] Reynolds also observes that the ideal of rational autonomy is actually illusory, since it assumes that the individual precedes its social environment, whereas we know that

---

[8] For the purpose of this brief chapter, I focus on Enlightenment developments, but the Western conception of reason had a long history before these thinkers. For a more complete survey, including Plato and Descartes, see Val Plumwood, *Feminism and the Mastery of Nature* (Routledge, 1993); for another critique of Descartes's influence, see Antonio R. Damasio, *Descartes' Error: Emotion, Reason, and the Human Brain* (Quill–HarperCollins, 1994).

[9] Thomas E. Reynolds, *Vulnerable Communion: A Theology of Disability and Hospitality* (Brazos Press, 2008), 84, 81.

42 SUSAN McELCHERAN

human beings originate in a situation of interdependence.[10] Cognitive science shows that human learning is deeply embedded in a network of relationships with others and with the environment.[11]

Feminist Val Plumwood argues that reason has been distorted in Western consciousness and allied with power and control.[12] Plumwood's analysis presents our conception of reason as a historically conditioned construct. While there are many possible alternative conceptions of rationality, the mainstream Western conception of reason forms part of a dualistic framework of power and of domination, implicating this view of reason in the dynamics of subjugation and control. Plumwood defines this dualism as a denial of dependency on a subjugated other, which creates a region of devalued otherness. This kind of relationship forms a logical structure in which the relationships of domination and subordination, as well as the denial of dependency, determine the identities of both parties. Plumwood argues that reason and emotion have been set in dualistic opposition to each other, as have male and female, mind and body. On the dominating side of this framework are the concepts of reason, culture, male, mind, master, freedom, civilization, subject, and self. Opposing these are emotion, nature, female, body, slave, necessity, primitive, object, and other. The framework of opposition means that reason is also opposed to nature and to the body, since each term on the dominating side is opposed and superior to all those on the subjugated side.[13] While she does not mention people with intellectual disabilities, the stigma associated with lack of autonomous rationality would place them in the marginalized category opposed to reason. This framework of dualism illustrates the violence of a system in which some achieve ascendancy through the suppression and subjugation of others, and a superficial and violent form of flourishing is maintained through the denial of interdependency with those who are vulnerable.[14] A kind of dualism that opposes mind to matter has been thoroughly debunked by an increasing amount of research that links

---

[10] Reynolds, *Vulnerable Communion*, 88.

[11] Gallagher, "Embodied Rationality."

[12] Plumwood, *Feminism and the Mastery of Nature*.

[13] Plumwood, *Feminism and the Mastery of Nature*, 42–43.

[14] Plumwood's thesis accords with stigma theory, which has established that stigmatized categories are created by dominant groups to consolidate the security of their position by defining their identity in opposition to a despised Other. See Erving Goffman, *Stigma: Notes on the Management of Spoiled Identity* (J. Aronson, 1974).

bodily and social processes to the workings of the brain. The discovery of mirror neurons that enable us to imitate the actions of others, and even to imagine that we are performing the same actions as we watch others, has shown that many cerebral processes are linked to bodily, social, and environmental cues. When we watch someone else perform an action, these neurons activate within us the same neural activity as if we were performing the action ourselves.[15] This enables us to imitate the actions of others and to participate in their feelings when watching a video or reading a book. The science of embodied cognition has refuted the conception of the mind working in an abstract, mechanistic way. Some varieties of embodied cognition reject the idea of mental representations altogether, and those that retain the idea of mental representations propose that they derive from sensory, motor, interoceptive (visceral), and affective sources.[16] Increasingly, cognitive science scholars find evidence that cognition is thoroughly entangled with the experience of having a body that operates through sense and motor capacities that these capacities themselves depend on and are derived from biological, psychological, and social contexts.[17]

The Cloud of Unknowing and Knowledge of God: Affect and Embodiment

In offering *The Cloud of Unknowing* as one source for an affective and embodied knowledge of God, I will explore just a few points here: first, the way the *Cloud* author emphasizes the primacy of the will over the intellect in the knowledge of God; second, the central role of desire in the *Cloud*; third, the author's vision of a harmonized body/spirit union. Finally, I apply the *Cloud*'s way of knowing to the situation of people with intellectual disabilities in the church.

First, *The Cloud of Unknowing*, a text written for the purpose of helping a disciple to advance in prayer, considers the question that was much debated in medieval circles: Do we come to know God more

---

[15] Giacomo Rizzolati and Corrado Sinigaglia, *Mirroring Brains: How We Understand Others from the Inside*, trans. Frances Anderson (Oxford University Press, 2023), 64–67.

[16] Petracca, "Embodying Bounded Rationality.

[17] Lawrence A. Shapiro, "Conceptions of Embodiment," in *Embodied Cognition* (Routledge, 2011), 58–59.

44 SUSAN McELCHERAN

fully through the intellect or through the will? Along with other writers in the Middle Ages, the *Cloud* author was deeply immersed in the thought of Pseudo-Dionysius the Areopagite (hereafter Dionysius),[18] who maintained that intellect could only lead up to a certain point in the search for God. At the point where intellect failed, Dionysius said that God was known in a darkness to the human mind that was full of divine light: "[T]he most godlike knowledge of God is that which is known by unknowing."[19] While for Dionysius it was wholly in the darkness of the intellect that union with God took place, later scholars such as Hugh of St. Victor in the twelfth century and Hugh of Balma and Thomas Gallus in the thirteenth added that the darkness of the intellect allowed for the faculty of loving will to complete the soul's union with God.[20] Bonaventure also interpreted Dionysius in this way, saying that the Areopagite's most important teaching was about "the ecstatic love that transcends the knowledge of faith" and the unitive state in which all intellectual activities are left behind while the "*apex affectus totus*" is transformed into God.[21] In Hugh of St. Victor's view, "love enters and approaches where knowledge stays outside."[22] The principle of affection was described as the soul's chief cognitive power by Thomas Gallus.[23] The *Cloud* author clearly agrees with those who claim primacy for the loving power of the will in the process of union with God. He is in accord with Thomas Aquinas that the intellect is unable to reach God's essence whereas charity can achieve direct union with God.[24] However, he goes beyond this position and is closer to Wil-

---

[18] Pseudo-Dionysius, originally thought to be Paul's Athenian convert in Acts 17, is now dated in the early sixth century: Sarah Coakley, "Introduction," in *Re-Thinking Dionysius the Areopagite*, ed. Sarah Coakley and Charles M. Stang (Wiley-Blackwell, 2009), 1, 7n1.

[19] Dionysius, *De Divinis Nominibus*, chap. vii, in Clifton Wolters, trans., *The Cloud of Unknowing and Other Works* (Penguin Books, 1961).

[20] Hugh of Balma, *The Roads to Zion Mourn*, trans. Dennis Martin (Paulist Press, 1996), 155–70; Hugh of St. Victor, *In hierarchiam caelestem S. Dionysii* (PL 175: 1038D); Thomas Gallus, *Glossa* (PL 122.272B, 274C, 279B, 282A).

[21] *Bonaventure: The Soul's Journey into God, The Tree of Life, The Life of St. Francis*, trans. Ewert Cousins (Paulist Press, 1978), 7.4.

[22] Hugh of St. Victor, *In hierarchiam caelestem S. Dionysii* (PL 175: 1038D).

[23] Thomas Gallus, *Glossa* (PL 122.272B, 274C, 279B, 282A).

[24] *S.T.* 2-2, q. 180, a. 5, ad. 2; also *S.T.* 1-2, q. 27. a. 2, ad 2; 2-2. q, 27, a. 4.

"UNKNOWING" GOD AND INTELLECTUAL DISABILITY   **45**

liam of Thierry who says that love confers its own knowledge of God.[25] As the *Cloud* author explains, human beings have "two faculties, the power of knowing and the power of loving. To the first, to the intellect, God who made them is forever unknowable, but to the second, to love, he is completely knowable, and that by every separate individual."[26] Although one may think of all other things, even of the works of God, "yet of God himself can no man think. Therefore I will leave on one side everything I can think and choose for my love that thing which I cannot think! Why? Because he may well be loved, but not thought. By love can he be caught and held, but by thinking never."[27]

The *Cloud* author teaches his disciple how to reach this kind of knowledge in love through attention to the movements of desire in the will. Here is my second point, the central role of desire in the *Cloud*. The author focuses on the desire of the human will as instrumental in knowing God rather than rational capacity. The affective knowledge of God in the *Cloud* is gained through the Spirit's transformation of desire. God has "called you and led you to him by the desire of your heart"; God "kindled your desire full graciously, and fastened by it a leash of longing"; "It all depends on your desire"; "All your life now must be standing always in desire"; "This desire must always be wrought in your will."[28]

The author coordinates the movements of desire in the will with a medieval understanding of time. He explains that the smallest units into which time can be divided are called atoms and that we have just as many movements or impulses of our will in one hour as there are atoms of time.[29] He urges the novice to direct each of these impulses Godward. Although attempts to reach God will encounter at first only "a darkness, and as it were a cloud of unknowing," the disciple must "strike that thick cloud of unknowing with the sharp dart of longing love, and on no account whatever think of giving up."[30] The reader is urged to continue in this work "until you feel list," which Bernard

---

[25] John P. Clark, "Sources and Theology in 'The Cloud of Unknowing,'" *Downside Review* 98, no. 331 (April 1, 1980): 104–5.

[26] Wolters, *Cloud*, 63.

[27] Wolters, *Cloud*, 67–68.

[28] Wolters, *Cloud*, 13–15.

[29] Wolters, *Cloud*, 62.

[30] Wolters, *Cloud*, 61, 68.

46   SUSAN McELCHERAN

McGinn translates as "to sense, feel, or experience desire."[31] The process of this kind of prayer occurs through desire.

The third and final aspect of the *Cloud* that I discuss as evidence of an affective and embodied way to image God is the way in which the author treats the body and physicality. The author's respect for the physical world is seen throughout the text. He continually mentions body and soul together: "God wants to be served with body and soul, both together, as it is right";[32] in heaven we will know God "both in body and soul."[33] The way he sees impulses of the will as corresponding to atoms of time shows an understanding of human being as deeply embodied in a corporeal existence within the flux and movement of experience in time. He constantly uses bodily images: "lift up the foot of your love"[34] toward God; when thoughts distract you in prayer you are to "tread them down under a cloud of forgetting"; "step over them resolutely and eagerly, with a devout and kindling love, and try to penetrate that darkness above you. Strike that thick cloud of unknowing with the sharp dart of longing love."[35]

It may seem counterintuitive to use the *Cloud* as an example of embodiment when the author spends so much time in his text warning the reader not to take his metaphors in a literal physical sense. He repeatedly urges his reader, "Be careful not to interpret physically what is meant spiritually,"[36] and he says that those who interpret God's call in a physical rather than spiritual sense strain their hearts unnaturally in their breasts and manufacture an unnatural glow or a spurious warmth within themselves.[37] However, these cautions should not be seen as a devaluation of the body, since the author also cautions those who approach this work as solely a work of the mind. He says that people understanding it only as a mental process can "manufacture an experience that is neither spiritual nor physical."[38]

The *Cloud*'s warnings against an overly physical interpretation can

---

[31] Bernard McGinn, *The Presence of God: A History of Western Christian Mysticism* (Crossroad Herder & Herder, 2012), 5:404.

[32] Wolters, *Cloud*, 117.

[33] Wolters, *Cloud*, 79.

[34] My own translation from Hodgson, *Cloud*, 14.

[35] Wolters, *Cloud*, 68.

[36] Wolters, *Cloud*, 121.

[37] Wolters, *Cloud*, 113–14.

[38] Wolters, *Cloud*, 65.

"UNKNOWING" GOD AND INTELLECTUAL DISABILITY   **47**

be seen in part as a response to a tendency toward extreme physicality in the thoughts of his contemporaries. The age in which the *Cloud* author lived was one in which there was a heightened awareness and appreciation of corporeality. Caroline Walker Bynum has researched the physical manifestations of devotion in writers preceding and contemporary with the *Cloud*, and she observes "a heightened concern with matter, with corporeality, with sensuality. Although . . . some ambivalence about matter, some sharp and agonizing dualism, remains in late medieval religiosity, no other period in the history of Christianity has placed so positive ... a value on the bodiliness of Christ's humanity."[39] The fact that the *Cloud* author spends so much time refuting a physical interpretation suggests that it must have been a common tendency. His mention of those who feel their breasts inflamed with an unnatural kind of heat and mistake this for the fire of the Holy Spirit could easily be a reference to Richard Rolle, a near contemporary, and his followers.[40] Rolle is most remembered for the emotion and enthusiasm of his writings, in which he speaks of "sensible feelings of heat and sweetness in the breast," among other physical manifestations of devotion.[41] The *Cloud*'s warnings against a physical construal of spiritual metaphors are often seen as a reaction to this overly physical interpretation.

John Burrow observes that the *Cloud* author moves back and forth between the physical and the spiritual, and that this zig-zag motion is one of the most characteristic qualities of the text.[42] The author compares the spiritual meaning of a physical metaphor to a sweet kernel within a husk. But he advises respect for the physical that carries the spiritual within it, not like "those mad folk whose custom it is when they have drunk from some beautiful cup to throw it at the wall and break it . . . we who feed on its fruit are not going to despise the tree, nor when we drink break the cup we have drunk from."[43] His attitude is of supreme respect for the integrity of both the physical and the

---

[39] Caroline Walker Bynum, *Holy Feast and Holy Fast: The Religious Significance of Food to Medieval Women* (University of California Press, 1988), 252.

[40] McGinn, *The Presence of God*, 5:413.

[41] John P. Clark, "The Cloud of Unknowing," in *An Introduction to the Medieval Mystics of Europe: Fourteen Original Essays*, ed. Paul E. Szarmach (State University of New York Press, 1984), 282.

[42] John A. Burrow, "Fantasy and Language in The Cloud of Unknowing," in *Essays of Medieval Literature* (Oxford University Press, 1984), 140.

[43] Wolters, *Cloud*, 131.

48 *SUSAN McELCHERAN*

spiritual.[44] He urges respect for one's particular physical nature and decries the tendency to adopt supposedly "holy" mannerisms such as speaking in a quavering, high-pitched voice, saying, "Where there are so many humble bleats without, there must be pride within."[45] Genuine humility of heart will be expressed according to the natural physical disposition of the speaker; someone with a deep voice should use that voice naturally, not distort it with false mannerisms.[46] Spiritual humility implies and requires bodily integrity. The movement back and forth between the physical and spiritual is not like a zipper joining two dissimilar sides but more like a relationship in which each transforms the other: "All who engage in this work of contemplation find that it has a good effect on the body as well as on the soul, for it makes them attractive in the eyes of all who see them. So much so that the ugliest person alive who becomes, by grace, a contemplative, finds that he suddenly (and again by grace) is different, and that every good man he sees is glad and happy to have his friendship, and is spiritually refreshed, and helped nearer God by his company."[47] This vision of the person reveals an inherent connection between the bodily and the spiritual.

In its promotion of affect and embodiment in relating to God, the *Cloud* suggests ways of knowing God that are accessible to people with intellectual disabilities. Although the kind of prayer promoted in the *Cloud* will usually be preceded by study and meditation, this is not necessary, since it is a gift of grace, and God can give this gift to anyone regardless of merit.[48] Returning to the beginning of this chapter with Liam and Rosie, can anyone be sure that God has not given this grace to them, since it is not dependent on words or mental concepts? We eventually found a priest who was happy to accept Liam as a candidate for reception of the sacrament of Holy Communion. On the day, dressed in his best suit and with all his family present, he was completely present in the moment. Normally fidgety and highly distractable, flitting from one thing to another, he became focused and attentive during the Mass and his face radiated joy.

Acknowledging other ways of knowing God is also transformative

---

[44] Burrow, "Fantasy and Language," 138–40.
[45] Wolters, *Cloud*, 126.
[46] Wolters, *Cloud*, 126.
[47] Wolters, *Cloud*, 125.
[48] Wolters, *Cloud*, 100.

for the community. Bethany McKinney Fox tells of her experience in the Beloved Everybody Church, where people with all kinds of disabilities have been welcomed in all roles, including leadership. She relates that the expectations of church members about what was valued in leadership were at first centered on verbal and organizational skills, but as they allowed people with intellectual disabilities to take more leadership roles, expectations were transformed to more relational, embodied, and affective ones.[49] This kind of transformation supports a flourishing that is not based on dualistic relationships of domination and subjugation but accepts interdependence with those who are vulnerable and with vulnerable ways of knowing.

---

[49] Bethany McKinney Fox, *Disability and the Way of Jesus: Holistic Healing in the Gospels and the Church* (IVP Academic, 2019), 151–52.

The Two-Fold Virtue Reconsidered

Humility, Magnanimity, and the Technocratic Paradigm

Katherine Tarrant

For a moment, imagine history through the lens of disaster. See the past—not as a series of singular events marching along a line—but instead as the rolling tides of peace and crisis, tumult and placidity. We might imagine that much of the time, the crashing wave of disaster would have caught people of the past unawares. Who can predict the onslaught of a drought or the invasion of strangers from across the sea? But surely there were other times, other moments in the past, when our forebears might have caught sight of a threat that loomed over them. Plagues do not consume populations overnight, and no tyrannical state was built in a day. What is one to do at such a time? Where does one find the strength and wisdom to act justly when the freezing, frenetic fear of change arises and we are faced with our own vulnerabilities?

We live in one such moment. The multifaceted threat of anthropogenic climate change to human and nonhuman creation alike is well understood, widely known, and of the greatest moral import. Nevertheless, most who live under the provisional protections of geopolitical power and affluence stand motionless before the tide of crisis, eyes closed in fear, sorrow, or hopelessness. At the same time, some members of our society's economic and technological elite are reacting to this moment of uncertainty with desperate attempts to extend their control over the Earth and its dynamic systems, rushing into frenzied action with little regard for the complex relational networks they might disrupt. While

THE TWO-FOLD VIRTUE RECONSIDERED 51

these two types of reaction to our global climate crisis may appear radically different at first blush—one is marked by insufficient action while the other is characterized by excess and disordered activity—they are two dimensions of a shared moral shortcoming, namely, the denial of our collective, creaturely vulnerability.

Human technological power has outpaced every other area of our development as a species. We often experiment, build, and innovate at a speed that cannot be matched by commensurate moral and social growth. As Pope Francis notes in the third chapter of the encyclical *Laudato Si'*, "There is a tendency to believe that every increase in power means 'an increase of 'progress' itself . . . The fact is that 'contemporary man has not been trained to use power well,' because our immense technological development has not been accompanied by a development in human responsibility, values and conscience."[1] While the fruits of these technological developments may give a lucky few the illusion of total independence from more-than-human networks of life and death, we remain reliant upon the smooth operation of ecosystemic balancing acts for our comfort and basic survival.

If some had forgotten this reality, the advent of this global climate crisis radically confronts us with the limitations of our bodies, of our status quo patterns of social organization, and of our past moral judgments. In the face of all this painful evidence of our finitude and fallibility, it has become clear that not all groups and individuals are responding productively to the revelation of their own ecosystemic vulnerability. Here we will consider two categories of response that sit at opposite ends of the spectrum of insufficient and excess action. On one hand, the quasinihilistic refusal to emotionally or morally engage with the realities of climate change sometimes called climate denialism and, on the other, a movement to escalate and intensify human manipulation of the global climate that we might characterize as ecomodernist. Informed by Pope Francis's instruction that "only by cultivating sound virtue will people be able to make a sound ecological commitment" and take responsibility for anthropogenic destruction, this chapter reframes the somewhat under examined Thomistic "two-fold virtue" of humility and magnanimity as so-called ecological virtues well suited to the address the distinct moral challenges faced by each of these two

---

[1] Pope Francis, *Laudato Si'* (2015), no. 105.

52 KATHERINE TARRANT

groups.[2] In conversation with the works of Francis, Leonardo Boff, and Daniel Castillo, the chapter demonstrates the applicability of these two Thomistic virtues to the pressing moral challenge of technocratic injustice, and explores the viability of an ecological virtue ethic grounded in the recognition of human vulnerability and potential.

Denial and Dissonance

While there was a time when the very notion of global warming was widely disbelieved, several sociological studies suggest that this is no longer the case in the so-called developed nations of the Global North.[3] For those living in the Global South, the tide is already rising too swiftly to be reasonably ignored. Given the immense gravity of this rapidly manifesting threat and our operational understanding of humanity's part in it, why haven't we done more? What keeps us from mounting a collective resistance against the forces that contribute to ecological destruction? What, in short, is wrong with us?

While there are any number of answers to that question, this section shall focus on one dimension of this particular problem: climate denialism. Colloquially, this term often references the outright rejection of any research that presents evidence of anthropogenic climate change. While this form of skepticism remains a pernicious impediment to the implementation of environmentally conscious legislation and education, I refer here to a different brand of denialism. In her significant article "Climate Denial: Emotion, Psychology, Culture, and Political Economy," sociologist Kari Marie Norgaard presents survey findings that reveal a dynamic far more pervasive and complex than straightforward disbelief in climate science. Defining "denial" in this context as the affective process wherein people "avoid acknowledging disturbing information in order to avoid emotions of fear, guilt, and helplessness," Norgaard asserts that abstract awareness about the reality of climate change does not generally translate into material resistance against

---

[2] Francis, *Laudato Si'*, no. 211.
[3] Kari Marie Norgaard, "Climate Denial: Emotion, Psychology, Culture, and Political Economy," in *The Oxford Handbook of Climate Change and Society,* ed. John S. Dryzek, Richard B. Norgaard, and David Schlosberg (Oxford University Press, 2012), 400.

ecological injustice.[4] To illustrate this point, she describes a particular ski town in Norway that was already experiencing warmer summers and diminished snowpack in the year 2000. Even though the residents of the town acknowledged the changes, bemoaned their economic consequences, and readily attributed them to climate change, Norgaard claims that "everyday life went on as though it [climate change] did not exist."[5] Here in the US in the year 2024, this observation is not so much unsurprising as it is self-evident.

To better understand the impetus for this odd and increasingly ubiquitous behavior, we should note the frequency with which Norgaard's subjects expressed a desire "not to know" the truth about climate change, to find momentary escapes into a kind of intentional ignorance that can shield the mind from fear, hopelessness, and guilt. Norgaard argues that her subjects live out a "double reality," wherein their thoughts/beliefs and their actions are at odds with each other and operating independently.[6] Rather than work toward a reconciliation of this cognitive dissonance, the subject lives with this tension so as to protect "coherent meaning systems" and "desirable emotional states."[7] Put another way, there seems to be a subconscious effort made to protect the individual or community from the consequences of confronting their vulnerabilities as agents and victims of climate change.

Lost in this cycle of cognitive dissonance that now entraps all who live in the overlapping worlds of knowledge and privilege, it can be difficult to imagine a different way forward. As Pope Francis notes in his broader explication of the technocratic paradigm, the social logic that exalts expansive human control over the Earth has become "so dominant that it would be difficult to do without its resources and even more difficult to utilize them without being dominated by their internal logic."[8] In this manner, the communal moral dissonance identified by Norgaard is supported by external, social conditions designed to uphold an unjust and increasingly ruinous status quo. If it feels impossible to effect tangible changes within a technocratic global economy that constrains both our labor and our consumption,

---

[4] Norgaard, "Climate Denial," 400.
[5] Norgaard, "Climate Denial," 403.
[6] Norgaard, "Climate Denial," 404.
[7] Norgaard, "Climate Denial," 405.
[8] Francis, *Laudato Si'*, no. 108.

54 KATHERINE TARRANT

the work of personal ecological conversion toward moral consonance may seem outright fantastical.

This tension is all the greater when an explicitly spiritual sense of dread or guilt is added to the equation of cognitive dissonance. While it is challenging to seriously look upon one's own faults and vulnerabilities in the context of the *physical* and *ethical* challenge of climate change, it is all the harder to face that challenge when it is compounded with a sense of *spiritual* failure before a Creator or divinized Earth. In a short text titled "We Scarcely Know Ourselves," Dorothy Day testifies to the deep theological roots of this dilemma, writing, "We do not really know ourselves . . . do we really want to see ourselves as God sees us? . . . we do not want to be given that clear inward vision which discloses to us our most secret faults."[9] We quake in the face of our own failures, all the more furiously when they are perpetuated by seemingly inescapable behavioral patterns that run counter to our love of life, justice, and beauty. We fear our dependency on all other living things and are unsettled by the revelation of our natural mutuality with creatures once named worthy of domination. In response, we reject the spiritual connections that gives us life and render us vulnerable, seeking to overcome our dependency through works of objectification, commodification, and destruction.

While the coemergent phenomena of climate denialism and moral cognitive dissonance are clearly quite complex in both their internal and interpersonal operations, I would argue that a lack of courage or, perhaps more accurately, an insufficient greatness of spirit is the fundamental deficiency behind this response. To be sure, the system is stacked against any individual or community that would seek to turn from denialism toward a more honest confrontation of the dire truth. As theologian Daniel Castillo points out in his book *An Ecological Theology of Liberation,*

> The embrace of ignorance is not simply tied to a generic fear of facing the emergency, nor can it be reduced to a generalized social inertia . . . the phenomenon of willful ignorance also must be understood in relation to the specific existential threat that it

---

[9] Dorothy Day, "We Scarcely Know Ourselves," in *Dorothy Day: Selected Writings*, ed. Robert Ellsberg (Orbis Books, 1983), 4.

provokes in the persons whose worldview and desires have been formed by the cultural mechanisms of consumerism.[10]

As Castillo notes, we have been molded in a capitalist, consumerist milieu that conditions not only our moral formation but also our most foundational fears and hopes: to overcome such a burden is no small task. To do so, those trapped in cycles of denialism will need to cultivate ecological virtues that move them into dynamic, conscientious action grounded in a deeply felt respect for human power and potential.

Ecomodernism

Before we turn to consider how these virtues might look in their moderate, justly actionable form, we must consider the opposite side of this moral equation, that is, excessive, disordered, and often imprudent forms of ecological action grounded in fearful recoil from the recognition of human vulnerability. We begin with a case study.

In the first weeks of 2021, reports began to circulate that billionaire entrepreneur Bill Gates had become a significant financial backer for an exciting new technology seeking to rapidly reduce the effects of global warming. It was soon confirmed that Gates was, in fact, working in collaboration with Harvard University's Solar Geoengineering Research Program to develop a new protocol provisionally named The Stratospheric Controlled Perturbation Experiment (SCoPEx).[11] Designed to artificially mimic the climate-cooling effect of ashy volcanic eruptions, the project aimed to functionally dim solar radiation by shooting sun-reflecting calcium carbonate particles into the atmosphere in hopes of cooling the Earth's surface at a rate to match the anthropogenic warming effects. While this project was ultimately canceled in March 2024 for reasons still subject to speculation, research like SCoPEx and similar endeavors to enhance the reflectivity of marine clouds, arctic ice, and even the surface of the ocean are still in development at various universities and for-profit firms.[12]

---

[10] Daniel Castillo, *An Ecological Theology of Liberation* (Orbis Books, 2019), 184.

[11] Ariel Cohen, "A Bill Gates Venture Aims to Spray Dust into the Atmosphere to Block the Sun. What Could Go Wrong?" *Forbes* online, January 11, 2021.

[12] James Temple, "Harvard Has Halted Its Long-Planned Atmospheric Geoengineering Experiment," *MIT Technology Review* online, March 18, 2024.

56   KATHERINE TARRANT

Though many in the scientific community and technology sector have expressed excitement about this area of research, others have demonstrated significant trepidation about the risks these projects entail. Beyond material concerns regarding the efficacy of global systems management, the threat of unforeseen ecosystemic consequences, and the basic dangers posed by insufficient regulation in this sector, both secular ethicists and moral theologians have raised pressing questions about the cultural and ethical implications of geoengineering projects like these. Do utopian visions of a technological "silver bullet" for the climate crisis give us license to continue extracting resources and emitting carbon into the immediate future? Do they simply buy us more time to put off the hard work of examining our collective ecological conscience and confronting our human vulnerability in this moment of crisis?

In many ways, the SCoPEx venture serves as an illuminating example of the guiding ethos and public aesthetics of ecomodernism. Defined by political scientist Jonathan Symons as "a call for state investment in mission-oriented research to accelerate the development and deployment of an array of breakthrough low-emission technologies," ecomodernism is founded on the basic premise that humanity's way out of this technologically generated climate crisis is "through."[13] Ecomodernists—who often characterize themselves as possessing a pragmatism and optimism that their critics lack—express a sense of comfort with the obviously anthropocentric character of the Anthropocene, asserting the belief that green technologies will allow humanity to flourish unhindered by the natural demands of their ecosystems. In a fascinating rhetorical turn, advocates of ecomodernism also associate their approach with a quality that is widely regarded as a vice, namely, hubris. In his discussion of the matter, Symons argues that, given the reality that the austerity measures needed to mitigate the effects of climate change *without* massive technological assistance would be undeniably taxing and world-altering, there is a certain emotional appeal to the idea of "turning to hubris in the face of catastrophe."[14] More pointedly, ecomodernist theorists Ted Nordhaus and Michael Shellenburg have

---

[13] Jonathan Symons, *Ecomodernism: Technology, Politics and the Climate Crisis* (Polity Press, 2019), 8.

[14] Symons, *Ecomodernism*, 52.

argued that simply facing the conceptual enormity of the climate crisis will require "a kind of greatness—even hubris."[15]

This hubris is generally framed by supporters of ecomodernism as a radical and righteous belief in the power of humans to rapidly innovate and survive against insurmountable odds. Nevertheless, it must be noted that the ecomodernists' brazen willingness to rhetorically center human development and flourishing also reflects a more conventional definition of this vice, an inordinate pride and self-importance grounded in the belief that human dominance over the naturally functional processes of the global biome represents an ideal condition. Ecomodernism does not view anthropogenic climate change as the result of ill-fated or immoral human attempts to control systems and structures we have never fully understood. Rather, the current crisis is framed as a growing pain, one which might be overcome to bring about a more perfect condition of human ecosystemic dominance.[16] This is undoubtedly consonant with the long-standing capitalism understanding of "progress" as the ultimate imperative of the human condition. As liberation theologian Leonardo Boff wrote in his landmark text, *Cry of the Earth, Cry of the Poor,*

> What was once obvious in collective consciousness is now called into question; namely, that everything must revolve around the idea of progress, and that such progress is advancing between two infinites: the infinite of the Earth's resources, and the infinite of the future. . . . Both infinites are illusory.[17]

For many critics of the ecomodernist agenda, the greatest concern emerges in reaction to the movement's apparent inattention to the delicacy of ecosystemic balances and the more-than-human networks of relationality to which we all belong. In *Laudato Si'* the pope argues that such attention is a necessary prerequisite to the formation of a wise and just approach to creation care, writing that the Earth "cries out to us because of the harm we have inflicted on her by our irresponsible

---

[15] Symons, *Ecomodernism*, 52.

[16] The Breakthrough Institute, "About Us," accessed June 26, 2024, https://thebreakthrough.org.

[17] Leonardo Boff, *Cry of the Earth, Cry of the Poor* (Orbis Books, 1997), 11.

58 KATHERINE TARRANT

use and abuse of the goods with which God has endowed her. We have come to see ourselves as her lords and masters, entitled to plunder her at will . . . we have forgotten that we ourselves are dust of the Earth."[18]

Here, we see the encyclical draw a clear line from the present suffering of the Earth and the multispecies poor back to the kind of hubris exalted by the most strident of ecomodernists. When we forget our own smallness, the finitude of our creaturely power, and the limitations to our collective powers of moral discernment, we may act out of turn in ways that imperil both ourselves and our Earthly neighbors. While I hope that the previous section demonstrated the danger of total inaction or excessive trepidation when it comes to confronting the challenges of the climate crisis, we must be mindful about the tools we use, who we allow to use them, and the spirit in which they are used. As Castillo reminds us, modern technocratic endeavors cannot and should not be regarded in isolation from the centuries-long capitalist colonial projects that preceded them:

> The aim of the project was to reduce the earth and human life at the periphery to the commodities of land and labor for the purpose of optimizing the extraction of wealth and power . . . These processes of extraction, governed by the instrumental logic intrinsic to the technocratic paradigm, initiated a centuries-long process of ecological degradation and socioeconomic exploitation.[19]

While many of the most powerful and wealthy individuals today ostensibly undertake ecomodernist projects like climate engineering toward the good end of preserving human life and culture, we must remember that solutions and approaches developed within the logics of the technocratic paradigm, which reject acknowledgment of human vulnerability in favor of the celebration of unchecked human power, are more likely to perpetuate the paradigm than to overturn it.

Humility and Magnanimity

Now that we have surveyed and critiqued these two starkly different responses to climate crisis united by a common unwillingness to

---

[18] Francis, *Laudato Si'*, no. 2.
[19] Castillo, *An Ecological Theology of Liberation*, 159.

THE TWO-FOLD VIRTUE RECONSIDERED

embrace humanity's creaturely vulnerability and fallibility, we may turn briefly to consider what manner of ecological virtue is suited to address these moral struggles. On one hand, we have the climate denialists, so deeply snared in cognitive dissonance and anxiety that they have chosen inaction and passive acceptance of the status quo over any active endeavors toward mitigation or healing. On the other hand, we have the hubris of the ecomodernists, who believe so deeply in the capacities of the human mind and free market to tackle any crisis that they may heedlessly rush us all to ruin. Surely, there is a virtuous zone of moderation to be found between the two.

I argue that we may find aid in the Second Part of the Second Part of Thomas Aquinas's *Summa Theologica,* wherein he discusses the virtues of humility and magnanimity. Thomas's treatment of these two traits can be found in his breakdown of the parts of temperance and fortitude, respectively. In his articles on humility, Thomas turns to the discussion of difficult goods—that is, truly desirable goods whose worth is made evident by the effort needed to attain them. In article 1, he writes, "The difficult good has something attractive to the appetite, namely the aspect of good, and likewise something repulsive to the appetite, namely the difficulty of obtaining it. In respect of the former there arises the movement of hope, and in respect of the latter, the movement of despair."[20] He goes on to argue that this double duality—the coexistence of hope for the good and fear of the struggle needed to attain it—necessitates virtues that will restrain inordinate desire for the former *and* unproductive trepidation about the latter, strengthening the will for a temperate pursuit of goodness. Given this, Thomas proposes that

> A twofold virtue is necessary with regard to the difficult good: one, to temper and restrain the mind, lest it tend to high things immoderately; and this belongs to the virtue of humility: and another to strengthen the mind against despair, and urge it on to the pursuit of great things according to right reason; and this is magnanimity.[21]

---

[20] Thomas Aquinas, *Summa Theologica*, trans. Fathers of the English Dominican Province (Benziger Brothers, 1947), II-II, q. 161, art. 1.

[21] Aquinas, *Summa Theologica*, II-II, q. 161, art.1.

60 KATHERINE TARRANT

Here we see a balancing of two impulses, two desires, two fears. As the human spirit has the capacity to become too lofty, too assured of its own capacities and inclined to disregard its creaturely smallness, it needs humility to restrain it. According to philosopher Martin Rhonheimer, Thomas understands this virtue as a kind of "living according to one's own truth," the recognition of one's powers and vulnerabilities in appropriate measure according to reason.[22] Alternately, as Thomas understands the capacity of the human mind to "fall into despair" in times of high crisis, he recommends magnanimity, which he defines in its own questions as a "stretching forth of the mind to great things."[23] While we must become cognizant of our vulnerabilities and the limits of our power, we cannot allow self-doubt to cripple our ability to act in a just and timely manner. In this sense, Thomas positions these two virtues not as opposites, but as complements, each urging the mind toward right reason and best suited to counter the corresponding vices of pride, presumption, and inordinate despair when cultivated in tandem.

Given this, I suggest that the dual virtues of humility and magnanimity might be embraced as key ecological virtues by those living under the protections of wealth, power, and privilege. While I do not suggest that the substance of this "twofold virtue" would objectively preclude or recommend specific pieces of geoengineering tech *or* green activism strategies, it can serve as a helpful guide in the work of moral discernment and judgment in these arenas. Confronting the climate challenges ahead will demand an incredible greatness of spirit, demand acts of bold imagination and experimentation in defense of our ecosystemic communities. Likewise, this moment calls us to develop our collective powers of wisdom and discernment, to embrace our creaturely vulnerability as dependent beings as we test the limits of our potential. As we are reminded in *Laudato Si'*, our human freedom and capacities for creative growth will be essential to the work of moving beyond the technocratic paradigm. Francis writes,

> We have the freedom needed to limit and direct technology; we can put it at the service of another type of progress, one which is healthier, more human, more social, more integral ... An

---

[22] Martin Rhonheimer, *The Perspective of Morality: Philosophical Foundations of Thomistic Virtue Ethics* (Catholic University of America Press, 2011), 89.

[23] Aquinas, *Summa Theologica*, II-II, q. 129, art. 1.

THE TWO-FOLD VIRTUE RECONSIDERED   **61**

authentic humanity, calling for a new synthesis, seems to dwell in the midst of our technological culture, almost unnoticed, like a mist seeping gently beneath a closed door.[24]

I propose that an embrace of the twofold virtues, an embrace of both our vulnerability and our immense capacity for flourishing, could be the first step in opening that door.

---

[24] Francis, *Laudato Si'*, no. 112.

Technocratic Eschatologies

Hope and Flourishing
amid an Artificially Intelligent Future

Stephen Okey

Since the release of Open AI's chatbot ChatGPT in November 2022, significant attention has turned to the role of artificial intelligence (AI). This has especially been the case within higher education, where there has been a flurry of articles and workshops about AI, often ranging in focus between safeguarding academic integrity against intrusions by AI perpetrated by students (and faculty), on one hand, and finding ways of incorporating AI into the classroom in useful and entertaining ways, on the other. This range reflects a deeper anxiety about the purpose and mission of higher education, especially within the humanities and liberal arts, that is pulled between a traditional, even romantic ideal of forming students to be well-rounded and intelligent persons and training students for well-paying jobs.

The higher education question is only one of the many public conversations about AI today. But the sense of anxiety, even threat, built into it is tied into a second, more overarching conversation regarding AI's potentially apocalyptic challenges to human flourishing. While faculty and administrators sometimes see in AI an asteroid that will finally render academic vocations extinct, many technologists and scholars think we ought to treat AI as an asteroid that could finally render all humanity extinct.

This chapter proceeds in three parts. The first part reviews public claims about potential for AI to be an "existential risk" to humanity.

TECHNOCRATIC ESCHATOLOGIES 63

In particular, it looks at the two main camps that have emerged in response to this issue, the so-called doomers and accelerationists, both of whom claim the promotion of human flourishing as the motivation for their concerns.

The second part argues that doomers and accelerationists share an implicit eschatological and anthropological vision that is fundamentally technocratic. Both are animated by concerns about human control of technology while offering apparently pessimistic and optimistic perspectives on that control. This technocratic worldview is framed through the lens of Pope Francis's encyclical *Laudato Si'*.

Finally, the chapter recalls Francis's shift from a technocratic paradigm to an integral ecology in order to sketch an "integral eschatology" in response to the doomer/accelerationist discourse. Such an eschatology requires a fuller vision of the human person, a recommitment to the divine role in eschatology, and ultimately a recovery of the theological virtue of hope.

Artificial Intelligence and Existential Risk

The basic idea that AI might present an "existential risk" to human existence and flourishing has a long history. The premise extends at least as far back as 1921's *R.U.R.* by Karel Čapek, in which the androids eventually rise up and wipe out the humans.[1] A far more widely known example of this genre is the film *The Terminator*, in which the terrifying, humanity-slaughtering AI of Skynet, which was originally created by humans as part of a military defense project before becoming self-aware, is personified by Arnold Schwarzenegger's relentless cyborg.[2]

These and other science fiction examples of AI as an existential risk typically assume certain shared features of these apocalyptic AI. First, the AI has achieved a sufficient level of intelligence that it becomes sentient and self-aware. Second, concomitant with that intelligence, the AI develops the capacity to make decisions completely independently of human persons. Third, the AI has some sort of capacity to act in the world beyond its immediate software and hardware in ways that are threatening to human survival.

---

[1] Karel Čapek, *R.U.R. (Rossum's Universal Robots)* (Penguin Classics, 2004).

[2] *The Terminator*, directed by James Cameron (Orion Pictures, 1984).

64 STEPHEN OKEY

While the fear of such AI has recurred in science fiction for decades, it has come to be taken seriously as a real possibility due to significant advances in AI in the last decade. For example, in 2014, physicist Stephen Hawking stated that "The development of full artificial intelligence could spell the end of the human race," noting that it could be capable of "re-design[ing] itself at an ever increasing rate" far outstripping human evolution.[3] The form and timeline for these threats are understandably vague. Yet that uncertainty has in part given rise to the diverse responses that people have to AI as an "existential risk." Broadly, these responses can be placed into two groups: doomers and accelerationists.[4]

Doomers

As the name suggests, doomers are those who have a pessimistic outlook on what are the likely outcomes of rapid technological advancement, especially in AI.[5] These risks range anywhere from run-of-the-mill harm to individual persons to large-scale social, even global, catastrophes. A key concern among doomers is that AI development is often done without any form of governmental regulation or input; any regulation that exists is done by the venture capital markets. Moreover, doomers typically see no concrete evidence that the developers of potentially risky AI systems are guided by prosocial or moral principles.

Moreover, some doomers note that AI creates significant risk, even absent the above criteria of sentience and free will; what matters most is the capacity for the AI to cause harm. In their taxonomy of societal-level AI risks, Andrew Critch and Stuart Russell note that major, society-wide problems could result from interactions of a range of AI systems that were designed for benign purposes and had bigger than expected outcomes.[6] Such an array of systems could, for example, potentially cause catastrophic failure of power grids through design failures, not

---

[3] Rory Cellan-Jones, "Stephen Hawking Warns Artificial Intelligence Could End Mankind," *BBC News*, December 2, 2014, sec. Technology, https://www.bbc.com.

[4] Doomers are also referred to as "decelerationists" while accelerationists are also referred to as "boomers."

[5] Thom Waite, "Doomer vs Accelerationist: The Two Tribes Fighting for the Future of AI," *Dazed*, November 24, 2023, https://www.dazeddigital.com.

[6] Andrew Critch and Stuart Russell, "TASRA: A Taxonomy and Analysis of Societal-Scale Risks from AI," arXiv, June 14, 2023, http://arxiv.org/.

through an alleged achievement of sentience or free will.

However, it is worth noting that, in their most public interventions, the doomer camp has largely not called for a full stop on technological progress. Instead, in March 2023 there was a call for a six-month moratorium on some AI development while frameworks for responsible development were drafted.[7] The letter itself raises the variety of risks presented by AI: "Should we let machines flood our information channels with propaganda and untruth? Should we automate away all the jobs, including the fulfilling ones? Should we develop nonhuman minds that might eventually outnumber, outsmart, obsolete and replace us? Should we risk loss of control of our civilization?" It goes on to offer some ways forward for regulating (either through self-regulation or government regulation) the development of AI. It is worth noting that neither the moratorium nor the frameworks have, to date, occurred.

A few months later, in May 2023, the Center for AI Safety (or CAIS) released an even briefer statement, signed by hundreds of technologists and academics, that stated, "Mitigating the risk of extinction from AI should be a global priority alongside other societal-scale risks such as pandemics and nuclear war."[8] For the most part, doomers are not opposed to AI development in principle, but rather are concerned with the threat that its rapid, careening evolution poses to human flourishing.[9]

Accelerationists

By contrast, accelerationists think that rapidly developing AI will greatly increase the intelligence on the planet and in the universe, improve our chances of bettering society, and ultimately mitigate or even eliminate some of the greatest challenges to human flourishing.[10] As

---

[7] "Pause Giant AI Experiments: An Open Letter," Future of Life Institute, March 22, 2023, https://futureoflife.org. Signatories include Steve Wozniak, Elon Musk, Andrew Yang, Yuval Noah Harari.

[8] "Statement on AI Risk," Center for AI Safety, May 30, 2023, https://www.safe.ai.

[9] One exception to this is Eliezer Yudkowsky, an AI researcher, who called for a far more extensive, immediate, and long-term moratorium, even writing that governments should "be willing to destroy a rogue datacenter by airstrike." Eliezer Yudkowsky, "The Open Letter on AI Doesn't Go Far Enough," *TIME*, March 29, 2023, https://time.com.

[10] Waite, "Doomer vs Accelerationist."

such, there is a moral obligation to continue, and even accelerate, the development of AI. Indeed, Colby Cosh writes that for accelerationists, "any delay in creating a world that uses AI to radically enhance human welfare would be a profound disaster."[11]

A paradigmatic version of the accelerationist argument can be found in software engineer and investor Marc Andreessen's "The Techno-Optimist Manifesto."[12] For Andreessen, the long-term good of human civilization depends on growth: "We believe everything good is downstream of growth." He identifies three primary sources of growth: population (which he overall sees as shrinking), natural resources usage (which has significant negative externalities), and technological development. Thus, the best way to ensure growth and human progress is technology, which we must commit to developing at full tilt. In what is perhaps the most instructive example of his beliefs in the entire manifesto, he writes not only that "We believe Artificial Intelligence can save lives—if we let it," but also that "We believe any deceleration of AI will cost lives. Deaths that were preventable by the AI that was prevented from existing is a form of murder."

For the accelerationists, continuous development of AI is a moral obligation as part of the strategy to promote human flourishing and to stave off catastrophic futures.

The Technocratic Eschatology of AI Existential Risk

There are numerous links between the doomer and accelerationist camps. First, both camps are invested, both ideologically and financially, in ongoing development of AI. Sam Altman, a signatory to the CAIS statement, is the CEO of OpenAI, the company behind ChatGPT, DALL-E, and many other AI projects. Marc Andreessen, in addition to writing the manifesto quoted above, raised over two billion dollars in 2024 through his venture capital fund for investment in AI com-

---

[11] Colby Cosh, "AI Divides Humanity into Two Camps—Doomers vs. Accelerationists," *National Post*, November 24, 2023, https://nationalpost.com.

[12] Marc Andreessen, "The Techno-Optimist Manifesto," Andreessen Horowitz, October 16, 2023, https://a16z.com.

panies.[13] The differences between doomers and accelerationists on AI development is much more about the pace of development and the need to have, or to eliminate, regulations on AI.

A second link is that both camps are quite explicitly concerned about human well-being. Both make moral arguments predicated on their ideas of human flourishing and survival, claiming that either restricting or unencumbering AI is necessary for our species. However, both doomers and accelerationists tend to share a fundamentally materialist view of the human person and a technocratic vision of the future.

To understand the "technocratic" aspect here, it is helpful to turn to Pope Francis's 2015 encyclical *Laudato Si': On Care for Our Common Home*. A crucial part of his argument about the ecological challenges faced by humans and the wider world is the "technocratic paradigm," which Francis describes as

> Exalt[ing] the concept of a subject who, using logical and rational procedures, progressively approaches and gains control over an external object. This subject makes every effort to establish the scientific and experimental method, which in itself is already a technique of possession, mastery and transformation. It is as if the subject were to find itself in the presence of something formless, completely open to manipulation.[14]

Similarly, Francis said in his 2014 Address to the European Parliament that

> We see technical and economic questions dominating political debate, to the detriment of genuine concern for human beings. Men and women risk being reduced to mere cogs in a machine that treats them as items of consumption to be exploited, with the result that—as is so tragically apparent—whenever a human life no longer proves useful for that machine, it is discarded with few qualms.[15]

---

[13] George Hammond, "Andreessen Horowitz Raises \$7.2bn and Sets Sights on AI Start-Ups," *Financial Times*, April 16, 2024, https://www.ft.com.

[14] Pope Francis, *Laudato Si'* (2015), no. 106.

[15] Pope Francis, "Address of Pope Francis to the European Parliament" (2014).

For Francis, the technocratic paradigm views technology and technical processes as self-evident goods and maintains a relentless optimism that not only can existing human problems be solved by new technologies, but that even the problems created by new technologies can be solved by further, newer technologies.[16]

Both doomers and accelerationists exhibit this technocratic mindset. For doomers, the check on AI to be pursued now is simply new protocols and principles for guiding and restraining the development of AI. There is rare consideration that the real risks of AI, which this group fully acknowledges, might in fact mean it ought not to be pursued. Rather, the conviction is that better protocols and regulations will protect humans from the risks of AI, and even from the risks of other humans who might choose to flout those rules.

For accelerationists, the confidence is much more fully grounded in technocratic optimism: problems raised today by AI can be solved by future developments in AI.

Undergirding this technocratic view is a particular materialism of the human person. This is clearest in Andreessen, who writes in his manifesto that "Technology is the glory of human ambition and achievement, the spearhead of progress, and the realization of our potential."[17] He notes Milton Friedman's claim that "human wants and needs are infinite"; yet, like Friedman, he only sees this infinite chain in terms of economic production and material consumption.[18] Andreessen makes two brief references to the "human soul" and "human spirit," but these are only in the context of how technology can liberate them and expand our idea of what it means to be human.

This combined vision of a valuable, but not apparently transcendent, human person, coupled with an instrumentalist and in-control perception of technology, contribute ultimately to the "technocratic eschatology" of the existential risk discourse in AI. The existential risk identified by the doomers is human extinction by means of AI. For the accelerationists, the existential risk is the suffering and death of humans, especially future humans, due to the failure to build better and better AI.

---

[16] Stephen Okey, "What Comes After the Failure of Technocracy?," *Church Life Journal*, September 28, 2021, https://churchlifejournal.nd.edu.

[17] Andreessen, "The Techno-Optimist Manifesto."

[18] Intriguingly, Andreessen makes one reference to "fallen humanity" in the context of the not-quite Utopianism of his manifesto but does not further elaborate.

Neither of these apocalyptic visions considers in any significant regard anything more than (1) the relative number of humans living and (2) the financial situation of those persons. This is not to say that these are unimportant aspects of thinking about the human future or that we should not consider material well-being when discussing human flourishing. Nonetheless, the doomers and accelerationists present a narrowly construed vision of human flourishing and of the eschaton. By and large neither group considers seriously nontechnological aspects of human creativity or the potential impacts of AI on human relationships and community formation/decline. Even on the material level, they generally ignore the environmental impact of AI beyond the accelerationist optimism that future technology can fix that, too.[19] It might be unsurprising that deeper, transcendent questions about the purpose of the human person or human destiny is absent from an AI discourse dominated by AI developers and investors, but it nonetheless seems to be a truncated and reductivist vision.

In this regard, the technocratic eschatologies abundant in AI discourse are simply new expressions of the "myth of progress" in modern thought. They are, as Richard Bauckham writes, grounded "on the immanent possibilities of the historical process itself" rather than "the transcendent possibilities of God's action in and on the world."[20] It might thus seem easy to dismiss these technocratic visions, which are not particularly curious or literate in theological terms, but this would be to abandon a Christian responsibility to engage with the signs of the times and see how they might be challenged and reframed in ways that better illuminate the reality of both human persons and God.

AI presents both a challenge and an opportunity to theological reflection on the human person. Most, though not all, consideration of AI emphasizes intelligence as the narrow and relevant concept, which one can see emphasized in Andreessen's manifesto. Intelligence or rationality has long been a distinguishing feature of humans in Christian theology, but it is importantly not the *only* distinguishing feature, nor is it the only *necessary* feature. AI presents renewed opportunities to consider how embodiment is part of the human person, as is the

---

[19] For more on the environmental impact, see Kate Crawford, *Atlas of AI* (Yale University Press, 2021), 23–51.

[20] Richard Bauckham, "Conclusion: Emerging Issues in Eschatology in the Twenty-First Century," in *The Oxford Handbook of Eschatology*, ed. Jerry L. Walls (Oxford University Press, 2010), 674.

analogous "embodiment" of AI systems themselves. The narrow focus on intelligence also brings into relief human affectivity, charity, and care. The utilitarian calculus that underlies both doomers and accelerationists is predicated on an unstated and uncritiqued set of values, including a version of "care," but without thematizing them.

Second, an eschatological vision driven solely by human choices can only ever be an immanent eschatology. It overlooks the Christian belief that "the eschaton [is] the result of a mighty act of God."[21] Again, it is not surprising that the discourse has by and large not followed Christian theology in doing so; it is part of a larger myth of progress. However, the lack of any transcendent insight helps to keep the project within the realm of human control and the attendant assumption that it is only human control that can determine the future. Moreover, it presumes that technologies created by human persons can always be controlled by humans and will pursue prohuman ends in ways deemed acceptable by humans.

To sum up, the technocratic eschatologies of the AI crowd are predicated on a truncated human and an absent God.

Toward an Integral Eschatology

Pope Francis's critique of the technocratic paradigm leads him to call for "another type of progress, one which is healthier, more human, more social, more integral."[22] Thus, in contrast to the widespread "technocratic ecology" at the root of the crisis, he proposes an "integral ecology" that "clearly respects its human and social dimensions."[23] Here Francis builds on the idea of "integral human development" in Catholic Social Teaching that comes out of Paul VI's *Populorum Progressio*: "the development we speak of here cannot be restricted to economic growth alone. To be authentic, it must be well rounded; it must foster the development of each man and of the whole man."[24] Connecting this "integral" idea to ecology emphasizes that the ecological challenge

---

[21] Stephen T. Davis, "Eschatology and Resurrection," in *The Oxford Handbook of Eschatology*, 394.

[22] Francis, *Laudato Si'*, no. 112.

[23] Francis, *Laudato Si'*, no. 137.

[24] Pope Paul VI, *Populorum Progressio* (1967), no. 14.

ahead is not merely a material or technical one, but a social and personal one that, like all challenges in Catholic Social Teaching, requires concern for the individual and the group and transformation of both the heart and the society.

Analogously, contemporary discourse about AI as an existential threat to human flourishing suggests the need to move from a technocratic eschatology to an integral eschatology. In this preliminary sketch of what that would mean, three key features emerge in response to the technocratic eschatology of the AI crowd. First, an integral eschatology would push for a more complete, more authentic vision of the human person. Like integral development or integral ecology, it would be concerned with the whole person, and thus it would not share the truncated vision of human flourishing that attends simply to the number of humans and their material well-being. In its consideration of the human person, it would recognize that as important as intelligence is to our understanding of humanity, intelligence (especially intelligence narrowly construed in AI terms) is not the ultimate end for human beings or for creation more broadly. Rather, it would recall the theological claim that human beings are ultimately fulfilled in eternal life with God rather than in the fulfillment of material needs and desires. It would reframe for us that technology is not the fulfillment of human glory, but rather an important aspect of human persons and communities that should be supportive of human flourishing, not idols of the same.

Second, an integral eschatology reframes the eschatological question to recognize the role of divine agency in human beings coming to their end. Human persons have a role to play, but humans are not fully in control of their destiny, either individually or as a species. An integral eschatology recalls not only that God is the ultimate end for the human person but also that God is the central agent in the entire eschatological drama.

Third, much as Francis advocates for cultivating "ecological virtues" as part of an integral ecology, so, too, does an integral eschatology need the theological virtue of hope. Cultivating hope, with its emphasis on yearning for that ultimate union with God, helps also to contextualize more effectively the promises and perils of AI within this life. It is reasonably easy to read the contrast between doomers and accelerationists as being between pessimists and optimists, and this is often the way they are portrayed. However, it is perhaps more accurate to read them as despairing and presumptuous, the vices that traditionally stand astride hope. Reading the doomers and accelerationists in this way further highlights that, in fact, hope itself, authentic hope, is absent from the conversation. There is no union with God to look forward to, there is only the endless effort to fulfill the infinite desires of humans with finitely satisfying intermediaries. Treating AI discourse through a lens of hope suggests a hedge against being drawn into that discourse on its own terms.

Conclusion

On the surface, contemporary discourse about AI as a potential existential threat to human flourishing has a certain resonance. It recalls the plotlines of popular science fiction, and it fits with other potentially apocalyptic concerns such as climate change and the proliferation of nuclear weapons. Those working on science fiction presume a certain vision of human flourishing, one fundamentally defined by the limits of exciting and emerging technologies.

Yet deeper analysis of this discourse reveals an implicit eschatology and anthropology. These are framed by a technocratic worldview that hinges on questions of human control of technology, the environment, and even of one another. While the doomer and accelerationist camps have different estimates of what that control looks like and what risks must be considered, they both ultimately perceive a human end that is defined more by numbers than actual human flourishing.

A more authentic, more human, more integral eschatology would provide greater theological insight to the problems evident in AI discourse. It would emphasize a fuller understanding of the human person than is on offer from the main AI camps, and it would recall the necessity of hope, a hope that is more than simple optimism and that recalls the ultimate end for which human beings exist. Recovering this hope can help elicit a healthier view of AI and its potential role in human life.

A Franciscanized Ecology
of Technology

Cristofer Fernández

What we might consider the "Franciscan Roots and Shoots" of Francis's magisterium are the fundamentals of Franciscan creation theology and the emergent Franciscan ecotheology being constructed today. Here, I apply this emergent thought to the growing ethical conversation on technology[1] and in search of an integral ecological technology. From the Franciscan Intellectual and Spiritual Tradition (FIST) I employ a twofold ethic as a scope for assessing the growing case of artificial intelligence (AI), naming technocratic vulnerabilities, and reimagining ecosocial flourishing. Drawing on intersectional studies on ecology, technology, and society, primarily reflecting on harmful vulnerabilities in generative AI vis-à-vis technocracy, this chapter argues for a theological response to these systematized vulnerabilities in technologizing and a corrective to the supremacy of colonial anthropocentric epistemologies over Creation.

Franciscan Ethics: Foundations and Principles

The FIST is a gospel-based wisdom tradition shaped in the way of Saint Francis and Saint Clare of Assisi in the High Middle Ages. The

---

[1] From here on, technology is understood generally as the application of (scientific) knowledge for practical purposes, including tools/devices, techniques, and systems; broadly, this knowledge and application interplay with sociocultural and environmental contexts.

73

74 CRISTOFER FERNÁNDEZ

gospel life of the friars and sisters is lived in community, with the ideal of being in communion with the poor and all Creation. Franciscanism was shaped by the virtue of *minoritas* (lesserness or poverty), in solidarity with the poor and Crucified Christ, living vulnerably and working earnestly among the lowest caste of society. Professed members are active contemplatives, called to works of peace and penance in the missionary spirit of repairing the church.[2] Francis was a "true materialist" in the sense of seeing all material reality as a gift from God's overflowing gratuitousness. In this respect, Francis permitted and encouraged the brothers to make use of tools and materials necessary for work and the cultivation of community—using technologies for practical ministerial uses.

The Franciscan ethical horizon[3] has been pivotal to ecological theology and spirituality today.[4] This chapter considers a joint planetary ethic and ethic of Lady Poverty characteristic of an emergent Franciscan ecological vision.[5] Two key ecosocial ethical realms of this joint ethic resemble what we familiarly refer to as *integral ecology*, both hinged together by a spirit of poverty.

The Joint Ethic: The Planet and Lady Poverty

The metaphor of "Lady Poverty" is used in Franciscan tradition as an allusion to the feminine God–Wisdom of the book of scripture (i.e., Logos or Spirit Sophia). An ontological poverty emerged from Francis and Clare's response to God's gratuitous love and beauty and their defense of the "Privilege of Poverty" in their religious life—oneness with

---

[2] See Regis J. Armstrong, OFM Cap., JA Wayne Hellman, OFM Conv., and William J. Short, OFM, eds., *The Saint*, annotated edition, vol. 1, Francis of Assisi, Early Documents, especially *The Earlier Rule* and *The Later Rule* (New City Press, 2002).

[3] Thomas Nairn, OFM, ed., *The Franciscan Moral Vision: Responding to God's Love* (Franciscan Institute, 2013); Martín Carbajo Núñez, OFM, *Sister Mother Earth, Franciscan Roots of the Laudato Si'* (Tau Publishing, 2017), chap. 3.

[4] See, for example, Dawn M. Nothwehr, ed., *Franciscan Theology of the Environment: An Introductory Reader* (St. Anthony Messenger Press, 2003).

[5] See the other principles of this vision (a kinship cosmology and paradigm, a decolonial sense of catholicity, and an integrative spiritual and moral "cosmography") in Cristofer Fernández, OFM Conv., "An Emergent Franciscan Ecology for an Evolving Earth: Catholicity, Integrity, and Common Homemaking in a Stochastic Cosmos" (master's thesis, Catholic University of America, 2023), 149–51.

A FRANCISCANIZED ECOLOGY OF TECHNOLOGY

the poor and commitment to a fraternal gift economy. What developed in the FIST is a *spiritual poverty* emphasizing solidarity (a committed, vulnerable, and freely entered interdependence) and a "generosity in action."[6] Poverty of spirit was expressed as a nonproprietary stance in living material simplicity and divesting from temporal power and capital, giving rise to a "penitential humanism" that practices mutual aid, minimalism, pride in local culture and community, and overcoming divisions for the common good.[7] In this regard, FIST sees vulnerability as a necessary precondition for Christification and spiritual flourishing.

This vision also challenges us to expand our circle of kinship to the rest of the family of Creation. However, the wide acceptance of (theo-anthropocentric) dominion cosmology and the capitalistic myth of progress—making humans self-entitled "real-estate brokers" of God's green Earth—commodifies and terraforms Sister Mother Earth into humanity's image and likeness for the sake of societal development.[8] The same absolute and linear thought schema of Western science and economics that led to the exploitative 500+ year technocratic globalization project[9] of commodified technology and consumerism is the same Western cosmovision that "universalized" an abstract and theologically false imperial ecology. The Franciscan response to the ecological crises embraces again the poverty of our nothingness or finitude; it embraces the gratuitous love and beauty that is central to the constitution of all Creation *ex nihilo*.

Franciscan ecotheology contributes to a weaker or nonanthropo-centric theology because of its vision of solidarity across all Creation; it corrects the subjugating coloniality over non-Western knowledge

---

[6] Nairn, *The Franciscan Moral Vision*, chap. 7.

[7] Dana Bultman, "Waste, Exclusion, and the Responsibility of the Rich: A Franciscan Critique of Early Capitalist Europe," *Religions* 13, no. 9 (September 2022): 13, https://doi.org/10.3390/rel13090818.

[8] Enrique Dussel, "Epistemological Decolonization of Theology," in *Decolonial Christianities: Latinx and Latin American Perspectives*, ed. Raimundo Barreto and Roberto Sirvent, New Approaches to Religion and Power (Springer International Publishing, 2019), 37; Daniel P. Horan, *Francis of Assisi and the Future of Faith: Exploring Franciscan Spirituality and Theology in the Modern World* (Tau Publishing, 2012), 106–7; Daniel P. Horan, *All God's Creatures: A Theology of Creation*, reprint paperback edition (Fortress Press, 2020), 64.

[9] For more on technocracy and the technocratic paradigm see Pope Francis, *Laudato Si'* (2015), nos. 106–14.

76 CRISTOFER FERNÁNDEZ

and particularity; and it redirects what we identify as the source of alterity in nature to the Creator—the *Wholly Other*—"the 'origin of this animating gift of animation.'"[10] Leonardo Boff and others like Dan Horan offer a basis for an emergent post/decolonial Franciscan theology that rereads "the master narratives about creation and humanity's place within it, which have been written and reinforced by means of a hegemonic discourse."[11] Because all species' existence and flourishing is entangled, a Mother Earth or planetary ethic reenvisions our human species within the Creation community of diverse subjects and challenges us to contemplate what it means to be theocreatiocentric[12]—to hold a kinship cosmology centered on a more-than-human God at the center of a more-than-human cosmos—as is St. Francis in his Canticle of the Creatures.

This joint ethic complicates the call to intellectual humility. In our philosophical and theological knowledge productions, how are we other-centered? How else do we reconstitute "alterity" beside reckoning with the Triune God?

Technocracy, Critical Realism, and Reimagining Our Technological Relations

Franciscan wisdom befits the reflexivity needed in the operations of remaking or repairing Catholic ecosocial thought. Our guardianship of our common home parallels our guardianship of each other as an integral objective, not an optional one; both an integral ecology and fraternal politics are indeed needed.[13] The challenge of technocracy[14] in this regard is complex, given its intractable origins in coloniality that

---

[10] Horan, *All God's Creatures*, 191, 195.

[11] Horan, *All God's Creatures*, 187.

[12] In contradistinction to being theoanthropocentric, where our "God-centered" theology emphasizes God's human qualities, or Jesus's humanness masks his createdness.

[13] Pope Francis, *Fratelli Tutti* (2020), nos. 1–4, 17.

[14] Technocracy is constitutive of the technocratic paradigm; it is the concept and praxis of reliance on scientific technical experts or highly skilled specialists to regulate and govern decision making, often aligned with meritocracy; it is driven by big data, efficiency, and empirical "rationality."

impinge upon all aspects of life.[15] The task of an ecology of technology concerned with "interrelationships between technology and the world" is to reintegrate "advanced human craft with the [Creation] it sprung from."[16] Therefore, it is valuable to distinguish between necessary, unitive, and transformative forms of vulnerability that are possible with technology from the scourge of harmful vulnerabilities imposed by supremacist technocracy. From ancient mystic wisdom, necessary vulnerability might entail any form of discomfort, pain, suffering, or grief that is unavoidable and grounds us in our creaturely and human existence—it paradoxically challenges us to grow from falsehood to authenticity, nurtures holy longing and communion. On the other hand, harmful vulnerability detracts from human or creaturely flourishing; it is avoidable in the sense that it is purposeful and often unjust. Modern tech in its instrumental efficiency, problem solving, and life-enhancing capabilities must aim to be whole-making—to improve human and environmental well-being while also retaining the checks and restraints of traditional tools and technologies in consideration of potential risks and unintended consequences on society and the environment. It follows that technological vulnerability is the capacity for technology to moderate potential harm and consequences to socioecological well-being, for example, privacy, space, time/speed, content constraints, smart sensors, automated shut-down, emissions-control, wildlife-safeties, etc. Technocratic vulnerability is the capacity for technology under technocracy and its related sociocultural infrastructure to cause harm, disenfranchisement, or marginalization and to neglect social, ethical, or ecological complexities, for example, socioeconomically biased algorithms, lack of transparency/mistrust, efficiency before safety, profit before ecosocial responsibility, etc.

In technological development, we positively note many contributions to the fields of medical diagnostics, energy optimization, monitoring of biodiversity, access to education, and more. Yet, as the deputy secretary general of the United Nations, Amina Mohammed, has noted, "these technologies also pose grave risks. They can displace jobs, exploit

---

[15] Walter D. Mignolo and Catherine E. Walsh, *On Decoloniality: Concepts, Analytics, Praxis* (Duke University Press, 2018), 10.

[16] James Bridle, *Ways of Being: Animals, Plants, Machines: The Search for a Planetary Intelligence* (Farrar, Straus and Giroux, 2022), 14, 19.

gaps in global governance, and exacerbate bias, discrimination, and misinformation . . . [and] on a monumental scale."[17] Our technological systems are only as influential as they are helpful to those most vulnerable and at risk of human rights violations. As Pope Francis notes, "the ideological context of [the] technocratic paradigm[,] inspired by a Promethean presumption [of mastering the world, is the rocky soil from which] inequalities [can continue to] grow out of proportion, knowledge and wealth accumulate in the hands of a few, and grave risks ensue for democratic societies and peaceful coexistence."[18] The "regardless power" wielded in modern technocratic culture socializes us to prioritize individual "self-sufficiency, ease, and convenience,"[19] to idolize our own capacities, while augmenting the "metafication of reality"[20]—which together overstimulates and numbs the mind, increases conspiracism and other posttruth blunders, disorients historical consciousness, critical thinking, and interpersonal and interspecies relating. Alone, neither will science and technology in themselves solve all our problems, nor will they bring about the fullness and abundance of a life in Christ. Under technocracy, science and technology limit our engagement with life to the anthropocentric, temporal, and instrumental. Because the dignity of our social and environmental relations is delicately intertwined, Franciscans through integrative justice and peace ministries have decried globalization as a vehicle for neocolonialism, criticizing the continued erasure of the subaltern and the destruction of their environments at the convenience of the privileged and powerful.[21]

Franciscan thinkers must be prepared to lean into the growing conversations around technology and AI to help overcome harmful

---

[17] Amina Mohammed, "Deputy Secretary-General's Remarks at the Opening of the ECOSOC Special Meeting" (Speech, Harnessing Artificial Intelligence for SDGs, UN Headquarters, May 7, 2024), https://www.un.org/sg/en/content/.

[18] Pope Francis, "Message of His Holiness for the World Day of Peace on Artificial Intelligence and Peace" (January 1, 2024), no. 4.

[19] Christine Ledger, *Towards a Theology of Technology: A Theological Inquiry into Technological Culture and the Koinonia of the Church* (Charles Sturt University, 2004), 125.

[20] Term coined by Nathan D. Oglesby to describe the obfuscation of the metaverse with lived reality (e.g., fake AI images of Pope Francis wearing a Balenciaga coat).

[21] See, for example, Astrid Puentes Riaño and Franciscans International, "The Right to a Healthy Environment: From Recognition to Implementation," October 21, 2024, www.franciscansinternational.org/.

A FRANCISCANIZED ECOLOGY OF TECHNOLOGY 79

technocratic vulnerabilities and foster possible ecosocial flourishing. Because rapid technological innovation heightens existential overwhelm via "VUCA forces" (volatility, uncertainty, complexity, and ambiguity),[22] we must be prepared to address its paradox and novelty. Theologians and pastoral leaders ought to help make sense of this overwhelm as it compounds with ecoanxiety, endeavoring to form an ecotheology of technology shaped by a trinitarian sense of relationality-with-otherness and reciprocal gratuitousness as its basis.[23] Since Franciscans are called to see technologies as an extension of our material home and as necessary to the work of caring for our common home, and because technology always models the constitutive power relations of its developer, it must be inspected. Technology itself is neutral in value; how we use it is not. Mindful of the powerful asymmetries, moral escapism, and trespasses of technocracy on the dignity and welfare of all Creation, we must pursue the highest good in technological development by embracing what Benedict XVI called "gratuitousness as an expression of kinship," breaking spirals of conceit, "disarming violence, [and] demilitarizing the heart."[24] We must look for opportunities for technological vulnerability that keep the human-in-the-loop and offer virtuous fail-safe mechanisms that prevent inequitable digital divides in generative AI such as the coding of "algorithms of oppression," the "automation of inequalities," the "coded gaze" of gender and racial bias, and the development of dangerous "weapons of math destruction."[25]

Our sense of spiritual poverty must even put into check the epistemic limits of concepts such as "technology" or AI. Since the recent history

---

[22] Coined by Amy Webb in Brene Brown, "Futurist Amy Webb on What's Coming (and What's Here)," Dare to Lead, accessed May 7, 2024, www.brenebrown.com /.

[23] Ledger, "Towards a Theology of Technology," 129; Celia Deane-Drummond, "Technology, Ecology, and the Divine: A Critical Look at New Technologies Through a Theology of Gratuitousness," in *Just Sustainability: Technology, Ecology, and Resource Extraction*, ed. Christiana Peppard and Andrea Vicini, SJ (Orbis Books, 2015), 153.

[24] Pope Benedict XVI, *Caritas in Veritate* (2009), no. 34; Pope Francis, "Homily of His Holiness at Holy Mass at the Bahrain National Stadium" (Apostolic Journey to the Kingdom of Bahrain, Bahrain Forum for Dialogue: East and West for Human Coexistence, 2022).

[25] See these terms from Safiya Noble, Virginia Eubanks, Cathy O'Neil, and technologists of the Algorithmic Justice League used in Joy Buolamwini's poem "To the Brooklyn Tenants," in *Unmasking AI: My Mission to Protect What Is Human in a World of Machines* (Random House, 2023), chap. 16.

80　　　　　*CRISTOFER FERNÁNDEZ*

of AI finds its origins in the Turing test deployed during World War II, we might ask if the right foundation of AI is a binarized and deceptive human intelligence as the benchmark for automated computational machinery. If such AI emerges from tyrannic technocratic militarism, and the form of solipsistic anthropocentrism schemed by White men conspiring about the decidability and deception of heteronormative identity, then, it is unsurprising that the limits of our thinking on AI have blinded us and wreaked violence in the domination and reduction of the "beauty of the world to numbers."[26] Therefore, a gratuitous approach to artificial developments ought to keep creation-in-the-loop instead of ignoring or erasing the analog complexity of biogeochemical reality. Like natural open systems our technological systems must allow the cybernetic undecidability and communal individuality of ecosystems to impress upon our understanding of intelligence—being more concerned with adapting to the changing planet than trying to preprogram or control it, with sensory feedback integration and the unknowable rather than discrete/concrete answers and certainty, with a system of interrelating, self-regulating, multispecies minds rather than a singular superbrain entrapped in a system.

When reinspecting *intelligence*, it is important to scrutinize our own creational contingency through our *umwelt*, a preunderstanding Jakob von Uexküll describes as the particular framing of socioenvironmental experience by a species, that is, their subjective environmental point of view.[27] Plants and nonhuman animals have distinct experiential perceptions of the world and, we might add, of the Creator, given their creational phenotype and genotype in evolutionary natural history.[28] Those traits that make other animals seem intelligent to us are contingent on them being trained and socialized into our *umwelt*, "on humans being able to read non-human signs."[29] The intelligence of all creatures in the tapestry of creation reflects the Wisdom of God. Intelligence is not simply the collection of abstractions we can test for in the lab (affectivity, self-awareness, etc.). Rather, as technologist James Bridle puts it, "intelligence is a stream, even an excess of all these qualities, more

---

[26] Bridle, *Ways of Being*, 29, 176–79.

[27] Bridle, *Ways of Being*, 24.

[28] Daniel P. Horan, *Catholicity and Emerging Personhood: A Contemporary Theological Anthropology* (Orbis Books, 2019), 113–15; Bridle, *Ways of Being*, 24.

[29] Bridle, *Ways of Being*, 47.

A FRANCISCANIZED ECOLOGY OF TECHNOLOGY

and less, manifesting as something greater, something only recognizable to us at certain times, but immanent in every moment, every gesture, every interaction of the more-than human world."[30]

If, as it appears, all intelligence is ecological, then we have some rather serious reconciliation to do as the species designated to be the cultivators and guardians of our common home. How are Christians undergoing an ecological conversion that repairs the church, rebuilds society, and reedifies catholicity in the earthly *kindom of God*?[31] How are we engaged in an *intersubjective exchange of being* with the wider Creation community, observing, sensing and listening to, and allowing "the alterity of the other to transform us"?[32] How might we apply a Franciscan ecology of technology to Catholic ecosocial ethics, attentive to the colonial power geometries at play?

Tasked with discerning paths for repairing the human and interspecies divide in a truly cocreative manner, we are invited to help devise an atlas for an "algorethics."[33] Our exercise of technological creativity must be tested and tried to prevent programming structural sins in the form of harmful vulnerabilities and human idolatry and separatism from the wider family of Creation. I conclude by proposing the following conditions for integrating Franciscan wisdom with Bridle's starting points for ecological technology.[34]

First, we should prioritize the *unlearning* or deconstruction of privileged anthropocentric epistemologies and the reconstitution of a cosmotheology and cosmography spiritually adequate for living faith in a stochastic and interconnected world. Doing so, we must encode a nonbinary quality into technology by respecting nonhuman agency, while decoding moral dualism and closing the zero-sum game. Second,

---

[30] Bridle, *Ways of Being*, 57.

[31] "Kin-dom" was coined with Georgene Wilson, OSF. Ada María Isasi-Díaz, "Kin-Dom of God: A Mujerista Proposal," in *In Our Own Voices: Latino/a Renditions of Theology*, ed. Benjamin Valentin (Orbis Books, 2010), 171–89.

[32] Leonardo Boff and Mark Hathaway, "Ecology and the Theology of Nature," in *Ecology and Theology of Nature*, vol. 5, Concilium, ed. Linda Hogan, João Vila-Chã, and A. E. Orobator (SCM Press, 2018), 50.

[33] Pope Francis, "Address of the Holy Father at the G7 in Borgo Egnazia" (2024); also see the work of the pope's Franciscan adviser on AI/Tech Paolo Benanti, "The Urgency of an Algorethics," *Discover Artificial Intelligence* 3, no. 1 (March 27, 2023), http://dx.doi.org/10.1007/s44163-023-00056-6.

[34] Bridle, *Ways of Being*, 207–11, 272, 281.

82   *CRISTOFER FERNÁNDEZ*

we must decenter the privileged human subject (including subsets of privileged humans and advantaged social systems)[35] and the increased inclusion of alterity in all its forms of creational intelligence. This includes the decentralization and sharing of power, knowledge, and materials, and the restructuring of digital networks (see, e.g., mycorrhizal networks and Mother Trees). Additionally, the insights of the intelligence and agency in the lives and societies of nonhuman beings and natural ecosystems should be integrated into our growing project of generative AI, into the lifecycle of machine learning, so that these systems can have built-in warning signs of fragmentation, oppression of alterity, or ecological degradation in Creation. Third, we ought to embrace the mystery of Creation by integrating the *unknowing* into our intellectual, moral, and spiritual formation—where God speaks from interstices, uncertainties, and the peripheries of Creation. Such a posture demands a healthy sense of contingency and firm faith in the Creator who created out of love a "complex, ever-shifting [planet] over which we do not, and cannot, have control."[36] This might be aided by study and education on wisdom theology, the promise of practical wisdom in more-than-human Creation to help instruct us, the dialogue between science and theology, and constructive theology emerging from dialogues with Indigenous cosmovisions.

It is important to acknowledge the constant challenge of vulnerability in the wilderness of the human condition. Technological ethics must experience a "sting of conscience" amidst the many vices of capitalist socioeconomics. After all, the technocratic vulnerabilities of today are systemic dominations over the potential for life to flourish. Because the ecosocial crises of our times are rooted foremost in a spiritual crisis of life in the Anthropocene,[37] it is fitting to harness the FIST for a thriving kindom formed by interrelational solidarity and interspecies mutuality. Perhaps we will be better suited to prevent environmental injustices—violence to lands and peoples—by designing better integrated infrastructure and technologies inspired by the wisdom of all creatures. It is in freely and boldly being technologically

---

[35] White Christian privilege, caste/apartheid/racism, colorism, ableism, misogyny, etc.

[36] Bridle, *Ways of Being*, 210.

[37] The age of humans.

vulnerable that we will sustain an ecology of technology inspired by Francis of Assisi and his penchant for *giving right praise* with and through Creation—instead of living over-and-against it all.[38] May this vision of the flourishing of all creatures toward a Symbiocene[39] on this side of heaven expand the exercise of imaginative cognition unto our collective destination in the New Creation.

---

[38] Horan, *All God's Creatures*, 209.

[39] The age of mutuality, when humans are reintegrated with the rest of Creation.

Gun Violence, Vulnerability, and Flourishing

Tobias Winright

As we awaited our food in a restaurant near our new home in Ireland during a late lunch at 3:12 p.m. on October 24, 2022, my wife and I received the following text: "There is a lockdown right now." The message was from one of our daughters, who was 3,897 miles away, where it was only 9:12 a.m. A senior in high school, she had decided to stay in St. Louis, Missouri, to graduate in December rather than to move with us and her younger sister across the Atlantic earlier that summer. Not only did distance separate us, the six-hour time difference did so, too. Thus, to our dismay, thirteen minutes had already elapsed before we even noticed her initial message as well as a subsequent one in which she added that this was not a drill—she heard yelling—and that she loved us. There was an active shooter in the building. We panicked, imagining that the worst had already happened to her. We replied that we loved her, and we asked for an update. To our relief, she immediately responded that she was hiding with her teacher and classmates in their barricaded classroom, but our dread remained as did our sense of helplessness. We continued texting, and it seemed like an eternity as we waited for each additional message from her. Several minutes later, she informed us that she could see through a window that the police had arrived outside and that she heard more gunfire. After a few more slow-motion minutes, at 9:34 (3:34 for us), we finally read the welcome words, "We're out."

This was one of 308 school shooting incidents that killed and

GUN VIOLENCE, VULNERABILITY, AND FLOURISHING

wounded 273 persons in the US during 2022.[1] According to the K–12 School Shooting Database, which includes any incidents at schools "when a gun is brandished, is fired, or a bullet hits school property for any reason, regardless of the number of victims, time, or day of the week," there were 256 such occurrences that wounded and killed 189 persons in 2021 and 349 more that wounded and killed 249 persons in 2023.[2] The mass shooting at Robb Elementary School in Uvalde, Texas, five months earlier, where nineteen children and two adults were killed, was on our minds as we awaited each text from our daughter.[3] Unbeknownst to us at the time, the shooter had expressed his intention in a note left in his car to murder more students, faculty, and staff than at other schools such as in Littleton, Colorado, in 1999, and in Parkland, Florida, in 2018.

Although it was one of the most secure buildings in the city's school system—with locked doors, metal detectors, and security officers—a nineteen-year-old alumnus of the school, armed with an AR-15 (Armalite) style rifle and six hundred rounds of ammunition, shot his way through the entrance. Unlike what happened in Uvalde, though, nearby law enforcement officers quickly responded and engaged the shooter. While our daughter was being evacuated by the police, she had to walk past the body of a fifteen-year-old girl who had been killed in the hall. As a former law enforcement officer, I have seen gunshot victims. My wife, an ICU nurse, also has seen too many herself. A sixty-one-year-old teacher was also slain, and seven other people were injured. On that terrible day, our daughter, her classmates, the teachers, administrators, and staff—as well as their loved ones and families—were traumatized.

As for the shooter, who was shot and killed by the police, his family during the months preceding this tragedy had grown concerned about his mental health, gotten treatment for him, and taken other precautionary measures. Yet, the note left in his car said, "I don't have any friends. I don't have any family. I've never had a girlfriend. I've never had

---

[1] David Riedman, K–12 School Shooting Database, 2023, https://k12ssdb.org/all-shootings.

[2] Riedman, K–12 School Shooting Database.

[3] Sneha Dey, "21 Killed at Uvalde Elementary in Texas' Deadliest School Shooting Ever," *Texas Tribune*, May 24, 2022, https://www.texastribune.org/2022/05/24/uvalde-texas-school-shooting/.

86   *TOBIAS WINRIGHT*

a social life. I've been an isolated loner my entire life."[4] Like 98 percent of mass shooters, he was a young male experiencing a mental health crisis, including a profound sense of alienation and loneliness.[5] I believe his mother when she says that she is "so heartbroken over the families that paid for his episode,"[6] and I know that she, too, has paid a price.

Several months later, during a summit on gun violence hosted by the Archdiocese of St. Louis, I sat with an agent from the ATF (Bureau of Alcohol, Tobacco, Firearms, and Explosives) who was one of the first two law enforcement officers to arrive at the school.[7] After he told me he was in the hall where my daughter was being evacuated, I thanked him for doing his part to save lives, including my daughter's. Both of us with tears in our eyes, I realized that he, too, was traumatized. When I worked in law enforcement, I responded to 911 calls of "shots fired" and saw the aftereffects of shootings. I am thankful that I never had to respond to an active school shooting. As another former police officer writes, "From a law enforcement perspective, responding to 911 calls involving multiple child victims, massive trauma and the loss of life is one of the most psychologically challenging events for police officers. It is unlike any other 911 call, because of the *vulnerability* of children and school staff who are unequipped to deal with active shooter incidents."[8] In addition to active shooter drills, many schools now conduct "vulnerability assessments" to mitigate against, if not to eliminate entirely, the threat of gun violence to students and staff.[9] Thus, the first word

---

[4] Nouran Salahieh, Holly Yan, and Rebekah Riess, "St. Louis School Shooter's Family Sought Mental Health Treatment for Him and Had His Gun Taken Away, Police Said. Yet Tragedy Still Unfolded," CNN, October 26, 2022, https://edition.cnn.com/2022/10/26/us/st-louis-school-shooting-wednesday/index.html.

[5] Michel Martin and Emma Bowman, "Why Nearly All Mass Shooters Are Men," *All Things Considered*, NPR, March 27, 2021, https://www.npr.org/2021/03/27/981803154/why-nearly-all-mass-shooters-are-men.

[6] Salahieh, Yan, and Riess, "St. Louis School Shooter's Family."

[7] Valerie Schremp Hahn, "Hundreds Gather for Gun Violence Summit Hosted by St. Louis Archdiocese," *Catholic Health World*, September 1, 2023, https://www.chausa.org/publications/catholic-health-world/archive/article/september-1-2023/hundreds-gather-for-gun-violence-summit-hosted-by-st.-louis-archdiocese.

[8] Jarrod Sadulski, "Responding to School Shootings: A Former Police Officer's Viewpoint," *Police 1*, July 21, 2022, https://www.police1.com/police-products/fitness-mental-health-wellness/articles/responding-to-school-shootings-a-former-police-officers-viewpoint-pa5XiRIHqfLjZRGp/. Italics added.

[9] Editors, "School Safety Drills Alone Won't Prevent Shootings. We Must Assess Our Vulnerabilities," *San Diego Tribune*, November 29, 2023, https://www.

GUN VIOLENCE, VULNERABILITY, AND FLOURISHING   **87**

in the title of this present annual volume, vulnerability, immediately came to mind for me in connection with the problem of gun violence.

Regarding the other word in this volume's title, if the purpose of human life is flourishing, happiness, and well-being, which is how Brian Stiltner translates the Greek term *eudaimonia*,[10] then gun violence in our schools violates it. Drawing on the work of Martha Nussbaum, Stiltner identifies ten central human capabilities that "are a way of specifying areas of flourishing . . . and the resources needed for the pursuit of flourishing."[11] For example, in addition to the "ability to live a normal lifespan," there are also the correlative abilities to "being safe from violence" and to "attain education."[12] Vulnerability to gun violence impedes and impairs each of these, thereby undermining flourishing. Moreover, if the purpose of ethics, as Stiltner claims, also is flourishing,[13] and if, as Stanley Hauerwas holds, "the question of violence is the central issue for any Christian social ethic,"[14] then it is striking that gun violence has been a lacuna.[15] Thus, I welcomed the Statement on Gun Violence (the Statement) issued by the Board of the College Theology Society (CTS) during our 2023 Annual Convention at Sacred Heart University in Fairfield, Connecticut, which urges CTS members to study

---

sandiegouniontribune.com/2023/11/29/school-safety-drills-alone-wont-prevent-shootings-we-must-assess-our-vulnerabilities/.

[10] Brian Stiltner, *Toward Thriving Communities: Virtue Ethics as Social Ethics* (Anselm Academic, 2016), 54, 73.

[11] Stiltner, *Toward Thriving Communities*, 85.

[12] Stiltner, *Toward Thriving Communities*, 83.

[13] Stiltner, *Toward Thriving Communities*, 72.

[14] Stanley Hauerwas, *The Peaceable Kingdom: A Primer in Christian Ethics* (University of Notre Dame Press, 1983), 114.

[15] Todd David Whitmore and I noted the problem of school shootings during the 1990s in our essay, "Children: An Undeveloped Theme in Catholic Teaching," in *The Challenge of Global Stewardship: Roman Catholic Responses*, ed. Maura A. Ryan and Todd David Whitmore (University of Notre Dame Press, 1997), 161–85. Among the few theological ethicists who have addressed gun violence are William P. George, "Guns and the Catholic Conscience," *Chicago Studies* 35, no. 1 (April 1996): 82–95; Richard C. Sparks, C.S.P., *Contemporary Christian Morality: Real Questions, Candid Responses* (Crossroad, 1996), 136–37; and Patrick T. McCormick, "Weapons of Self-Destruction," *U.S. Catholic* 74, no. 1 (January 2009): 42–43. Some theological ethicists have published blog posts; for my earliest attempt, see Tobias Winright, "*Pacem in Terris*, The US Gun Legislation Debate, and Rights," *Catholic Moral Theology*, April 11, 2013, https://catholicmoraltheology.com/pacem-in-terris-the-us-gun-legislation-debate-and-rights/.

88   *TOBIAS WINRIGHT*

"gun violence in ways proper to our disciplines" and to "use whatever resources we possess—as scholars, teachers, ministers, and activists—to shed light on the causes and effects of gun violence and foster a praxis of life that interrupts and seeks to end this terrible reality."[16]

As a theological ethicist, I thus attempt to "shed light" on gun violence, especially as it impacts the vulnerable, using some of the "ways proper to" my discipline. One of these "ways" has to do with beginning with the "signs of the times" alluded to in the Statement and, as Patrick T. McCormick and Russell B. Connors Jr. emphasize, "first listening to the voice, or rather the voices of experience," and especially "those with the least protection or power and thus most likely to be harmed by our choices."[17] While the Statement mentions some who are vulnerable to gun violence, there are additional persons at risk whose voices should be included. Next, I suggest that the Statement's neglect of these others may be due to its main form of moral discourse—a prophetic approach—and that employing additional modes of moral discourse would bolster its persuasiveness and reception. Finally, while some theological ethicists recently have advocated an "ethics of vulnerability," I echo Ellen Ott Marshall's caveat about a "virtuous vulnerability," which I note may be associated with the prophetic approach, and "its implications for vulnerable people . . . in the context of gun violence."[18]

The Statement begins with three biblical quotations: Cain's murder of his brother Abel (Genesis 1:9–10), the prophetic vision of peace when weapons are converted to farming tools (Isaiah 2:4), and the absence of fear in love (1 Jn 4:18). In its opening paragraph, the Statement notes "an unprecedented surge in gun violence" in the United States, including the number of mass shootings that "has nearly doubled since 2016" and the fact that gun violence has become "the leading killer of children in the United States, with more children dying from gun

---

[16] The College Theology Society Board, "Statement on Gun Violence," June 1, 2023, https://www.collegetheology.org/resources/Documents/CTS%20Board%20 Statement%20on%20Gun%20Violence%20_%20Adopted%20June%201,%202023. pdf. This statement is two-and-one-half pages long, and subsequent quotes from it are from the first two pages.

[17] Patrick T. McCormick and Russell B. Connors Jr., *Facing Ethical Issues: Dimensions of Character, Choices and Community* (Paulist Press, 2002), 19–20.

[18] Ellen Ott Marshall, "Christian Arguments for Gun Violence Prevention: Reflections on Moral Claims in the Context of Advocacy," *Journal of Moral Theology* 12, Special Issue 2 (2023): 134, 149.

violence than motor vehicle accidents or cancer." While the Statement calls gun violence a "pandemic," it should perhaps be viewed more as an *epidemic* because the problem is especially acute in the US, which leads the world when it comes to firearms ownership and gun deaths.[19] Indeed, there are more guns than there are people in the US; whereas, in Ireland, with a population of just over five million people, there are only around 200,000 licensed gun owners, and most of these firearms are shotguns rather than rifles or handguns.[20] Although gun violence is a problem in many other nations around the world, it is not present in all countries.[21]

According to the second paragraph of the Statement, this "terrible reality" of the "deaths of persons made in God's image with an inalienable dignity and the right to flourish as beloved children of God" is one of the "signs of the times" that CTS members "as scholars [are] committed to reading . . . in the light of the Gospel proclamation of love and peace." In the rest of this paragraph and the remaining two paragraphs of the Statement, the "reality of gun violence" is described more sweepingly. The "structural roots of gun violence" are the primary problem to be examined and addressed, and the Statement foregrounds the firearms industry, the gun lobby, "a logic of violence and domination," a "culture of death," "a false narrative," and "any association of this system with the Christian faith," especially "white Christian nationalism." More than once, and invoking the words of Martin Luther King Jr., the Statement says that silence and indifference are forms of complicity with the evils of gun violence, and it calls on CTS members to "speak and act, denouncing social and ideological forces that fuel gun violence and diminish human life, and announcing a radical message of peace."

Among its recommendations, the Statement highlights "listening to and elevating the voices of those communities most affected by gun violence," including BIPOC (Black, Indigenous, and People of Color)

---

[19] Shane Claiborne and Michael Martin, *Beating Guns: Hope for People Who Are Weary of Violence* (Brazos, 2019), 39.

[20] Conor Gallagher, "Ireland's 100,000+ Gun Owners: Who Are They, Where Are They and What Firearms Do They Own?," *Irish Times*, August 6, 2022, https://www.irishtimes.com/life-style/2022/08/06/gun-ownership-in-ireland-dont-call-it-a-weapon-whatever-you-do-call-it-a-firearm/.

[21] Editorial, "Understanding Global Gun Violence, and How to Control It," *The Lancet* 402, no. 10411 (October 21, 2023), https://www.thelancet.com/article/S0140-6736(23)02347-4/fulltext.

90 TOBIAS WINRIGHT

communities that are disproportionately impacted. It expresses the CTS's "solidarity with other groups and communities" and the "solutions proposed by organizers and advocates engaged with these communities." Again quoting Isaiah 2:4—"They shall beat their swords into plowshares"—the Statement calls on Christians to "radically recommit ourselves to peace and justice" and to "the creation of a new world of peace founded on justice."

While I concur with the Statement's criticisms of gun violence, its call for solidarity with those most affected by it, and its exhortations to promote a just peace, I wish that it were more comprehensive in both its consideration of whom else to include among those vulnerable to gun violence and its mode of moral discourse. On the first, I appreciate the attention the Statement gives to the consequences of gun violence on children, as well as its recognition of the disproportionate impact of gun violence on BIPOC communities. As the Centers for Disease Control and Prevention (CDC) reports, "some groups have higher rates of firearm injury than others," and among these are both children up to the age of nineteen and members of BIPOC communities.[22] Concerning the latter, according to the Giffords Law Center, 50 percent of firearm-caused homicide victims are Black men,[23] and Everytown for Gun Safety reports that Black men and women combined constitute 68 percent of gun homicides.[24] These homicides occur at higher rates in urban areas, such as downtown St. Louis, where most of my family's neighbors were Black persons who inordinately experienced gun violence.[25]

---

[22] Centers for Disease Control and Prevention, "Fast Facts: Firearm Injury and Death," July 5, 2024, https://www.cdc.gov/firearm-violence/data-research/facts-stats/index.html.

[23] Giffords Law Centre, "Statistics," giffords.org/lawcenter/gun-violence-statistics/.

[24] Everytown for Gun Safety, "Impact of Gun Violence on Black Americans," everytownresearch.org/issue/gun-violence-black-americans/.

[25] Monica Obradovic, "Missouri's Black Homicide Victimization Rate Again Highest in US," *Riverfront Times*, April 27, 2023, https://www.riverfronttimes.com/news/missouris-black-homicide-victimization-rate-again-highest-in-us-39941072. I often posted on social media my videos of gunfights near our apartment and photos of bullet casings that I saw while jogging on the city's streets and sidewalks. One time while I was jogging, I was the victim of a drive-by shooting; fortunately, I realized as I fell over and grabbed my chest that the liquid on my shirt was paint rather than blood—but for a moment I definitely believed I was shot by a real rather than a paintball gun.

GUN VIOLENCE, VULNERABILITY, AND FLOURISHING 91

Also of significance, the firearm homicide rate is especially high for Black children, who are doubly vulnerable by being both a child and a Black person. In an article appearing in the September 2023 issue of *Pediatrics*, published by the American Academy of Pediatrics, from 2018 to 2021, there was a 41.6 percent increase in the firearm death rate amongst US children, with Black children during 2021 accounting for 67.3 percent of firearm homicides and White children comprising 78.4 percent of firearm suicides.[26]

That last statistic is notable about gun suicides and White children. Curiously, the Statement does not mention persons who are vulnerable to firearm suicide. Although mass shootings, as the Statement mentions, have increased in number from 272 in 2013 to 656 in 2023, most gun deaths are suicides.[27] According to the Giffords Law Center, 60 percent of gun deaths are suicides, primarily by White men, especially in poor rural areas.[28] The CDC, too, notes that non-Hispanic White persons are particularly vulnerable to suicide.[29] The Gun Violence Archive (GVA) reports that between 2014 and 2022, while the number of willful, malicious, and accidental firearms deaths increased from 12,356 to 20,390, the number of firearm suicides increased from 21,386 to 27,038.[30] As Conor M. Kelly notes, in 2019, the US, which is 4 percent of the world's population, "was home to forty-four percent of the planet's firearms suicides."[31] This fact should be included in the "signs of the times" when it comes to gun violence. Surely those who are experiencing severe mental health crises should be counted among those who are vulnerable to gun violence. In his article, Kelly comprehensively considers firearms suicides in different US states, as well as the rural–urban divide regarding firearms homicides, and he provides

---

[26] Bailey K. Roberts et al., "Trends and Disparities in Firearm Deaths Among Children," *Pediatrics* 152, no. 3 (September 2023): 1–8, https://doi.org/10.1542/peds.2023-061296.

[27] Gun Violence Archive, https://www.gunviolencearchive.org/. The GVA defines a mass shooting as four or more persons shot or killed, not including the shooter.

[28] Giffords Law Center, "Statistics," giffords.org/lawcenter/gun-violence-statistics/. Nearly four decades ago, when I was in my early twenties, during one night of despair I almost became one of these statistics.

[29] Centers for Disease Control and Prevention, "Fast Facts: Firearm Injury and Death," https://www.cdc.gov/firearm-violence/data-research/facts-stats/index.html.

[30] Gun Violence Archive, https://www.gunviolencearchive.org/.

[31] Conor M. Kelly, "Gun Laws and Gun Deaths: An Empirical Analysis and Theological Assessment," *Journal of Moral Theology* 12, Special Issue 2 (2023): 11.

a careful empirical analysis taking into account many variables that, while structural in scope and having a lot to do with the availability of guns, cannot be attributed merely to what the bulk of the Statement indicts as "the logic of violence and domination that drives America's obsession with gun ownership and violence."

To be fair, the Statement is an asseveration, not an article. It invites CTS members to do the scholarly work and to conduct "intersectional analysis of gun violence and religion, race, class, etc." It does not purport to do any of this itself. Still, its omission of a large group of US citizens who are vulnerable to being killed by firearms is conspicuous. Drawing on one of the "ways proper to" my discipline of theological ethics, I suggest that this oversight may be due to the Statement's reliance on what Cathleen Kaveny calls "the rhetoric of prophetic indictment."[32] The main approach throughout the Statement is "prophetic denunciation" rather than "deliberative assessment."[33] While the Statement solicits the latter, it mostly employs unequivocal "prophetic indictments" that may, warns Kaveny, "function as instruments of the culture wars" and exacerbate "the heated battles of the American public square."[34] I worry that the Statement "preaches to the choir" and fails to engage others who might be persuaded through a more deliberative approach. For Kaveny, *both* the prophetic and deliberative approaches were exemplified by Martin Luther King Jr. While prophetically condemning social evils, we must deliberatively engage the perspective and arguments of those with whom we disagree. The Statement's sweeping condemnations of "a logic of violence and domination" that is fueled by "ideological forces" and the "industry of gun manufacturing and sales," apparently lumping all gun ownership and use under this indictment, and its failure to attend to any arguments that are given by citizens, including Christians, to justify gun ownership, may not be as helpful as hoped to prevent and reduce gun violence.

According to a 2023 Pew Research Center survey, "72% of U.S. gun owners say protection is a major reason they own a gun."[35] In other

---

[32] Cathleen Kaveny, *Prophecy Without Contempt: Religious Discourse in the Public Square* (Harvard University Press, 2016), 2.

[33] Kaveny, *Prophecy Without Contempt*, 8.

[34] Kaveny, *Prophecy Without Contempt*, x, 6.

[35] Pew Research Center, "For Most U.S. Gun Owners, Protection Is the Main Reason They Own a Gun," August 16, 2023, https://www.pewresearch.org/

GUN VIOLENCE, VULNERABILITY, AND FLOURISHING 93

words, these citizens justify their ownership of a firearm by claiming they may need to defend themselves and others, usually their family, and perhaps their property. Indeed, women, African Americans, and LGBTQ+ persons in recent years increasingly have been purchasing firearms for protection too.[36] Although the Statement does not mention this within the "reality of gun violence," the GVA includes "defensive gun use," which is defined as the "reported use of force with a firearm to protect and defend oneself or family."[37] During my experience working in law enforcement, but also for a few years afterward, I owned a handgun for only this reason: to defend myself or other persons (family or not), but *not* property, from threats against life. In other words, like many other citizens, I could give a moral justification for owning and possibly using a firearm, a rationale that perhaps should not be sweepingly condemned and dismissed as part of the ideological "logic of violence and domination."

Indeed, 81 percent of gun owners say owning a firearm makes them "feel safer."[38] Although this attitude may be attributed ultimately to the ideological forces circulating in society, including the gun lobby, this claim about protection, safety, and defense of lives should be taken seriously. After all, according to the *Catechism*, "Legitimate defense can be not only a right but a grave duty for someone responsible for another's life."[39] This moral grounding for possible gun ownership ought to be acknowledged and then addressed. Doing so, however, requires more than the approach of prophetic indictment can achieve alone. As the influential ethicist James M. Gustafson has noted, while the prophetic approach may use evidence to support its indictment, few "prophetic

---

politics/2023/08/16/for-most-u-s-gun-owners-protection-is-the-main-reason-they-own-a-gun/#:~:text=Gun%20owners%20in%20the%20United%20States%20continue%20to,%2881%25%29%20say%20they%20feel%20safer%20owning%20a%20gun.

[36] Chauncey Alcorn, "The Fight Against Gun Control Has Some Surprising New Allies," CNN Business, May 18, 2021, https://edition.cnn.com/2021/05/18/business/gun-control-debate-women-minorities.

[37] Gun Violence Archive, "The Explainer," https://www.gunviolencearchive.org/explainer.

[38] Katherine Schaeffer, "Key Facts About Americans and Guns," Pew Research Center, July 24, 2024, https://www.pewresearch.org/short-reads/2024/07/24/key-facts-about-americans-and-guns/.

[39] *Catechism of the Catholic Church*, no. 2265.

94 TOBIAS WINRIGHT

voices take counterevidence into account and develop arguments."[40] Hence, in her friendly critique of prophetic indictment, Kaveny draws on Gustafson's insights about forms of moral discourse, including the observation that any single mode, such as the prophetic, is insufficient, which is why she advocates "prophecy without contempt" in tandem with deliberative assessment.[41]

Gustafson identifies four forms of moral discourse commonly employed by ethicists: prophetic, narrative, ethical, and policy.[42] Kaveny's deliberative assessment includes Gustafson's ethical and policy forms of moral discourse. Other theological ethicists, such as Bernard V. Brady and William Schweiker, have utilized these four forms, too.[43] Lisa Sowle Cahill expands on Gustafson's work by adding a fifth mode, participatory discourse.[44] These ethicists agree that no single mode is sufficient and that "they often overlap and supplement each other."[45]

Prophetic discourse "jars" people and institutions from "blind acceptance of the status quo" by using powerful metaphors and symbols "that are directed to the 'heart' as well as to the 'head.'"[46] In addition to indictment, prophetic discourse offers a utopian vision of peace and justice that contrasts with how things are in society; however, the path for getting from the present reality, including the "resources for the modest increments of improvements," toward the ideal future is not as clearly marked.[47] The Statement mostly manifests this prophetic approach, with its strong criticisms of the "logic of violence and domi-

---

[40] James M. Gustafson, *Intersections: Science, Theology, and Ethics* (Pilgrim Press, 1996), 41.

[41] Kaveny, *Prophecy Without Contempt*, 422.

[42] James M. Gustafson, *Varieties of Moral Discourse: Prophetic, Narrative, Ethical, and Policy* (Calvin College, 1988); James M. Gustafson, "Moral Discourse About Medicine: A Variety of Forms," *Journal of Medicine and Philosophy* 15 (1990): 25–42; James M. Gustafson, *A Sense of the Divine: The Natural Environment from a Theocentric Perspective* (Pilgrim Press, 1994), 111–38.

[43] Bernard V. Brady, *Essential Catholic Social Thought*, 2nd ed. (Orbis Books, 2017), 12–15; William Schweiker, "The Rhetorics of Ethics: To Convince the Mind and Move the Heart," in *Ethics and Advocacy: Bridges and Boundaries*, ed. Harlan Beckley et al. (Cascade, 2022), 3–24.

[44] Lisa Sowle Cahill, *Theological Bioethics: Participation, Justice, and Change* (Georgetown University Press, 2005), 34–42.

[45] Gustafson, *Intersections*, 52.

[46] Gustafson, *Intersections*, 54; Gustafson, *Varieties of Moral Discourse*, 11.

[47] Gustafson, *Varieties of Moral Discourse*, 13; Gustafson, *Intersections*, 42.

GUN VIOLENCE, VULNERABILITY, AND FLOURISHING 95

nation" permeating US culture and its call for speaking and acting in support of "a radical message of peace."

Often connected with prophetic discourse, the narrative form features inspirational stories from scripture and accounts of saints and other exemplary persons, such as Martin Luther King Jr., whom the Statement mentions.[48] As Gustafson puts it, "the principal line of argument is that we are members of moral communities, and the outlooks, values, and visions of these communities are shaped by their stories."[49] After a mass shooting, when someone says, "That's not us," or "That's not America," they are appealing to a narrative. Of course, a counternarrative, or myth, exists also about the place of guns in the American story. Like prophetic discourse, narratives illumine while stirring imagination, emotion, and heart.[50] I would include the stories of victims and survivors of gun violence that, as Ellen Ott Marshall has witnessed, are shared during vigils and prayer services.[51] Indeed, the opening paragraphs of this present chapter are mostly in narrative form. I would also add the ethnographic research that Michael Grigoni has conducted through interviews with Christian gun owners, as well as in his own reflections on his experience taking a course on concealed carry.[52] Still, while helpful, this mode is insufficient, for as Gustafson notes, "Narratives are not arguments in the sense that ethical discourse provides arguments."[53]

The ethical form of moral discourse focuses on moral justification, clarifies and categorizes an issue, and gives reasons for a position on it.[54] It considers theories, principles, duties, intentions, circumstances, consequences, and alternatives, as well as norms like justice and action-guiding criteria.[55] While this approach is necessary, it can tend to concentrate on the "micro" and, "if moral discourse is excessively limited to it," it risks becoming "myopic."[56] As noted earlier, to date there are

---

[48] Brady, *Essential Catholic Social Thought*, 13.

[49] Gustafson, *Intersections*, 49.

[50] Cahill, *Theological Bioethics*, 38; Brady, *Essential Catholic Social Thought*, 13.

[51] Marshall, "Christian Arguments for Gun Violence Prevention," 154–56.

[52] Michael R. Grigoni, "The Christian Handgun Owner and Just War," *Journal of Moral Theology* 12, Special Issue 2 (2023): 108–32.

[53] Gustafson, *Intersections*, 49.

[54] Brady, *Essential Catholic Social Thought*, 13.

[55] Gustafson, *Intersections*, 39.

[56] Gustafson, *Intersections*, 41.

only a few examples of ethical discourse by theologians regarding gun violence. Luis Vera, for instance, engages those who refer to defensive use for justifying their gun ownership, and he interrogates their assumptions about agency, intentionality, and responsibility.[57] Vera's attention to and critique of "situational awareness," in my estimation, is nuanced, careful, and thorough as he questions the accuracy of gun owners' perception of "reality," along with what this habituation does to their personhood.[58] A similarly thoughtful analysis is provided by William P. George, who drills down on intentionality and how it "cannot be totally isolated from act and circumstances," including not only the intention of the gun owner but also the firearm and the ammunition themselves.[59] Thus, while defensive use is posited as the main reason justifying gun ownership, there is also intentionality built into a weapon, such as the AR-15 style rifle, which Eugene Stoner, who invented it, intentionally designed to replace the M14 rifle during the Vietnam War in order to kill quickly as many enemy soldiers as possible.[60] As George observes, "Guns (and bullets) apparently do kill people, and are in fact sometimes *intended* by the manufacturer to do just that, the good or evil intentions of the user aside."[61]

In his ethnographic study of Christian gun owners, Grigoni uncovers an "everyday form of just war reasoning" about the defensive use of a firearm.[62] In the course on concealed carry that he took, Grigoni learned, "Your first priority is not to shoot. If you have to shoot, you shoot to stop, not to kill."[63] This defensive approach to gun ownership "places limits on [one's] use of lethal force" through robust adherence to strict criteria—for example, last resort, right intention, proportionality, discrimination, etc.—and thereby goes beyond the requirements of the

---

[57] Luis Vera, "Concealed Carry, Agency, and Attention in a Technocratic Context," *Journal of Moral Theology* 12, Special Issue 2 (2023): 58–83.

[58] Vera, "Concealed Carry, Agency, and Attention in a Technocratic Context," 75–81.

[59] George, "Guns and the Catholic Conscience," 91, 93.

[60] Zusha Elinson and Cameron McWhirter, "The Creator of the AR-15 Didn't See This Coming," *The Atlantic* (September 27, 2023), https://www.theatlantic.com/ideas/archive/2023/09/ar-15-rifle-gun-history/675449/.

[61] George, "Guns and the Catholic Conscience," 93; italics his.

[62] Grigoni, "The Christian Handgun Owner and Just War," 113.

[63] Grigoni, "The Christian Handgun Owner and Just War," 110.

law such as stand-your-ground laws.[64] Indeed, when I explain the strict guidelines for "legitimate defense" in the *Catechism* (nos. 2263–67) to students and others, they soon realize how different such an approach is from what the Statement calls the "logic of violence and domination."

Gerald W. Schlabach also takes "defensive gun culture" and its reasons justifying gun ownership seriously even as he notes how gun ownership tends to do exactly the opposite of what they claim. Instead of protecting family, gun owners are putting their families in greater danger of accidental death or suicide; or instead of stopping a threat, guns escalate it and intensify the violence.[65] Such concerns were on my mind when I decided to no longer own a handgun, especially when my wife and I began to have children. I would add that, as a former law enforcement officer, I know how thorny threat assessments can be and how difficult using a firearm in real life, split-second circumstances is. After all, even with all their training, police officers make mistakes; plus, some research on implicit bias has found that, when compared to police officers, "community members were overall more likely to shoot black targets than white targets."[66] I share Schlabach's concern that, "whatever the overall statistics regarding the dangers of gun ownership," some will nevertheless consider themselves as exceptions to these precarities.[67] While the ethical mode is necessary, it is insufficient.

The policy mode of moral discourse focuses on institutions, including governments and corporations, and persons working within them. It assesses practices and provides procedures. Policy discourse is "concerned with what is possible given the realities of the social situation,"[68] with what works, the doables, the lower as well as the higher hanging fruit. The Statement does not employ policy discourse. An example of

---

[64] Grigoni, "The Christian Handgun Owner and Just War," 112. This is not to say that I completely agree with Grigoni's interpretation of just war or with his interviewees' implicit application of its moral reasoning and principles. See Tobias Winright, "Firearms and Moral Theology: A Response," *Journal of Moral Theology* 12, Special Issue 2 (2023): 193–96.

[65] Gerald W. Schlabach, "Gun Culture, Free Riding, and Nothing Short of Conversion," *Journal of Moral Theology* 12, Special Issue 2 (2023): 158–84.

[66] Katheryn Russell-Brown, "Making Implicit Bias Explicit: Black Men and the Police," in *Policing the Black Man: Arrest, Prosecution, and Imprisonment*, ed. Angela J. Davis (Vintage, 2017), 145.

[67] Schlabach, "Gun Culture, Free Riding, and Nothing Short of Conversion," 163.

[68] Brady, *Essential Catholic Social Thought*, 14.

98　　　　　　　*TOBIAS WINRIGHT*

this mode may be found in statements and other documents from the United States Conference of Catholic Bishops, such as its 2022 "Backgrounder on Gun Violence: A Mercy and Peacebuilding Approach to Gun Violence," which calls for a ban on assault weapons, the implementation of universal background checks, provision of improved access to and increased resources for mental health care and earlier interventions, and efforts to increase gun safety such as gun locks.[69] This last policy recommendation has been implemented, for example, at St. Louis Children's Hospital, where thousands of gun locks have been made available to patients' families and a study has shown that two-thirds of them use the lock to make their children and their homes safer.[70] In addition to the Statement's prophetic mode of moral discourse, with its utopian call for nonviolence and "beating swords into plowshares," there needs to be this sort of policy discourse in the interim.

A fifth form of moral discourse is suggested by Lisa Sowle Cahill. Participatory discourse focuses more on actions and practices than words and statements.[71] Rather than concentrating on public policy, participatory discourse attends to political and activist movements, associations, churches, and democratic institutions within civil society. Advocacy groups and organizations such as Moms Demand Action for Gun Sense in America, with which Marshall volunteers, and Pax Christi USA, with its gun violence prevention resources, especially the DC Area Interfaith Gun Violence Prevention Network's Interfaith Gun Violence Prevention Toolkit, exemplify participatory discourse.[72] The Statement rightly calls on CTS members to engage "solutions proposed by organizers and advocates engaged with these communities."

In her experience volunteering with Moms Demand Action, Marshall has come to see that theologians should "center those most vulnerable to gun violence in moral reflection."[73] What is required,

---

[69] United States Conference of Catholic Bishops, "Backgrounder on Gun Violence: A Mercy and Peacebuilding Approach to Gun Violence," January 2020, https://www.usccb.org/resources/backgrounder-gun-violence-january-2020.

[70] Emma Tucker, "Pediatricians Are Giving Out Free Gun Locks to Approach the Gun Violence Epidemic as a Public Health Crisis," *CNN*, January 22, 2023, https://edition.cnn.com/2023/01/22/health/pediatricians-gun-locks-public-health-crisis/index.html.

[71] Cahill, *Theological Bioethics*, 253.

[72] See https://paxchristiusa.org/gun-violence-prevention/.

[73] Marshall, "Christian Arguments for Gun Violence Prevention," 150.

she argues, is "a shift in attention from one's own moral claims about guns to the needs of those who have experienced and are most likely to experience gun violence."[74] While homing in on vulnerability, Marshall also worries that "references to vulnerability" in arguments about gun violence may "bring significant moral confusion."[75] For this reason, she distinguishes between "actual vulnerability to gun violence, existential vulnerability as finite creatures in a fragile creation, and a virtuous vulnerability that voluntarily assumes risk as a sign of faith in God."[76] The first includes children, persons struggling with mental illness, and those belonging to BIPOC communities, who Marshall recognizes "are more vulnerable than others," and whose vulnerability increases with the availability of firearms.[77] Next, existential vulnerability is "related to the seeming randomness and pervasiveness of gun violence" that is conveyed when, for instance, there is another mass shooting at a shopping center.[78]

The third type, and about which Marshall has reservations, is virtuous vulnerability. She associates it with some activists, such as Shane Claiborne and Michael Martin, who call for "a literal practice of changing guns into tools . . . and the call to nonviolence."[79] Like Marshall, I worry that the Statement's prophetic exhortation, invoking Isaiah 2:4, and for radical nonviolence, may inadvertently encourage this sort of vulnerability. Indeed, while identifying as a pacifist, Marshall is unsettled by Claiborne's and Martin's apparent expectation that Christians should refuse to take up arms to protect themselves or others vulnerable to attack. "Commending vulnerability as a mark of faith in the context of gun violence," Marshall suggests, "carries the same pastoral and ethical dangers as commending meekness to the margin-

---

[74] Marshall, "Christian Arguments for Gun Violence Prevention," 150.

[75] Marshall, "Christian Arguments for Gun Violence Prevention," 132.

[76] Marshall, "Christian Arguments for Gun Violence Prevention," 132.

[77] Marshall, "Christian Arguments for Gun Violence Prevention," 147, 149.

[78] Marshall, "Christian Arguments for Gun Violence Prevention," 148.

[79] Marshall, "Christian Arguments for Gun Violence Prevention," 144, 146. To be fair, in *Beating Guns*, Claiborne and Martin use more than the prophetic mode, with narratives especially prominent, as well as empirical data. They write, "We hope to engage both the head and the heart in this book" (13). They also recognize that "an overwhelming majority of gun owners are concerned about gun violence" (18). Nevertheless, they ultimately expect nonviolence, saying, "We would rather die with a cross in our hands than a gun" (158).

alized and simplicity to the poor."[80] I also am troubled that by making vulnerability virtuous, students like my daughter are encouraged to be "martyrs" like Cassie Bernall and Rachel Scott, who were murdered at Columbine High School in Littleton, Colorado.[81] I think there should be, as implied by Ott Marshall, a distinction between voluntary and involuntary vulnerability when it comes to gun violence. I also share her concern that this expectation of nonviolence "unnecessarily limits the field of faithful responses to gun violence," but also focuses "on the moral character of the activist [while also pitting] the latter against the needs of those statistically vulnerable to gun violence."[82] Thus, while I welcome the Statement from the Board of the CTS, I wish that it did not limit itself to using the prophetic mode of moral discourse, which possibly promotes this problematic virtuous vulnerability. As Gustafson warns, "if too exclusive attention is given to any one of the types, significant issues of concern to morally sensitive persons and communities are left unattended."[83]

Irish ethicist Linda Hogan has proposed an ethics of vulnerability in which theologians "generate a new kind of conversation: about how we act in the world; about our ethical obligations towards each other; about how to oppose the conditions under which some lives are more vulnerable than others."[84] Her recognition that some lives are, as Ott Marshall puts it, *actually* vulnerable is significant. It supports Ott Marshall's call for "changing the frame from a focus on guns to a focus on victims" and saving people's lives.[85] An ethics of vulnerability should contribute to an ethics of flourishing. And because no single form of moral discourse is sufficient, I recommend the use of all modes to shed light on gun violence and to move from vulnerability to flourishing.

---

[80] Ott Marshall, "Christian Arguments for Gun Violence Prevention," 149.

[81] Alissa Wilkinson, "After Columbine, Martyrdom Became a Powerful Fantasy for Christian Teenagers," *Vox*, April 17, 2019, https://www.vox.com/culture/2017/4/20/15369442/columbine-anniversary-cassie-bernall-rachel-scott-martyrdom.

[82] Ott Marshall, "Christian Arguments for Gun Violence Prevention," 149.

[83] Gustafson, *Intersections*, 37.

[84] Linda Hogan, "Vulnerability: An Ethic for a Divided World," in *Building Bridges in Sarajevo: The Plenary Papers of Sarajevo 2018*, ed. James Keenan et al. (Orbis Books, 2019), 219. See James F. Keenan, SJ, "The World at Risk: Vulnerability, Precarity, and Connectedness," *Theological Studies* 81, no. 1 (March 2020): 132–49.

[85] Marshall, "Christian Arguments for Gun Violence Prevention," 151.

There Is a Balm

Vulnerability, Challenge, and Hope

C. Vanessa White

I am happy to have this time to journey with members of the College Theology Society and the National Association of Baptist Professors of Religion as we reflect together on vocation and the experience of being a scholar and theological educator in an institution of higher education. I specifically was invited to share with you my own journey as one who has strived to maintain and sustain a healthy wholistic and joyful life as a theological educator, minister, and academic. Rooted in the African American storytelling tradition, as caretaker of this story, I will be using my own life experience and story as a source for theology and praxis as I try to illustrate the journey of vulnerability, challenge, and hope. The story that I will tell will utilize aspects of the past for use in this present-day circumstance.[1] This chapter will focus on the journey as academics and theologians living in authenticity and freedom in the midst of various challenges that threaten their own spiritual, psychological, and ministerial life. I will also highlight the role of self-care and embodiment in the journey of teaching in the academy. How do we care for these bodies as temples of the Holy Spirit? How are we

---

[1] For further sources on African American storytelling tradition, see timone davis, *Intergenerational Catechesis: Revitalizing Faith Through African-American Storytelling* (Lexington Books, 2021); Henry Louis Gates, "Narration and Cultural Memory in the African American Tradition," in *Talk That Talk: An Anthology of African American Storytelling*, ed. Linda Goss and Marian E. Barnes (Simon & Schuster/Touchstone, 1989).

102 C. VANESSA WHITE

mindful of ourselves as *imago dei*? Before reading further, I invite the reader to take several moments and become mindful of your breath as well as your body. Let us breathe.

I choose the title of this chapter based on an African American spiritual that speaks to that sense of nurture and care—"A Balm in Gilead." This song is taken from the African American religious tradition and is known as one of the Spirituals—the sorrow songs (of the enslaved African) that were described by W. E. B. DuBois in his seminal classic, *The Souls of Black Folk.*[2] The title of the song, "A Balm in Gilead" is taken from scripture—in Jeremiah 8:22, which asks, "Is there no balm in Gilead? Is there no physician there?"[3] For our enslaved ancestors and even today, song has been a balm for healing, song has power, and the spiritual practice of singing allows us to prepare this vessel to receive the Holy Spirit. The sorrow songs gave my ancestors the strength to continue to endure in times of immense struggle. If you have the opportunity, I even encourage the reader to find this song on a social media platform and listen to the words, specifically in the context of your journey as a theological educator in today's context.

> There is a balm in Gilead
>   to make the wounded whole.
> There is a balm in Gilead
>   to heal the sin-sick soul.
> Sometimes I feel discouraged,
>   and think my works in vain,
>   but then the Holy Spirit
>   revives my soul again.
> There is a balm in Gilead
>   to make the wounded whole.
> There is a balm in Gilead
>   to heal the sin-sick soul.

Take a moment and reflect on this song. Where is that balm of Gilead to be found in our communities and within the academy? Where is

---

[2] See W. E. B. DuBois, "Of the Sorrow Songs," in *The Souls of Black Folk* (1903). Various publishers are available for this book. You may also use the link below for immediate access to the chapter that refers to the spirituals in the book. https://teachingamericanhistory.org/document/the-sorrow-songs/.

[3] Jeremiah 8:22 (African American Catholic Youth Bible–NAB).

THERE IS A BALM   **103**

there need for healing? Before I respond to this question, I need to take a moment and address our current social situation, which in many ways impacts the theological educator and students in the classroom and requires the need of a healing balm.

These few years have been a time of immense crisis, chaos within our world that has shaped our teaching, research, and writing. As we prepare our students to encounter this world, to live as persons of faith and justice, we ourselves also cannot separate our spiritual life, our emotional, psychological wellbeing from what is taking place in our world. One cannot separate our spiritual life from our current context. In fact, for many of us, our current context is continually addressed in our teaching and our writings. It is hard to make the choice to find good news. But that is what I am going to ask you to do at this moment. Over the past few years, we have had to cope with the violence inflicted upon unarmed Black bodies by police. The horrific deaths of Breonna Taylor and George Floyd instantly come to mind. The impact of the COVID-19 pandemic still affects many in our communities. There is xenophobia in all its forms, and how we treat our immigrants and migrants in this nation and in our cities is a sorry testament to the US being the land that welcomes all. While many deny there is climate change, we cannot ignore the increase in wildfires, contaminated water in many communities, and the increase in hurricanes and other storms. I recently returned from a pilgrimage to the Equal Justice Initiative's legacy museum in Montgomery, Alabama, where I was once again confronted by unequal justice and incarceration of Black and Brown bodies. Finally, our current political climate in the US, the spewing of hate and racism by some who are running for public office, has created an environment that is a breeding ground for stress and other ills.

Focusing on the increasing negative influences in our society also negatively impacts our health. Dr. Andrew Weil, a Harvard-educated physician, in 1995 wrote of the negative impact of all the events that surround us. He suggested taking a news fast once a week where you do not read, watch, or listen to any news for a day and see how you feel.[4] In fact, why not change your focus to reflecting on the good news that also surrounds you? What you focus on is what you give power to. Focusing on the negative aspects of your journey gives them power, and therefore just imagine if you change your focus. Imagine how that

---

[4] Andrew Weil, *Spontaneous Healing* (Random House, 1995), 212.

could change your outlook and even your own spiritual and emotional health. Focusing on the negative breeds further negativity, while focusing on God's presence and grace in the midst of the chaos can in fact give one the spiritual strength to endure. In my journey of health and healing, God's grace can be found in the mentors and words of advice that have sustained me for the past forty years of active ministry and theological education. Those mentors include M. Shawn Copeland, Ana Maria Pineda, Jamie T. Phelps, O.P., and Cyprian Davis, OSB. My teaching and writing have been shaped by the legacy of Sr. Thea Bowman and Fr. Cyprian Davis of happy memory. My words of experience and caution in navigating in the academy are fueled by the words of African American poet Mari Evans, who eloquently admonishes us to speak the truth to the people in love, courage, and honesty to free their minds.[5]

Today, I wish to speak my truth and my experience of journeying in theological education and the academy as a BIPOC (Black Indigenous Person of Color) who identifies as a cisgender woman. In my journey, I have been confronted with the loss of many ministers who died too soon. African American scholars and ministers as Sr. Thea Bowman, Archbishop James Patterson Lyke, musician extraordinaire Kenneth Louis, and religious education scholar Nathan Jones were instrumental to my own formation as a minister but who also succumbed to an early death. I also encountered many who continued in ministry and theological education who are unhappy, overwhelmed by stress and "pastoral hostility." Some of my fellow academics are engaged in the theological work but are constantly angry, frustrated, and depressed. As I journeyed, the words of Rev. Dr. Martin Luther King came to mind. Dr. King has often been quoted saying, "Our lives begin to end the day we are silent about things that matter."[6] I found that like the Rev. Dr. Martin Luther King, I must speak out and address the unhealth that I have witnessed and have personally experienced in my own journey as a scholar, minister, and theologian.

---

[5] Mari Evans, *Continuum: New and Selected Poems* (Black Classic Press, 2007), 22–23.

[6] Rev. Dr. Martin Luther King. Paraphrase of sermon that Dr. King gave in Selma, Alabama, on March 8, 1965. His actual quote was, "A man dies when he refuses to stand up for that which is right. A man dies when he refuses to stand up for justice. A man dies when he refuses to take a stand for that which is true."

My Journey—Seeking the Balm

Before I share suggestions for navigating in the academy, I need to begin with my own journey as a scholar, minister, and theologian. In fact, my story in many ways is a common one among BIPOC faculty. When I began at my institution over twenty years ago, I had the role of formation director for Black Catholic lay students at a graduate school of theology and ministry. In a faculty consisting of twenty-five members, there were no regular African American/Black faculty and only one adjunct Black religious male who taught a pastoral ministry course every two years. Fifteen years later, I became the first and only tenured, Black lay faculty at an institution that is known globally for forming men and women to minister in a diverse church. In the time since, we have hired four Asian faculty, three Latin@ faculty, one Nigerian faculty member, and one African American faculty. I have been at my institution now for over twenty-five years. The current faculty of twenty-four includes two Latin@ faculty, four Asian faculty members (three males and one female—who will be leaving in the next two months), one African American faculty, and one Nigerian faculty member. Except for one, all are tenure-track faculty. Almost all the BIPOC faculty hold dual faculty and administrative appointments. I, in fact, for several years held a tenured faculty position as well as the director of six graduate degree programs, founding director of one graduate certificate program, and chair of the department. How do these numbers compare to recent data from both the National Center for Education Statistics and the Association for Theological Schools?

National Center for Education Statistics (2021)

In the fall of 2021, of the 1.5 million faculty at degree-granting postsecondary institutions, 56 percent were full time, and 44 percent were part time.[7] Faculty includes professors, associate professors, assistant professors, instructors, lecturers, assisting professors, adjunct professors, and interim professors. Considering full-time faculty only,

---

[7] National Center for Education Statistics. "Race/Ethnicity of College Faculty. Fall 2021–2022."

in fall 2021, 73 percent of all full-time faculty in the US were White (non-Hispanic), specifically 35 percent White female and 38 percent White male. Twelve percent of faculty were Asian, specifically 5 percent Asian female and 7 percent Asian male. Seven percent of faculty were Black, specifically 4 percent Black female and 3 percent Black male. Six percent of faculty were Hispanic, specifically 3 percent each, Hispanic female and Hispanic male. One percent were of two or more races, while less than one-half of 1 percent were American Indian/Alaska Native; and less than one-half of 1 percent were Pacific Islander.

Association for Theological Schools

The Association for Theological Schools also collects data that are focused on the statistical information of full-time faculty by race/ethnicity/rank and gender in the US and Canada.[8] Among the faculty listed, there is a noticeable disparity in numbers for women faculty and faculty of color versus White male faculty. The fact that male faculty, across the board, are in higher teaching positions at the rate of almost three times as high as their female counterparts is particularly interesting: 491 to 233 assistant professors, 688 to 265 associate professors, 1,209 to 270 professors, and 195 to 101 others in 2019, for example.[9] When analyzed on gender lines in 2019, 2020, 2021, 2022, and 2023, the total number of male faculty, regardless of rank, ranged from a low of 2,156 in 2023 to a high of 2,583 in 2019.[10] For female faculty in those same years, the census ranged from a low of 813 in 2023 to a high of 879 in 2022.[11] The disparity is also true when looking at White male faculty in comparison to any of the BIPOC faculty data presented, with a White male faculty census ranging between 1,495 and 1,950 across ranks.[12] No BIPOC demographic group in that same time period had a census higher than the 215 Asian or Pacific Islander male faculty of 2022.[13]

---

[8] Association for Theological Schools, *2023–2024 Annual Data Tables*, published digitally, Table 3.1.

[9] Association for Theological Schools, *2023–2024 Annual Data Tables*, Table 3.1.

[10] Association for Theological Schools, *2023–2024 Annual Data Tables*, Table 3.1.

[11] Association for Theological Schools, *2023–2024 Annual Data Tables*, Table 3.1.

[12] Association for Theological Schools, *2023–2024 Annual Data Tables*, Table 3.1.

[13] Association for Theological Schools, *2023–2024 Annual Data Tables*, Table 3.1.

Scholars who have done research on faculty of color as well as women faculty have stated that faculty from underrepresented communities also spend more of their academic time mentoring and doing other forms of service for the institution.[14] This was my experience. As a tenure-track assistant professor, I also held an administrative position as director of five master's degree programs and sat on twelve committees for the institution. During this time, I was also expected to be actively pursuing my research and writing. For many schools, service is not as highly valued in the academy as writing and research. Unfortunately, there is a penalty for lack of writing, publications, and research, and this lack can impact tenure and promotion. "This gender gap is largely due to greater service and administrative responsibilities women assume or are assigned, which takes away from what really matters for promotion—research and publication."[15]

Several studies highlight the role gender plays in academia, and particularly the realities of women and their scholarship. "According to the American Association of University Professors, on average, male associate professors spent 37% of their time on research, while women associate professors spent 25% of their time on research. While women associate professors spent 27% of their time on service, men spent 20% of their time on service."[16] The study does not address the added time that BIPOC faculty also spends mentoring, advising, and listening to students, particularly those students who themselves are BIPOC.

This journey as an academic can lead to numerous challenges as one tries to pursue one's vocation. Bryan Massingale authored an essay in 2010 that described the challenges of the Black theologian.[17] In reviewing that essay, I realized that it spoke in many ways to the challenges faced today by those faculty, particularly BIPOC and women who must navigate treacherous landscape to thrive in the academy.

---

[14] For further study, see *APA Task Force Report on Promotion, Tenure and Retention of Faculty of Color in Psychology* (American Psychological Association, 2023).

[15] Pearl Stewart and cmaadmin (EDU), "Female Faculty Putting Productivity in Writing," *Diverse Issues in Higher Education* online (November 2, 2016).

[16] Stewart and cmaadmin (EDU), "Female Faculty Putting Productivity in Writing."

[17] Bryan Massingale, *Racial Justice and the Catholic Church* (Orbis Books, 2010), 167–69.

Depression and Despair

Massingale asks the question, "Why do I keep doing what I am doing for a church (institution) that would be more comforted by my absence or silence?"[18] For years, as an emerging scholar, I remained silent or spoke in very measured tones when issues of racism or sexism within the academy needed to be addressed. Also, the phenomena of sexual abuse of minors within the Catholic Church has been one that needs constant attention and vigilance. The constant bombardment of these issues, along with many others, leaves one physically, emotionally, and spiritually exhausted, and there are weeks that go by when I do not have space to rejuvenate.

Temptation to Fit In Like Everyone Else

We are rewarded for conducting ourselves in accordance with certain norms. When I arrived at my institution, I was challenged and tempted to shape my teaching style in a linear fashion like the professors who taught me in the academy. I was trying to teach like everyone else and ignoring my own value as a trained catechist, storyteller, and one who had learned a style of integrative teaching at a historically Black institution. For me, the question becomes, how can one spend four years in theology school and remain unchanged? How are we providing an environment where transformation takes place? In many of our institutions, the style of teaching that had been encouraged is lecture and memorization. For me, the question became how does that change hearts and minds? The stress for years to teach in this fashion rather than in one that involves more engagement and integrative reflection was causing harm to my psyche and health. I also wonder how it may impact some of our students who come from diverse backgrounds and communities. I remember a student sharing with me after graduation how she wished she had had the opportunity to reflect and pray more in her classes rather than only take tests and draft papers. Having minored in education in college and later as a trained catechist, I had met many adult learning models of teaching that focused on engagement

---

[18] Massingale, *Racial Justice and the Catholic Church*, 167.

and reflection as two modes of learning. Over the years, I gradually included these various teaching methods in my classroom (shared reflection, engagement in prayer practices, journaling) to enhance the teaching environment. Only in changing and valuing my own style and not trying to fit in did I see change in my health as well as an added benefit in how my students received the course material.

Fear and/or Cowardice

The theological vocation, as lived by many scholars, does not prepare one with a decision to defy conventional understandings of faith and human experience. But for those coming from many marginalized and underrepresented communities, it is the opposite. The theological calling of a Black Catholic entails a struggle against fear: of being misunderstood; of making a false start in developing a new voice and perspective; of self-revelation, of self-doubt, of self-censorship; of retaliation both personal, professional, and communal; of ecclesiastical penalty and censure; of ecclesial alienation and estrangement. How often are women and BIPOC scholars forced to remain silent because if they speak, their job is in danger or their ability to financially support themselves is threatened?

Overextension and Overwhelmed

Massingale stated three challenges to the vocation of the theologian. As one who has taught and ministered in the Catholic Church for over forty years, I would include another challenge: that of becoming overextended or overworked. Because we do not rest, we lose our way. And for want of rest, our lives are in danger. Thomas Merton states,

> There is a pervasive form of contemporary violence and that is activism and overwork. The rush and pressure of modern life are a form, perhaps the most common form, of its innate violence. To allow oneself to be carried away by a multitude of conflicting concerns, to surrender to too many demands, to commit oneself to too many projects, to want to help everyone in everything is to succumb to violence. The frenzy of our activism neutralizes our work for peace. It destroys our own inner capacity for peace.

110 *C. VANESSA WHITE*

It destroys the fruitfulness of our own work, because it kills the root of inner wisdom which makes work fruitful.[19]

This overextension can also be seen in the amount of time and energy that is placed in student advising, independent study work, guiding students through dissertations and research papers, family time, time with religious communities, and preparing for tenure.

Battle Fatigue and Burnout

The aforementioned challenges can also lead to battle fatigue. Battle fatigue in the workplace can be described as the cumulative stress of working in a hostile environment and experiencing daily devaluation and disrespect. It can exhibit itself as an inability to focus, extreme tiredness and fatigue, and a feeling of being overwhelmed. An additional form of battle fatigue that is now being researched is the fatigue related to navigating stressful racial environments. Racial battle fatigue is described as a cumulative result of a natural race-related stress response to distressing mental and emotional conditions. These conditions emerged from constantly facing racially dismissive, demeaning, insensitive, and/or hostile racial environments and individuals.[20] People of color experience daily battles of attempting to deflect racism, stereotypes, and discrimination in predominately White spaces, and must always be on guard or weary of the next attack they may face. Both the anticipation and experiences of racial trauma contribute to racial battle fatigue (RBF). RBF can cause BIPOC faculty to suffer various forms of mental, emotional, and physical strain that can lead to psychophysiological symptoms. The symptoms of RBF are suppressed immunity and increased sickness, tension headaches, trembling and jumpiness, chronic pain in healed injuries, elevated blood pressure, and a pounding heartbeat. When people of color with RBF anticipate racially motivated conflicts, they may experience rapid breathing, an

---

[19] Thomas Merton, *Conjectures of a Guilty Bystander* (Image Books/Doubleday, 1966), 108.

[20] Morgan Goodman, "Racial Battle Fatigue: What Is It and What Are the Symptoms," JustJasmineBlog.com. See also Sherry C. Wang and Rebecca R. Hubbard. "Overcoming Racial Battle Fatigue through Dialogue," *Training and Education in Professional Psychology* 14, no. 4 (2020): 285–92.

upset stomach, or frequent diarrhea/urination.[21] Ultimately the one experiencing RBF feels emotionally, physically, and spiritually drained.

Sustained battle fatigue and /or RBF over a period of time can lead to burnout in the academy, which is described as chronic workplace stress that has not been successfully managed.[22] Symptoms of burnout include: (1) feelings of energy depletion or exhaustion, (2) increased mental distance from one's job, (3) increased negativism or cynicism related to one's job, and (4) reduced professional efficacy.

Having experienced both RBF and burnout in my journey as a theological scholar and minister, I realized that at some point I needed to make a change. Midway through my time as a member of the faculty, I began exhibiting many of the symptoms mentioned earlier. I experienced periods of anxiety, difficulty sleeping (which further exhibited itself in waking up extremely tired), headaches, fatigue, and mental disengagement from my teaching responsibilities. The latter was particularly disturbing for me, since my identity and joy had been found in my teaching vocation. Upon visiting my physician, I was also diagnosed with being borderline diabetic, having high cholesterol, and having high blood pressure. A change needed to take place.

Fortunately, after engaging in a hermitage retreat before beginning a new school year, I took a moment to take a life inventory, which a friend shared with me. This inventory consisted of asking myself lifestyle questions and then reflecting on my answers with the hope of gaining insight that would lead to a healthy change in my behavior. I have adapted this inventory over the years and wish to share with you my most recent adaptation. We are not willing to change until the pain becomes worse than the pleasure. In other words, we can become comfortable in our pain, or inability to function, and until it becomes unmanageable, we will not change. Only when we have that *aha* moment will change begin to happen. So here is the inventory. Feel free to adapt and adjust.

---

[21] See also Nicholas D. Hartlep and Daisy Ball, eds., *Racial Battle Fatigue in Faculty: Perspectives and Lessons from Higher Education* (Routledge, 2019); Jennifer L. Martin and Richard Milner, eds., *Racial Battle Fatigue: Insights from the Front Lines of Social Justice Advocacy* (Praeger, 2015).

[22] For more information about faculty burnout, see Rebecca Pope-Ruark. *Unraveling Faculty Burnout: Pathways to Reckoning and Renewal* (Johns Hopkins University Press, 2022).

Life Inventory

Do I find myself saying or feeling, "I don't have time"?

What do I surround myself with?

Am I finding it hard to concentrate, find things, etc.?

What are my sleep habits like?

Do I have trouble getting up in the morning?

What am I reading?

Do I have trouble focusing?

What words are coming out of my mouth?

Do I find myself complaining more?

Are people around me just irritating me more?

Do I take time each day for reflection, prayer, personal or spiritual reading?

Do I exercise? How am I treating my body as a temple of the Holy Spirit?

Have I been experiencing colds, flu, laryngitis, and other ailments on a regular basis?

Do I find it hard to get out of bed in the morning?

How would I rate my tiredness level (high, low)?

What am I hopeful about?

When was the last time I took some time just for myself?

When was the last time I went on a personal retreat?

When was the last time I really did something fun?

What am I hopeful about?

Can I honestly say that I am happy?

There is an Ethiopian proverb that states the one who conceals his (her) illness cannot hope to be cured. The time comes when the one who is immersed in this fatigue/burnout must name what is taking place and begin the movement toward health and wholeness. So, let's begin to change the course. Let us begin the healing process.

THERE IS A BALM
Navigating in the Academy—Changing the Course

The rest of this chapter focuses on the four guideposts that are needed to move toward a healthy journey in academia and the specifics within each that can help to sustain and nurture a healthy environment. These guideposts include being proactive in your insitution, knowing your institution, documenting what occurs at your institution, and caring for yourself.

Be Proactive

Many times, we wait for things to happen to us instead of realizing we have within us the power to make changes and make decisions for our own health and well-being. As BIPOC and women faculty, we tend to see ourselves in a tenuous position, and we find ourselves saying yes to tasks and duties that cause greater strain and distress. For example, instead of scrambling to complete necessary tasks and projects at the last minute, be realistic about what needs planning and also realize that not everything will get done in a particular timeframe. Value yourself and your goals, and define what you want. For example, I reached a point in my journey where I had been adjunct faculty for a period of time. The institution had the benefit of my skill set but I did not have the security of whether my position was long-lasting. I finally made an appointment with the dean and stated that it was time that I begin the process to become a tenured member of the faculty. While the dean expressed hesitation and stated that there was not a position available, I also shared that I would begin looking and at present already had two other job offers. Interestingly enough, I was soon given the opportunity to apply for a tenure-track position on the faculty. I caution the reader not to fall into the trap of feeling guilty in making a request. You are worth the respect and need to value yourself as you value your students and others.

Know Your Institution

There are times that we accept a position at an institution without knowing if that institution would really be a good fit for us. Do your research. Are you a good fit? Know your own history and family influ-

114　　　　　*C. VANESSA WHITE*

ence. For example, I am teaching at an institution that is primarily a male religious order institution. My background has been working with male religious orders since my young adult days. Many of my colleagues have had difficulty at this institution because that has not been their history, so they do not have an understanding of the unwritten rules and ways of being that shape the daily function of this institution. Other questions to ask are, How is your institution organized? Who has the title and who has the power and influence to make decisions within your institution? They may not always be the same person. What are the rules of the institution: such rules as office hours; how much time are you as faculty expected to be on campus; what meetings/events are you expected to attend; what are the gender rules (such as does it appear that the women faculty are expected to do certain tasks that men faculty are not asked to perform); what are the race rules (such as being the only BIPOC, you are expected to be on almost every committee—because your "voice" is so important)? Finally, where can you go for support or trust? Do not journey alone. Know who are your allies and ask for support when needed.

Document What Occurs

The one rule I highly recommend for all new faculty is to document what occurs in the academy. If you attend a meeting, keep a log, and always respond in writing to your supervisor with your own synopsis of what took place in the meeting. This guideline has been invaluable for my own journey and ability to work in the academy. There have been numerous times when faculty in power who did not support me have tried to go to my dean and/or president to share negative information about me. In one instance, I was able to show how I had over four pages of documentation that included instances of verbal abuse, lies, advising students to avoid taking my classes, and not receiving information that I needed as department chair to show how this faculty member had continually disrespected me. It was only that I had kept this documentation, which included emails, that protected me from a faculty member who had tenure and had a position of authority and power. Documentation is extremely important when communicating with faculty who have not been supportive and those in power. For women in this #METOO era, this is doubly important and vital.

THERE IS A BALM

Care for Self

Caring for yourself is not being a narcissist, but rather loving. Care of self is rooted in the greatest commandment of loving God and your neighbor as yourself. Jesus's commandment to his disciples as stated in the Gospel of Mark 12:30–32 is to love God, our neighbor, and ourselves. We focus on loving others and loving God, but if we do not practice love of self, then we are out of balance and our journey as ministers and scholars cannot be effective. There are many books and essays written on self-care, and I encourage you to pick up one and begin practicing loving yourself. One practice that I have found indispensable has been the practice of taking Sabbath. In our daily lives we may not be able to take an entire day, but I encourage you to take a morning, afternoon, or evening of prayer, refreshment, and renewal. Turn off the computer and do something you enjoy doing. It may be something you haven't done in months or years, but the engagement of that activity will be indispensable to your own thriving. Take some time during your Sabbath to be grateful. What has happened this day that gives evidence of the grace of God in your life? What we focus on is what we give power to and our focus on the negative has begun to sap our strength, our ability to be joyful missionary disciples and scholars. As Pope Francis states in *Evangelii Gaudium*—"A committed missionary knows the joy of being a spring which spills over and refreshes others."[23]

A Balm in Gilead

As highlighted earlier in this chapter, "Even as women have consistently achieved higher levels of education than men, men still continue to occupy most tenured positions." "This gender gap is largely due to greater service and administrative responsibilities women assume or are assigned, which takes away from what really matters for promotion—research and publication."[24]

Over the years, I have shared the insights that I have gained with

---

[23] Pope Francis, *Evangelii Gaudium* (2013), no. 272.

[24] Stewart and cmaadmin (EDU), "Female Faculty Putting Productivity in Writing."

116 C. VANESSA WHITE

my colleagues at my home institution. As a result of reflecting on their own status and experience at their institution, my fellow women faculty decided to become proactive. Our faculty had become increasingly stressed and fatigued as a result of the events of COVID-19; a sustained hiring freeze of faculty; as well as the racism, sexism, homophobia, and xenophobia evident in our country. Rather than continue to complain and disengage, we began gathering to see what we needed to do. With this gender gap in mind, three members of the women faculty at our institution took the initiative to write a grant proposal for monies to develop a year focused on women faculty engagement with the hopes to offer intentional space for the faculty to support and encourage one another in their research and publication, and to also foster relationships of support and mentoring. The year would include times for gathering in the fall and spring semester as well as accountability partners for support and writing and would culminate in a Women's Faculty Writing Retreat. The members of the women faculty were diverse and included people of color and different religious traditions—Jewish, Catholic, Episcopalian. Members were LGBTQ, tenured, not tenured, and multigenerational. The guidelines were as follows:

1. Individual faculty grant monies were put together to have a retreat. We wanted all to feel welcomed and included.
2. Each had an accountability writing/prayer partner.
3. Monies were dispersed to include two lunches/dinners in the academic year culminating in a weeklong faculty writing retreat.

Not everyone could attend all week, some came for a few days, some with young children drove to the retreat facility every day where they focused on writing, research, and self-care that included rest, enjoyment of life, social interaction, etc. On the one day that the Orthodox Jewish member could attend, we catered in a kosher meal. Those members who were out of town or out of the country but wanted to participate were Zoomed in for some of the evening sessions. We took the time to pause, share our stories, pray for one another, and offer support. As faculty, we were also given the choice of two books that were specifically chosen in light of our shared experience and story: *Unraveling Faculty Burnout* by Rebecca Pope-Ruark and *Presumed Incompetent II—Race, Class, Power and Resistance of Women in the Academy*, edited by Yolanda Flores Niemann, Gabriella Gutierrez Y. Muhs, and Carmen G. Gonzalez. An evaluation was given at the end of the grant year, and we shared what we had learned with the rest of the faculty in the following academic semester at a faculty seminar.

The benefits of the yearlong experience included transformation, healing, and productivity. The experience transformed our relationships and helped us to remember we are not alone. The experiences helped to build trust among all the members who participated. It was a time of healing, and that healing continues to emerge from the power of women coming together in support, in truth telling, in memory. Pastoral care is not only something we teach. It must be evident in how we care for one another as theologians, scholars, and academics. Because many faculty members were given the time needed to complete important writing and research projects, productivity increased. One member completed work on a manuscript that was later published, and several members were able to complete book chapters, including some who were able to use the time to finish academic papers for conferences.

As we continue the journey, I encourage all to be mindful of how you are navigating through the academy. Reach out to others if you feel neglected, overwhelmed, hassled, or powerless. We, as faculty in theological settings, are called to model what we preach and teach to our students. If our well is dry, how, then, can we refresh others? How can we be a balm in Gilead that heals the sin-sick soul?

Not Enough Time to Flourish

Vocation, Work, and Leisure in Catholic Higher Education

Christopher Welch

It is hard to imagine an observer of higher education who has not noted a significant number of students who are time-poor, exhausted, and, for many reasons, scattered in their attention. These symptoms are manifested not only in academic performance but also in lower levels of engagement in other activities, on and off campus. Drawing on a mixed-methods study of undergraduates, which I undertook at Rivier University, I found paid employment was often a deterrent to the students' productive leisure. While the human person develops through work, the human person also develops through leisure. Unfortunately, the marketing messages to which students are often exposed leave them binding themselves to certain levels of consumption that require they work more hours. In other cases, their financial circumstances necessitate working more to pay for their education. In either situation, students often find leisure to be elusive, to the detriment of their flourishing. It is essential, then, that institutions of Catholic higher education be attentive to these needs and seek ways to promote the flourishing of students, which includes promoting their productive leisure.

Work and Leisure in a Vocational Framework

Part of the mission of Catholic higher education is to help awaken in students an attentiveness to vocation—where vocation, to use the

NOT ENOUGH TIME TO FLOURISH 119

work of theologian Edward Hahnenberg, is broadly understood as an invitation from God, but through others, to live a life of meaning and purpose.[1] It is a graced invitation, and the idea that one might have a vocation depends on a belief that there is some chance of being drawn toward meaning beyond oneself. Notably, it is a notion that, despite the religious history of the term, seems to have traction even in secularized spaces. Students are open to the possibility and language of vocation whether or not they have ever heard of the Incarnation or the sacraments.

Vocation is complex, layered, and multiple. It is about character, family, community, relationships, work, and leisure. It is, as the Lutheran scholar Caryn Riswold describes it, about deep humanization in a profoundly de-humanizing culture.[2] We might summarize the Christian notion of vocation as an invitation both to personal flourishing and to contributing to the common good. It is among the goals of the whole university to provide, as religious scholar David Cunningham puts it, the time and the place in which students may explore vocation.[3]

If we are to help students explore vocation, we need to be thinking of course about work. For the purposes of the rest of this chapter let me confine "work" to work as paid employment or some other effort that is seen as obligatory.[4] In the tradition of Catholic Social Thought, John Paul II's encyclical *Laborem Exercens* remains canonical in its description of the good work to which we are called if we are to be cocreators with God, the good work that we as persons should strive for, and to which society ought to be oriented: it provides for physical needs, enhances solidarity among workers, and fosters the worker's growth in skill and creativity while contributing to the common good.[5]

While John Paul II writes eloquently about the human person as a worker, we should not truncate our anthropology. The human person

---

[1] Edward P. Hahnenberg, *Awakening Vocation: A Theology of Christian Call* (Liturgical Press, 2010).

[2] Caryn Riswold, "A Pedagogy of Humanization," in *At This Time and in This Place: Vocation and Higher Education*, ed. David Cunningham (Oxford University Press, 2016), 72–95.

[3] David Cunningham, "Introduction: Time and Place," in *At This Time and in This Place: Vocation and Higher Education*, 1–19.

[4] "Study" is a form of work, but herein will be treated as its own category.

[5] Pope John Paul II, *Laborem Exercens* (1981).

is not *only* a worker. Leisure, too, is both formative and expressive of who we are, and therefore is a way in which we live out a calling and are shaped within our vocations. The moral theologian Conor Kelly helpfully distinguishes between leisure, which is effortful but done for its own sake, and recreation, which is only restorative.[6] Kelly, like the philosopher Josef Pieper, holds leisure in great esteem; it is not time wasted, but is in fact an attitude of accepting one's truest self in a world of meaning.[7]

The students with whom I spoke used the term more colloquially. They used "leisure" broadly to include both what Kelly would call leisure and recreation. That being said, they differentiated among types of leisure and saw some as higher than others, even if they found themselves not always willing or able to put in the effort or time to engage in the "higher" types. For instance, students tended to call scrolling social media "useless" or "mindless," even if, for restoration, they "just need time to sit on my phone."

Rivier Students' Time Use
in Work and Leisure

This particular study engaged with students at Rivier University, where I teach.[8] Context is important, and so I present a few facts about the school here. Roughly one thousand of Rivier's students are traditional "day" undergraduates, most of those in the eighteen- to twenty-four- year-old age range. Roughly a quarter of Rivier students are Pell eligible.[9] Nursing students comprise half of the day undergraduate body. About 30 percent of undergraduate students participate in varsity sports. The undergraduate student body is roughly evenly split between campus residents and commuters.[10]

---

[6] Conor M. Kelly, *The Fullness of Free Time: A Theological Account of Leisure and Recreation in the Moral Life* (Georgetown University Press, 2020).

[7] Josef Pieper, *Leisure, the Basis of Culture* (Pantheon Books, 1952).

[8.] This research was conducted with the approval of Rivier University's Institutional Review Board.

[9] The federal Pell Grant program offers grants to students based on income. Pell eligibility is a useful indicator of the percentage of students from low-income households.

[10] National Center for Education Statistics, "College Navigator—Rivier University," accessed July 1, 2024, https://nces.ed.gov/collegenavigator.

There were two elements to this empirical study: an anonymous survey of one hundred full-time day undergraduate students, and then, partly framed by the results of the survey, small-group interviews with fifteen students. Both the survey and the interviews were mostly, but not exclusively, with sophomores and juniors. Those sample sizes were enough to be meaningful, but probably not enough to reach saturation, so the following observations should be considered emergent.

Regarding the relationship among work, leisure, and vocation, a few answers from the surveys prompted further exploration. First, almost everyone surveyed said their leisure activities held significant meaning for them, but also most (88 percent) said their paid employment held significant meaning for them. However, only 75 percent said they expected that their paid employment would contribute to a meaningful future. They have lower expectations of their future work than they do of their current work.

Also, while only a quarter of the respondents said they had time to do everything they wanted, half the students wanted to work more hours for pay, and only a quarter wanted to work fewer hours. Yet, when asked what they would do if they had two extra hours in the day, with the proviso that they were "doing OK" financially, only two of the one hundred respondents said, "work more." Apparently, the desire to work more is financially driven. Work serves as more instrumental than aspirational for these students' lives. So, what meaning do students give to their employment and their leisure? Three particular themes emerged from the data.

Emerging Themes
from Student Thoughts on Leisure and Work

Squeezed Out: Restoration Precedes Active Leisure

In interviews, the feeling of never having enough time or energy was almost universal. Students were keenly aware of what had been squeezed out of their days filled with work, school, and sometimes sports or commuting. Few students claimed they had time or energy to spare. One student commented on a recent study noting that 58 percent of US adults state they do not get enough sleep, "Who are those other people who do [get enough sleep]? I don't know those people."

When asked why they worked for pay, students' answers mirrored those in national studies: to make money to support habits of consumption, to defray tuition costs, to pay for rent and groceries, and to reduce dependence on their family, among others.[11] Many students interviewed mentioned working multiple jobs. Of course, how much students worked and what they paid for on their own varied widely. Some claimed responsibility for their whole college costs, others just for expenses like auto insurance and gas, and a few stated that all of their money was saved or spent solely on entertainment and clothing. Regardless of circumstance, almost all of the students said they had to work, and most could not imagine cutting back on hours. Only one very exhausted student wished that she did not have to work at all.

It is noteworthy that students expressed a *desire* to engage in more "productive" or active leisure—crafts, cooking, picking up an instrument, or gardening—but they often expressed frustration that they neither had the time nor the energy for it. When offered the hypothetical two extra hours a day, quite a few students said they would "love to just read, you know, something NOT for school. A beach read." They wanted to watch TV, or play video games, or "chill." The restorative elements of leisure—what Kelly distinguishes more as recreation than leisure—took priority for many students.[12]

There is also, beyond the fatigue, something of a Catch-22 situation for many students. Some wanted to work because they did not have another activity that engaged them deeply, but they did not have an activity that engaged them deeply because their work (and school) schedules did not afford them the time to develop those activities. One heartbreaking reflection from Jeanette exemplified this bind: "I would love to have a hobby. I have too many things that require so much of my time and so much of my energy. I would love to find a hobby. . . . I just feel like I don't even have time to think about what a hobby would be because there's no time for it anyway."

If "hobby" here could be understood as meaningful leisure that is integral to vocation, then Jeanette's dilemma points to a significant problem in society. In the current ways we prepare children and young

---

[11] Lauren Dundes and Jeffrey Marx, "Balancing Work and Academics in College: Why Do Students Working 10 to 19 Hours per Week Excel?," *Journal of College Student Retention* 8, no. 1 (2006): 107–20.

[12] Kelly, *The Fullness of Free Time.*

NOT ENOUGH TIME TO FLOURISH

adults to become working (and spending) members of society, we have squeezed out of them the ability even to imagine leisure as a tool of exploration and discovery.

Several students, though, did note they had meaningful, effortful leisure experiences that included acquiring and using skills. For instance, one sophomore found herself excited to have successfully, with the tutoring of her mechanic boyfriend, replaced her car's brake pads and rotors. New dimensions of her self and her relationship with the world began to open for her. "I think I like the idea of building stuff and learning how things work, but I never had people in my life that did that. . . . I never knew I wanted to get into it."

She and others spoke to what philosopher Matthew Crawford refers to as the "mastery over one's stuff." It is, says Crawford, a sense of mastery that brings with it humility in grappling with the real world. This sustained, deep attention is "incompatible with self-absorption."[13] We may call this attention a form of mindfulness, and it is akin to the deep absorption in what the late psychologist Mihaly Csikszentmihalyi termed the "flow state."[14] The attention and effort pulled the car repairer out of herself, and she loved it. This "incompatibility with self-absorption" is also a solid foundation on which concern for others can be built.

The Priority of Relationships

Without exception, what students craved most, even more than rest, was time with friends and family. For some students, a number of those relationships were integrated into their college experience in ways that are time efficient. When student–athletes[15] talked about their teams, they emphasized playing, practicing, and hanging out with friends. One student reflected on his hockey career, with long hours on buses and early-morning rink times, saying "I made so many . . . relationships and friendships. . . . I met great people and I wouldn't

---

[13] Matthew B. Crawford, *Shop Class as Soulcraft: An Inquiry into the Value of Work* (Penguin Press, 2009), 82.

[14] Mihaly Csikszentmihalyi, *Flow: The Psychology of Optimal Experience* (Harper & Row, 1990).

[15] Intercollegiate athletics stood in nebulous relationship to "school," "work," and "leisure" for interview subjects. Their sports had elements of all of those categories.

change it for anything." His friendships on and off the ice were with teammates, such that they precluded his desire to participate in other on-campus activities. A different student, a senior on the women's soccer team, simply said, "I don't have to hang out with friends and be social, because that's what practice is for."

As for time at work, in keeping with the survey data that had students finding meaning in current employment at higher rates than they expected to have in the future, students expressed a desire to work jobs that paid well and were fun, less stressful, or more flexible than they expected in their future careers. "Fun" mostly meant good relationships with co-workers and clients. Several students spoke about spending one more summer working a "fun" job before looking for a job in their career field. Another sheepishly stated that she had a "silly job" selling bongs but then went on to rhapsodize about her "awesome" interactions with coworkers and with regular customers. In ice cream stands and country clubs, in retail and in day care facilities, relationships were frequently mentioned as first among the "goods" of the work.

At the same time, busy schedules tended to leave students craving time with friends and family during their leisure time. This is not surprising. If God is a God who is relational within Godself, then humans created in the image and likeness of God are called into and desire relationship. To return to Hahnenberg's description of vocation, it is a graced call that is both through and for others.[16] It is also a call to be *with* others.

Physical and Emotional Selves

The students at Rivier did not seem to fall prey to a docetist heresy. They took seriously their bodily selves, and so attentiveness to vocation must involve attentiveness to their whole selves. Students listed various types of exercise as preferred leisure activities, and many, when offered two extra hours a day, would choose to go to the gym, take a hike, play basketball, take an exercise class, or walk the dog. Part of the appeal of attention to the physical seemed to be its connection to the emotional and mental. The emotional and mental benefits of exercise and of time in nature are well established, and our students experience

---

[16] Hahnenberg, *Awakening Vocation*.

NOT ENOUGH TIME TO FLOURISH

those benefits. Varsity athletes talked about their sport adding stress because of the time commitment but also time at practice as being a period of attention to just one thing. As one field hockey player put it, "When I'm there at practice or during a game, I'm not thinking about everything else." It is restorative but also part of the habit of sustained, mindful attention that promotes the deep absorption that characterizes the state of flow[17] and makes leisure more meaningful.

Students also frequently referenced that physical and emotional connection when describing "self-care" as a preferred leisure activity and as something people would do with extra time if they had it. When asked what they meant by self-care, students spoke wistfully of long showers, scented candles, mani-pedis, and specific and elaborate hygiene regimes. Again, the emphasis was on connecting the physical and emotional in the restorative practices of "de-stressing." A question worth pursuing in future research is how much of the income students make from their work is then spent on the services and products that purport to restore them from the stress of their busy lives juggling work and school.

Implications for Rivier in Particular
and for Catholic Higher Education in General

If religious scholar David Cunningham[18] is right that vocational exploration requires time and space that colleges are uniquely placed to provide, then it is incumbent on Catholic colleges and universities to provide these. This is not a task for us that can wait while we let the rest of society fill our students' time, space, minds, and bodies with demands that may not promote their flourishing. Students are already now developing and perhaps solidifying the ways they think about and embody work and leisure. While students' time choices around work and leisure are partly conditioned by financial need, they are also vulnerable to a culture that glorifies the "grind" of earning in order to promote consumption. This culture deafens their ability to hear and respond to the God who calls them toward their vocation to personal flourishing and to contributing to the common good. Catholic insti-

---

[17] Csikszentmihalyi, *Flow.*
[18] Cunningham, "Introduction: Time and Place."

126   CHRISTOPHER WELCH

tutions of higher education vary widely in size, demographics, and academic focus, so some of what I suggest here is intended broadly, while some of it may not be applicable beyond institutions that are similar to Rivier.

Time and Skills

Time scarcity is among the barriers our students face, and, in this problem, they are in step with most of society and certainly with the culture of academia. We need to help them use time to engage in the experiments of vocational discernment, to ask big questions and dream worthy dreams,[19] and to imagine themselves in both work and leisure that promote human flourishing and the common good.

Students discussed needing time-management skills, and certainly executive function and practical strategies for managing time are part of what we can teach in first-year seminars and "Student Success" classes. At issue, though, is not just executive functioning but also procrastination. Time and again, students spoke with regret about the procrastination that had them spending more time worrying about tasks than actually doing them. Because procrastination is more about anxiety than about sloth, the skills of managing academic anxiety can free not only time but also psychic space. School work can become less of a chore, carving out room for more leisure in learning. Theologian Elizabeth Newman aptly describes this virtue of "studiousness" not as an attempt to possess knowledge, but rather a joyful exploration of and participation in the knowledge of God's world.[20]

However, what is at stake is not simply that students do not always manage time well and can be drawn into vicious cycles of academic anxiety and procrastination; it is also that that they have more to do than they can do wholeheartedly. Part of the issue is that they have not yet taken ownership of which commitments they should make and how to prioritize those commitments. For instance, most of my interview subjects agreed to spend the time simply because I asked them to, and so they responded with kindness. They take the extra shift at

---

[19] Sharon Daloz Parks, *Big Questions, Worthy Dreams: Mentoring Young Adults in Their Search for Meaning, Purpose, and Faith* (Jossey-Bass, 2000).

[20] Elizabeth Newman, *Divine Abundance: Leisure, the Basis of Academic Culture* (Cascade Books, 2018).

NOT ENOUGH TIME TO FLOURISH   **127**

work because a manager called. There is still an external force setting the agenda. It is hard in young adulthood to differentiate among tasks and to prioritize them internally.[21] Our students are at an age when they have been thoroughly socialized into a culture of busy-ness. One student used the metaphor of her life as trying to keep a bunch of balls in the air. She is beginning to realize, however, that some of the balls are made of glass, others of plastic, still others of rubber. It is alright to let some drop, but first she must discern which ones need to be kept in the air. Helping students develop this frame of mind requires both provision of an alternative to the culture of busy-ness and educating them into the habit of critically evaluating that culture.

Space to Imagine Differently

Students need space to imagine differently. This space of imagination includes not only the psychic and spiritual space to explore safely, but also physical space and material resources. Smaller schools like Rivier are especially challenged in meeting these needs. One psychology major shared that she could not easily indulge her passion for painting in her dorm room. I wondered if our school could have an art studio for leisure. Further, students who are not varsity athletes, especially if they are commuters, are unlikely to use the gym on campus if they do not have access to showers or to group classes. Could we make these things available for students who want to engage their full selves on campus? Moreover, what might that availability mean for the student who discovers an aptitude for leading group exercise classes? New ways of living their vocation can open up for students, but schools will have to examine the means by which they can facilitate these discoveries.

When it comes to teaching to imagine leisure as a space for vocation, in the current academic culture it is often hard to find any role models. Who am I to suggest to my students that leisure is at least as constitutive of vocation as is work? As professional academics, most of our days are overfull with the tasks of teaching, service, and research. Structurally, our continued employment depends on fulfilling this role. So, it is quite difficult for us to convince observant students that leisure

---

[21] Robert Kegan, *In Over Our Heads: The Mental Demands of Modern Life* (Harvard University Press, 1994).

matters. Students can often read their teachers and the surrounding culture quite well. In our individual behaviors but also in our institutional cultures, we need to be attentive to our own vocations to both work and leisure.

Practically, at Rivier, the small size and the large percentage of commuters makes initiating and sustaining programs difficult. Aside from participation in varsity sports, almost none of my interview subjects pointed to school clubs or sponsored activities as attractive to them. Commuters come to class, go to work, and go home. They rarely come back to campus. Even residential students largely do not have a habit of thinking of the school as providing meaningful activities. They might see a small group appearing to have fun at library trivia night, but they told me they would be unlikely to go anyway. None seemed able to imagine starting an outdoor club, despite their affinity for the outdoors. So, even though college is most transformative when the curriculum and cocurriculum reinforce each other, practically speaking, Rivier students may benefit from our bringing the vocational exploration of leisure first more fully into the curriculum. Paradoxically, perhaps we must assign leisure in class.

Conclusion

As always, it is part of the mission of Catholic higher education to invite students to see themselves as called broadly into personal flourishing and contributing to the common good. The shapes of their vocations will vary, manifesting in their work and leisure spaces, as well as in their families and communities. In an age of busy-ness and of maintaining exhausting levels of consumption, we as a society have placed our young adults in the position of normalizing the removal of leisure from vocational discernment. While the Rivier students surveyed and interviewed expressed hopes for living meaningfully in their work lives, they had perhaps even higher hopes of doing so in their leisure times. These hopes, for many, stand in contrast to their experiences. Having thoroughly learned to stay busy and to earn a paycheck, they are vulnerable to an imbalance that inhibits their flourishing. So, if Catholic higher education educates for vocation as an invitation to personal flourishing and contributing to the common good, our students require that we be attentive to their time use, their relationships, and their whole persons. This attentiveness must come not only from individuals at the university; it must also be woven into the culture of Catholic higher education as a witness to the broader society, if our students are to have the space to hear themselves called into the fullness of their humanity.

The Vulnerability
and Flourishing of Girls

Cynthia L. Cameron

Because academic theology tends to be written and read by middle-aged adults, the default human being under consideration in our systematic theologies tends to be the middle-aged adult. Indeed, our default theological assumption of White, middle-class, middle-aged, heterosexual, cisgender male adulthood in our theological anthropologies means that those who differ from this norm have to be consciously brought to the forefront of theological reflection. Feminist, Latine, Asian, and Black theologians, among many others, have worked for decades to bring women, people of color, and other marginalized people into theological view, decentering some of our default assumptions and centering the lived experiences and real contexts of those who have often been excluded from view.

I want bring into theological view one such overlooked and vulnerable group, looking at questions of vulnerability and flourishing through the lens of female adolescence, focusing on the experiences of White, middle-class, and cisgender adolescent girls. I take this focus not to exclude LGBTQIA adolescents or adolescents of color from consideration but to avoid lumping their experiences in with those of White, cisgender, and heterosexual adolescents. Of course, our contemporary North American culture shapes the experiences of marginalized adolescents in profound, troubling, and different ways, which would require a more fulsome discussion than I can do here.

In this chapter, I explore some of the contours of vulnerability and flourishing for girls, and I begin to think about what it would look like

THE VULNERABILITY AND FLOURISHING OF GIRLS   **131**

to take the flourishing of girls seriously in our theologies. If the goal of feminist and other contextual theologies is the flourishing of all those who have traditionally been marginalized or excluded from theological view,[1] then attention to the vulnerability and flourishing of girls can bring us closer to a theological anthropology that is capacious enough to speak to the reality of female adolescence. This, in turn, can lead us to theologies that include all those that the tradition has excluded from theological view—not just girls, but all those who differ from the norm of middle-aged, middle-class, straight, cisgender White maleness.

Defining Flourishing

Before turning to the ways in which adolescent girls are particularly vulnerable, I start with some thoughts on how we can define flourishing. Theologians are not the only ones who are considering the question of flourishing of adolescent girls. Indeed, research into what girls need in order to flourish in our contemporary culture is an interdisciplinary endeavor, involving medical professionals, social scientists, and pastoral ministers.[2] But, even with all these people focused on the question of supporting adolescent girls toward flourishing, it is a remarkably difficult category to define. Indeed, there is not agreement on what flourishing even looks like. Theologian Miroslav Volf and his colleagues name the problem this way:

> One of the major challenges in the current research about human flourishing—about the good life, happiness, well-being, the true

---

[1] See, for example, Elizabeth A. Johnson, *She Who Is: The Mystery of God in Feminist Theological Discourse*, 10th anniv. ed. (Herder and Herder, 2002), 30–31.

[2] See, for example, Richard M. Lerner, *Liberty: Thriving and Civic Engagement Among America's Youth* (Sage, 2004); Thema Bryant-Davis, *Multicultural Feminist Therapy: Helping Adolescent Girls of Color to Thrive* (American Psychological Association, 2019); Laura Choate, *Swimming Upstream: Parenting Girls for Resilience in a Toxic Culture* (Oxford University Press, 2015); Linda Spatig and Layne Amerikaner, *Thinking Outside the Girl Box: Teaming Up with Resilient Youth in Appalachia* (Ohio University Press, 2014); Anne Phillips, *The Faith of Girls: Children's Spirituality and Transition to Adulthood* (Routledge, 2016); Nicola Slee, Fran Porter, and Anne Phillips, eds., *The Faith Lives of Women and Girls: Qualitative Research Perspectives* (Routledge, 2016).

life, the life worth living, and other designations under which the topic is discussed—is lack of agreement on what we mean by "flourishing" and its many near synonyms. The disagreement is not surprising. For there is no way to determine "objectively" what it would mean for human beings to flourish. The reasons for this are many, but first among them is that flourishing is a normative idea; it names what kind of beings humans *ought to be* and provides the orienting criteria... for what they *ought to desire* and how they *ought to live*.[3]

Thus, one of the problems with using flourishing as a way to describe what we want for adolescent girls is that we run the risk of speaking prescriptively, of describing what we think flourishing should look like, based primarily on our own experiences of flourishing or failing to flourish. Therefore, to think theologically about the flourishing of girls, we need to define it in ways that do not assume the experiences of adulthood.

That said, Volf does give us some guidance for defining flourishing that seems helpful for thinking about adolescent girls. He suggests orienting our thinking around three axes: agency, circumstances, and affect.[4] While the choices that we make do influence our flourishing, the context in which we make those choices also plays a factor. Circumstances beyond our control—such as race, gender, age, class, family structures, safety, and so on—play a significant role in determining whether and how we can make good choices and, therefore, whether and how we can flourish. In addition, how we feel about how our life is going plays a crucial role in our sense of our flourishing. For example, an adolescent girl who is growing up in a middle-class family with parents and other adults who support her will find it easier to exercise her agency than the girl growing up in situations of poverty or violence. A girl who struggles with depression and anxiety may not feel like her life is going well, even though, from the outside, she seems to be flourishing. Volf's definition of flourishing reminds us that, as the

---

[3] Miroslav Volf, Matthew Croasmun, and Ryan McAnnally-Linz, "Meanings and Dimensions of Flourishing," in *Religion and Human Flourishing*, ed. Adam B. Cohen (Baylor University Press, 2020), 7.

[4] Volf, Croasmun, and McAnnally-Linz, "Meanings and Dimensions of Flourishing," 10.

adults who love and care for girls, we cannot support the flourishing of girls without attending to all three aspects: the context in which they are growing up, their ability to make choices, and the ways that they feel about their lives.

The Vulnerability of Girls

The vulnerabilities of female adolescents are different from those of other people, and these differences demand our attention. Vulnerability is a part of the human condition, an anthropological constant;[5] we are all susceptible to being harmed by others. Indeed, the fact that we are limited, mortal, and susceptible to physical and emotional injury provides the context in which human life and flourishing can happen. It is the very riskiness of opening ourselves up to another person that makes friendship and love possible, and it is our shared experiences of vulnerability that help us to identify those situations when suffering and pain must be named and resisted. That said, adolescent girls are not simply a subset of the larger category of women; their experiences are different because of their physical and cognitive immaturity. And they are not merely a subset of the category of adolescents; gender makes a difference in how they experience the world. In other words, being an adolescent girl is qualitatively different from being "adolescent" and from being "female." And an identity as an adolescent girl becomes further complicated when additional social locations, such as race, gender identity, or disability, are also considered.

To name an aspect of the vulnerability of girls, I use a conceptual framework offered by clinical psychologist Stephen Hinshaw, which he calls a triple bind. The triple bind is the set of conflicting and impossible-to-meet expectations that many girls, particularly in North America, confront in adolescence.[6] First, girls are expected to focus on build-

---

[5] Edward Schillebeeckx, *Christ: The Experience of Jesus as Lord* (Crossroad Publishing, 1980), 733. Schillebeeckx uses "anthropological constant" to refer to dimensions of life that seem to be constitutive of the human condition.

[6] Stephen Hinshaw with Rachel Kranz, *The Triple Bind: Saving Our Teenage Girls from Today's Pressures and Conflicting Expectations* (Ballantine Books, 2009), 7–10. Hinshaw's identification of the triple bind rests primarily on research done with White girls. For explorations of the effects of this toxic culture on other adolescent populations, see C. J. Pascoe, *Dude, You're a Fag: Masculinity and Sexuality in High School* (University of California Press, 2011); Danielle Dickens, *Psychology of Black*

ing and maintaining relationships with family, friends, and romantic partners, often putting someone else's needs before their own, all the traditional tasks of girls. Second, girls are expected to be ambitious, oriented toward competition and leadership, focused on getting into a good college and having a successful career, all the things that are traditionally expected of boys. And, third, girls are expected to do all this while being thin, fit, and effortlessly beautiful, conforming to society's expectations of female appearance. The insidiousness of the triple bind is that, amid the seeming proliferation of options available for girls today, girlhood is being defined more and more restrictively. As Hinshaw argues, girls "are confronted with a seemingly endless parade of options that are nonetheless relentlessly similar: all pretty, hot, and thin; all seemingly happy with perfect [partners] and children . . . ; all eagerly striving for power, money, and corporate success."[7]

A part of what makes the triple bind so difficult for girls to name and resist is that it has become a part of our social imaginary,[8] a part of our unreflected-upon milieu, the way we expect the world to work. And, importantly, it is a deeply sexist imaginary. Boys—particularly cisgender, heterosexual, White boys—are not expected to meet the same standards in their relationality or their physical appearance; however, girls, because they have to master all three aspects of the triple bind, do not become a threat to boys or White male privilege. Indeed, the messages of a sexist culture persist: women and girls must take care of others, particularly children; they must look and act the way men and boys want them to look and act; they must fashion themselves to meet the desires of a culture that objectifies and commodifies them.

All of this makes many girls vulnerable. Because the expectations of the triple bind are a part of the social imaginary in which girls are growing up, it both goes unremarked on and pervades the day-to-day experiences of girls, leading to significant stress and distress in adolescent girls. The incidence of maladaptive behaviors, such as

---

Womanhood (Rowman & Littlefield, 2024); Cristina L. Magalhaes, Richard A. Sprott, and G. Nic Rider, eds., *Mental Health Practice with LGBTQ+ Children, Adolescents, and Emerging Adults in Multiple Systems of Care* (Rowman & Littlefield, 2023).

[7] Hinshaw, *The Triple Bind*, 21. Hinshaw notes that these cultural expectations also impact boys and how they learn to express masculinity (xix–xx, 98). See also Rosalyn H. Shute, *Clinical Psychology and Adolescent Girls in a Postfeminist Era* (Routledge, 2018), 107–11.

[8] Charles Taylor, *Modern Social Imaginaries* (Duke University Press, 2004), 23.

THE VULNERABILITY AND FLOURISHING OF GIRLS   **135**

disordered eating or self-harm, are rising, as are diagnoses of depression and anxiety and the rates of suicidal ideation and suicide.[9] Even girls who do not come to the attention of medical professionals are stressed, overwhelmed, confused, and unsure of themselves.[10] Our contemporary culture is producing cohorts of girls who can seem like they are successful and coping but who are actually struggling, some just a bit and others quite a great deal.

The Flourishing of Girls

Given the definition of flourishing that we borrowed from Volf and given the triple bind as a way of conceptualizing an aspect of the vulnerability of girls, I want to turn to the work of Elizabeth Gandolfo as a way of thinking about how vulnerability and flourishing can operate together in the lives of girls. In her book *The Power and Vulnerability of Love*, Gandolfo takes on the challenge of thinking theologically about the twinned experiences of vulnerability and love, particularly in women's experiences of maternity and natality. In sketching a theological anthropology that takes vulnerability seriously, she balances the ways that vulnerability, as an anthropological constant, can lead to fear, anxiety, and violence while at the same time is a source of human experiences of love and caregiving.[11]

First, Gandolfo explores the implications of understanding vulnerability as the context in which flourishing happens. Taking human vulnerability seriously is important because, as she puts it, "human happiness—or flourishing—is only possible working within the confines

---

[9] Hinshaw, *The Triple Bind*, x–xi.

[10] Hinshaw makes this point with a helpful analogy: "Imagine what might happen if we forced our teenage daughters to remain for several hours each day in a room that was full of cigarette smoke. Distasteful (and unethical) though this would be, the vast majority would probably emerge relatively intact. Yes, some would develop lung cancer (probably those with genetic vulnerabilities), and a few more would develop emphysema, asthma, bronchitis, and other respiratory ailments as a direct or indirect result of the smoke . . . Most, however, would not require medical care or hospital treatment. But does that mean they would be truly okay?" (Hinshaw, *The Triple Bind*, xvi).

[11] Elizabeth O'Donnell Gandolfo, *The Power and Vulnerability of Love: A Theological Anthropology* (Fortress Press, 2015), 34.

136   *CYNTHIA L. CAMERON*

of our vulnerable condition."[12] Thus, the pursuit of flourishing—for ourselves or, in this case, for girls—is only possible because of our human vulnerability:

> The features of human life that expose us to misfortune are precisely those dimensions of our condition that *make possible* our experience of love and joy, beauty and truth. Our embodied, relational, (inter)dependent, changing, and ambiguous condition makes us vulnerable, but it also makes available to us a life of great power and possibility.[13]

This point about vulnerability as that which makes flourishing possible also draws our attention to the ways that flourishing is a human good and not just an individual one. Flourishing is not something that is realized by an individual under her own efforts alone; it is always going to be bound up with the flourishing of those who make up our families and communities.[14]

Gandolfo does not use Volf's language of agency, circumstances, and affect, but these theologians complement each other nicely. For Volf, our sense of the experience of flourishing (or the failure to flourish) is determined by the choices that people make, both individually and as communities, by the historical contexts and communities in which we find ourselves, and by our emotional responses to these choices and contexts.[15] For Gandolfo, vulnerability is one of those circumstances in our lives, one that is often beyond our control, that shapes our flourishing (or not); at the same time, vulnerability—or, better, our tolerance of vulnerabilities that are rooted in human sinfulness, like sexism and ageism—can be affected by the various choices that people and communities make, for good and for ill. Furthermore, our vulnerability shapes our emotional responses to the choices and circumstances in our lives. In this sense, the vulnerability of girls can be understood as a circumstance that they cannot control, as something that results

---

[12] Gandolfo, *The Power and Vulnerability of Love*, 35.

[13] Gandolfo, *The Power and Vulnerability of Love*, 96.

[14] Gandolfo, *The Power and Vulnerability of Love*, 100.

[15] Volf, Croasmun, and McAnnally-Linz, "Meanings and Dimensions of Flourishing," 10.

THE VULNERABILITY AND FLOURISHING OF GIRLS   **137**

from the collective choices of our society. Or, to put it another way, the triple bind makes girls vulnerable because it results from societal and individual decisions about how girls should be in the world. It shapes the lived experiences of actual girls and has a profound impact on their self-esteem and mental health.

Second, in a move that is helpful for our consideration of the vulnerability and flourishing of girls, Gandolfo argues that embodiment and relationality are two ways in which vulnerability can be experienced. Embodiment—that all humans have physical bodies—points to the fragility of human life, to the bodily harms, physical sufferings, and mortality to which all of us are subject. Girls experience this vulnerability acutely; not only are they embodied as female, shaped by the sexism, misogyny, and patriarchy of our contemporary Western culture, they are also undergoing the significant bodily changes of puberty, when their sense of their own bodies can seem foreign and in flux. Similarly, human relationality and our orientation toward the building of relationships points to the inherent vulnerability that comes with being in relationship with others. We can be hurt by those we love; we can suffer because of the sufferings of others. As Gandolfo puts it,

> As embodied and relational creatures, we need social bonds—political, cultural, economic, personal, and intimate bonds—in order to live a human life and attain to human happiness. Close ties of affection are part of this need. Love, in its many and varied forms, is a part of this need. But love is not something we can control and the beloved is not someone we can control. Our need for love, and our attachment to our loved ones, renders us intractably vulnerable to anguish and despair. And yet we cannot resist love's power, for it is on love that our happiness depends.[16]

And, because the formation of bonds of affection is one of the key developmental tasks of adolescence and because the prioritization of relationships and caregiving is a part of the socialization of girls and women, girls experience this vulnerability in particularly keen ways.

---

[16] Gandolfo, *The Power and Vulnerability of Love*, 65.

138 CYNTHIA L. CAMERON

Toward a Theology of Flourishing

All of this raises questions for how we, as theologians, can think about the flourishing of adolescent girls in the midst of a culture that is often arrayed against them. Putting adolescent girls at the center of our theological view reveals to us the ways that the "normal" human experiences of vulnerability are complicated when age is brought into the mix.[17] Adult women may find that, for example, their relationships are both a source of stress and of meaning, care, and love. Girls, because of their differing developmental capabilities, are not yet always able to step outside of their relationships to analyze the ways that relationality is both stressful and life-giving.[18] So, girls experience contradictory cultural expectations about how they are to manage intimate relationships—being asked to both form deep and caring relationships with a romantic partner and hook up for casual sex—and they are ill-equipped to manage these contradictions. To use Volf's language, in trying to navigate the circumstances of their lives, their agency is bound up in these conflicting expectations, with seemingly every choice disappointing someone. It is no wonder this leaves them feeling overwhelmed and unhappy.

Embodiment is likewise differently complicated for girls than it is for adult women. While both women and girls are pressured in our society to be thin, fit, and attractive, with the right makeup, hairstyle, and clothing, girls are navigating these pressures in the midst of the physical changes of puberty and in a culture that is obsessed with

---

[17] For a theological exploration of how adults can assist adolescents in navigating the complexities of relationships, see Theresa A. O'Keefe, *Navigating Toward Adulthood: A Theology of Ministry with Adolescents* (Paulist Press, 2018).

[18] Constructive-developmental psychologist Robert Kegan describes this using the language of subject/object theory. This is the epistemological structure to the ways that we make sense of our world and our relationships with the other things, people, and ideas in our world. Things, people, and ideas that are "object" to us are those that we are able to reflect on; we are embedded in those to which we are "subject." For example, an adolescent is often able to gush about their new significant other, but may not be able to reflect on the nature of the relationship itself. She can see herself as separate from the significant other but is too embedded in the relationship to be able to stand "outside" of the relationship and reflect on it. See Robert Kegan, *In Over Our Heads: The Mental Demands of Modern Life* (Harvard University Press, 1994), 32.

THE VULNERABILITY AND FLOURISHING OF GIRLS **139**

youthfulness and that prematurely sexualizes young girls.[19] Again, echoing Volf, amid the circumstances of a youth- and sex-oriented culture and the physical changes of puberty, girls can feel as if their bodies are wrong, do not meet expectations, do not fit in, leaving them feeling worried and leading them to potentially make poor choices about eating, exercise, and so on.

Girls are not simply immature women, and they experience their vulnerability very differently than adult women would. In fact, it is their very immaturity and inexperience that make them even more vulnerable and more likely to become stressed and distressed by our common vulnerable human condition. So, as we think about what girls need then to flourish in the context of these experiences of vulnerability, we need a theological approach to female adolescence that emphasizes their goodness. We need to acknowledge the lived experiences of adolescent girls and make space in our theologies for these experiences. Because, even if their experiences are different from adult women and men, they are the experiences of fully human people, created by God in the image of God and loved by God and others. To take liberties with the words of Karl Rahner, "The strange and wonderful flowers of [female adolescence] are already fruits in themselves, and do not merely rely for their justification on the fruit that is to come afterwards. The grace of [female adolescence] is not merely the pledge of the grace of [adult womanhood]."[20] Female adolescence is not merely a stage that one must pass through to reach some greater good or more complete construction of humanity in adulthood. Girlhood is an aspect of humanity that is both intended by God and, therefore, intended by God for flourishing. In other words, a girl is a full human being, already known and loved by God; she is a gift to the world and not a problem that needs to be solved. When we focus on the flourishing of girls, we must recognize the ways in which the world may be arrayed against them. But, instead of thinking only about how to fix girls, how to mitigate the pitfalls of adolescence, or how to help them get on the "right track," the idea of flourishing contains within it a recognition that girls are already good, loved, wanted, and worthy, regardless of the challenges and opportuni-

---

[19] Shute, *Clinical Psychology and Adolescent Girls in a Postfeminist Era*, 35–37.

[20] Karl Rahner, "Ideas for a Theology of Childhood," in *Theological Investigations, Volume VIII: Further Theology of the Spiritual Life*, trans. David Bourke (Darton, Longman & Todd, 1971), 37.

ties they might face and regardless of the kinds of adults that they will eventually become. This is not to say that we should be uninterested in helping adolescent girls to grow toward a healthy adulthood or in creating a more just society within which they can do so. Rather, it is to say that, in that process, we need to also pay attention to the lives they are currently living and to work to ensure that they are valued for who they are now, and not just for who they will become.

Gloria Dei, Vivens Homo

Vulnerability and Flourishing in Post-*Dobbs* "Hard Cases"

James T. Bretzke

Following the *Dobbs* decision, cases have arisen in several states where highly restrictive abortion legislation produced several legal proceedings in which women with medically problematic pregnancies found it nearly impossible to get the "best practices" medical care standard before the *Roe* reversal. This article considers cases such as the Ohio ten-year-old rape victim and the Texas woman whose court-approved abortion was reversed by the Texas Supreme Court. Evaluating these cases from different perspectives, such as traditional Catholic bioethics, feminist perspectives, and legal analyses, yields greater insights into both vulnerability and human flourishing in this highly controversial area.

Chief Justice John Roberts in his opinion on the 2022 *Dobbs* decision, in an effort to maintain part of the settled law of *Roe v. Wade* that had for a half-century protected women's reproductive health-care autonomy, invoked the legal principle of prudent judicial restraint to argue the Court should limit itself to decide only those items that absolutely needed adjudication and sidestep the temptation of any judicial activism to go beyond those limits. Roberts added that both sides of the *Dobbs* decision showed "a relentless freedom from doubt on the legal issue" that he could not share.[1] His Cassandra-esque

---

[1] See Chief Justice John Roberts, "Opinion on Thomas E. Dobbs, State Health

prophecy that the overturning of *Roe* would send significant shock waves through American culture has undeniably come true.[2] While most in the political "pro-life" sector continue to applaud *Roe*'s demise, nevertheless several unplanned consequences have arisen that merit closer attention. This article will consider some of these using the traditional genre of a *status quaestionis* (state of the question/dispute). Some may feel that such an approach lacks precision or focus, but for an issue that is so deeply contested, this effort to present in a fair and even-handed manner the range of conflicted positions may be helpful in coming to a common ground for dialogue—literally, following the Greek etymology, a "talking through" differences.

Our post-*Dobbs status quaestionis* must consider carefully the effects on the proper human flourishing of vulnerable women in medically problematic pregnancies, the majority of which prove to be nonviable. Individual state "trigger laws" resulted in denial or delay of clearly long-established "best care medical practices" for such pregnancies. Greater engagement with the bioethical principles of settled casuistry in the Catholic moral tradition certainly could improve this legislation.[3] However, in this article I probe a related bioethical issue, namely, to broaden the application of these related principles in cases that would not immediately be considered candidates for licit pregnancy termination under traditional interpretations of the *Ethical and Religious Directives for Catholic Health Care Services* (ERDs).[4]

Officer of the Mississippi Department of Health, et al., Petitioners v. Jackson Women's Health Organization, et al." *Justitia U.S. Supreme Court* (June 22, 2022), https://supreme.justia.com/cases/federal/us/597/19-1392/.

[2] See James T. Bretzke, SJ, "Annotated Bibliography on the Supreme Court Reversal of *Roe v. Wade*" (updated regularly), https://docs.google.com/document/d/1KgcJwgdTTdmOs5jVdI_SPIROLXCeCUKt/edit?usp=sharing&ouid=103519537108777764442&rtpof=true&sd=true.

[3] For a detailing of these laws and some illustrative accompanying medical cases, see James T. Bretzke, SJ, "Beyond the Binary: Religious Bioethical Analysis of Post Dobbs Abortion Legislation," *Journal of the Society of Christian Ethics* (forthcoming).

[4] For the sixth edition of ERDs, see U.S. Conference of Catholic Bishops, *Ethical and Religious Directives for Catholic Health Care Services*, 6th ed. (2018), https://www.usccb.org/resources/ethical-religious-directives-catholic-health-service-sixth-edition-2016-06_0.pdf.

"Quaestio Disputata":
Two "Hard Cases" in Ohio and Texas

A *status quaestionis* usually centers around the *quaestio disputata*[5] or "disputed question/issue." Here a careful consideration of some of these "hard cases"[6] will help us to see where some of the key disputed interpretations might lie. The first hard case involves a ten-year-old child in Columbus, Ohio, who was repeatedly raped and became pregnant. Denied access to legal abortion in Ohio, the child's parents took her to the neighboring state of Indiana where her pregnancy was terminated.[7] The second case involved Kate Cox, a Texas woman whose fetus was diagnosed with the untreatable genetic condition of trisomy 18.[8] Initially a judge ruled that Ms. Cox's medical condition qualified for a pregnancy termination, but this decision was quickly blocked by the Texas attorney general and the GOP-controlled Texas Supreme Court. Ms. Cox then traveled out of Texas for medical care.

Pregnancy termination in both of these cases would be rejected

---

[5] For a short description of the theological genres of the *quaestio disputata* and its related *status quaestionis,* see James T. Bretzke, SJ, *Handbook of Roman Catholic Moral Terms* (Georgetown University Press, 2013), 193.

[6] I take the term "hard cases" from Cathleen Kaveny's "Who Trusts the Pro-Life Movement? Abortion and a Child Rape Victim in Ohio," *Commonweal* (November 27, 2023), https://www.commonwealmagazine.org/abortion-ohio-kaveny-women-GOP-rape.

[7] For a succinct overview of the case as it first came to national attention, as well as some key initial political reactions, see Timothy Bella, "Man Charged in Rape of 10-Year-Old Girl Who Had to Travel for Abortion," *Washington Post* (July 13, 2022), https://www.washingtonpost.com/politics/2022/07/13/abortion-girl-rape-victim-arrest-ohio/?utm_campaign=wp_todays_headlines&utm_medium=email&utm_source=newsletter&wpisrc=nl_headlines&carta-url=https%3A%2F%2Fs2.washingtonpost.com%2Fcar-ln-tr%2F375e18e%2F62cfe954cfe8a21601eb85c5%2F5d82fccd9bbc0f783cfa627d%2F11%2F61%2F62cfe954cfe8a21601eb85c5&wp_cu=1b126712e1fab3d0be69d0f2738e0074%7C92E0EEAF6D812953E0530100007F7A9D.

[8] Trisomy 18 usually leads to miscarriage, stillbirth, or in fewer cases, the infant's death within the first year. As with the previous case, the bibliography is large. For an earlier report in the secular press, see J. David Goodman, "Texas Judge Grants Woman's Request for Abortion, in Rare Post-Roe Case," *New York Times* (December 7, 2023), https://www.nytimes.com/2023/12/07/us/texas-abortion-ruling-exception.html?te=1&nl=from-the-times&emc=edit_ufn_20231207.

144 *JAMES BRETZKE*

out of hand by conservatives who judge them as constituting a "direct abortion," since the physical life of the mother did not seem to be in great risk. Pregnancy termination here would be classed by some as an intrinsic evil of the sort explicitly condemned in Pope John Paul II's *Veritatis Splendor*. However, referencing *Gaudium et Spes* no. 27, Pope John Paul II "expands" our understanding of what constitutes an intrinsic evil as being anything that "is hostile to life itself" including

> whatever violates the integrity of the human person, such as mutilation, physical and mental torture and attempts to coerce the spirit; whatever is offensive to human dignity, [since . . .] all these and the like are a disgrace, and so long as they infect human civilization they contaminate those who inflict them more than those who suffer injustice, and they are a negation of the honour due to the Creator. [9]

This expanded list of "intrinsic evil" that includes "hostile to life itself" could be a good example of what anthropologist Clifford Geertz calls a "thick description,"[10] as it opens up a broader perspective of what genuinely promotes and contradicts human flourishing. This "thick description" does not "contradict" the traditional act-centered use of the term but simply makes it both broader and better matched to the realities that result in such evils. The traditional usage would employ what Geertz might call a "thin description," namely, a more narrow, deductive portrayal of the moral act that focuses chiefly on whether or not a viable fetus was aborted. This approach is often viewed through a physicalist paradigm, which concludes the moral meaning of the act simply in what physically occurs, for example, a pregnancy is terminated. Too often this abstract moral judgment is largely removed from the accompanying intentions and circumstances that comprise the integral human moral act.[11]

"Thick description" lines up better with inductive reasoning em-

---

[9] See Pope John Paul II, *Veritatis Splendor* (1993), no. 80. See also James T. Bretzke, SJ, "Intrinsic Evil in *Veritatis Splendor* and Two Contemporary Debates," in *The Concept of Intrinsic Evil and Catholic Theological Ethics*, ed. Nenad Polgar and Joseph A. Selling (Lexington Press, 2019), 55–66.

[10] See Clifford Geertz, "Thick Description: Toward an Interpretive Theory of Culture," in Clifford Geertz, *The Interpretation of Cultures* (Basic Books, 1973), 3–30.

[11] See the entries *Actus hominis* and *Actus humanus* in Bretzke, *Handbook of Roman Catholic Moral Terms*, 5.

ployed by the so-called personalist paradigm than the physicalists' reliance on abstract deductive reasoning.[12] Messy though it occasionally may be, a "thick(er)" description seen through the lens of a personalist paradigm does give us a fuller and morally more accurate picture of what is going on in the perspective of God's providential care for all, especially those who are most vulnerable.

To return to the question of pregnancy termination in Kate Cox's case, inasmuch as the viability of her fetus would be highly questionable, and injury to her own physical and psychological health likewise seemed to be quite probable, a strong case could be made on those health grounds to seek what medically would be termed an "abortion." Such a difficult decision would not be morally an elective abortion in which the fetus seems clearly viable and carries no other significant health risks to either the mother or child.

Here the application of the principle of the double effect to the Kate Cox case might not be persuasive for those who would argue that the "health" of the mother by itself could not be a determining factor, *unless* her physical life were also in serious question. However, it is precisely here where greater attention to the vulnerability of the mother's whole condition, body and soul, may open up a broader perspective that a simply life or death optic would eclipse from our moral view.

However, a narrowly focused deductive analysis may sidestep or even deny some of these critical morally relevant vulnerability features, such that even the very life of the mother is not deemed sufficient to a termination of a pregnancy if a live birth might occur (regardless of other quality of life considerations of the child or mother). Writing in this vein, Joseph Meaney, the president of the National Catholic Bioethics Center, asserts that, even in difficult pregnancy situations in which an abortion would be required to save the life of the mother, the genuinely "Catholic" position is that *both* mother and child must die:

> Some will immediately object that it is absurd to allow both a mother and baby to die when an abortion would allow the woman to live. Catholics hold the deepest reverence for the right to life,

---

[12] See the entry "Physicalism and Personalism" in Bretzke, *Handbook of Roman Catholic Moral Terms,* 176–78. See also the Introduction and Glossary for these terms in James T. Bretzke, SJ, *Moral Debates in Contemporary Catholic Thought: Paradigms, Principles, and Prudence* (Rowman & Littlefield, 2025).

146 *JAMES BRETZKE*

but we affirm that committing evil is too high a price to pay to preserve a person's physical life. ... Abortion is not the ethical answer to high-risk pregnancies.[13]

Meaney's narrow deductive framing of the ethical issues surrounding medically problematic pregnancies has been adopted by other allies. Celebrating an Arkansas 2024 report where literally no abortions took place in that state the previous year, Catherine Phillips, director of Respect Life in the Diocese of Little Rock, stated, "we know it's never medically necessary, so we do welcome that report," while Arkansas Right to Life Executive Director Rose Mimms said the Arkansas Department of Health's report of no abortions, even to save the life of the mother, shows abortion does not need to be available for any reason.[14]

In a companion piece, Meaney removes all doubt as to the practical meaning of his reading of moral obligation:

It is up to our science and skill to save mothers and their preborn children, and when this is just not possible, not to fall into the crime of the unjust killing of the innocent. It is beyond the power of medicine to cure every patient, but the ethical practice of medicine is always possible. The frequent success of the Catholic approach to refuse to simply sacrifice patients should be a shining example of good ethics to the world.[15]

"Sacrifice" is certainly involved here, but is it morally justified for human flourishing? Others have expressed a similar willingness to go this route. Writing in the wake of the notorious 2010 Phoenix case in which

---

[13] Joseph Meaney, "The Bioethics of High-Risk Pregnancy," *National Catholic Bioethics Center* (NCBC) (June 3, 2022; reposted May 11, 2024), https://www.ncbcenter.org/messages-from-presidents/highrisk.

[14] Adriana Azarian, "Zero Abortions in Arkansas for 2023: A Pro-Life Victory," *National Catholic Register* (June 6, 2024), https://www.ncregister.com/news/zero-abortions-in-arkansas-for-2023-a-pro-life-victory?utm_campaign=NCR&utm_medium=email&_hsenc=p2ANqtz-_Zr8fiLuGN2bQbgDwERLtxdmtL9ps-GsWexf9jH1DgtMIhamMxDmghR6bnxc4_20LFIMEp9mDqbhxhECTXmKUff-5tumg&_hsmi=310470025&utm_content=310470025&utm_source=hs_email.

[15] Joseph Meaney, "Save Them Both: Maternal-Fetal Conflicts," *National Catholic Bioethics Center* (May 7, 2024), https://www.ncbcenter.org/messages-from-presidents/savethemboth.

VULNERABILITY AND FLOURISHING IN POST-DOBBS "HARD CASES" **147**

Bishop Thomas Olmsted stripped the "Catholic" designation for St. Joseph's Hospital while declaring hospital administrator Sr. Margaret McBride excommunicated, philosopher Thomas Cavanaugh argued that the preventable death of the mother in this sort of case represents a "moral martyrdom" supported by *Veritatis Splendor*. In his view, the preventable death of the mother, along with unpreventable death of her child, represented a good exemplar of "the position that there are certain acts from which one ought to refrain, regardless of the outcomes" and that "[m]oral martyrs witness to justice, its ubiquitous reach, and its absolute demands."[16]

While certainly there are "certain acts from which one ought to refrain, regardless of the outcomes," such as genocide, attention to saving those vulnerable lives that can be saved indicate that these "hard cases" do not belong to that genus. As the Irish Bishops note in cases like these "it will be a matter of weighing risks, rather than certainties, of harm for mother and child when considering possible interventions. The aim is always to save whatever life can be saved."[17] Contrary to Meaney's vocabulary of "a shining example of good ethics," it is human flourishing of the vulnerable that is immolated on the high altar of "thin description" narrow deductive reasoning of what supposedly constitutes "direct" abortion.

Here St. Irenaeus's famous dictum *Gloria Dei, Vivens Homo*, which was used by Pope John Paul II, helps show that it is human flourishing that truly gives glory to the Creator.[18] How then could God be genuinely glorified by the needless, avoidable suffering and/or death of God's precious ones made in God's own image? Greater attention to the vulnerability of the women and children involved may help refocus our attention on a genuine human flourishing that will give witness to God's glory.

In this optic let us return to the "hard case" of the ten-year-old child

---

[16] Thomas A. Cavanaugh, "Double Effect Reasoning, Craniotomy, and Vital Conflicts: A Case of Contemporary Catholic Casuistry," *National Catholic Bioethics Quarterly* (Autumn 2011): 463.

[17] Irish Catholic Bishops Conference, *Code of Ethical Standards for Healthcare*, no. 2.29 (October 4, 2017), https://councilforlife.ie/wp-content/uploads/2023/09/20180425-Code-of-Ethical-Standards-for-Healthcare.pdf.

[18] I would more freely translate St. Irenaeus's *Gloria Dei, Vivens Homo* as "The glory of God is found in the full flourishing of men and women." Pope John Paul II quoted St. Irenaeus in his General Audience of April 5, 2000.

148 *JAMES BRETZKE*

rape victim. National Catholic Bioethics Center neuroscientist Rev. Tadeuz Pacholczyk maintains this case has a clear, undisputed answer: the raped child, and her parents, simply have no other ethical choice but to carry the rapist's child to term:

> When a 10-year-old girl becomes pregnant from rape, responding to her trauma by offering a second trauma makes no sense . . . It exacerbates the original act of violence with yet more violence . . . It plays off the emotional vulnerability we all feel whenever tragedy strikes home. . . . What a young woman needs in such a situation is the support of family and friends, along with the reassurance that "we can get through this together." . . . What she really needs is the love, hope and compassion that buoys up anyone facing uncertainty about her own future.[19]

Pacholczyk's narrow deductive methodology begins with an a priori conclusion grounded in moral principles that simply read back into the chosen features of the particular case. Any aspect that does not fit with the conclusion, or that may point to a different judgment, is brushed aside or reformulated in ways that will not challenge the predetermined conclusion. This "thin description" method largely governs what is and what is not "seen" in this case. Thus, no termination of a viable pregnancy could ever be ethically countenanced, unless (perhaps) the physical life of the mother was in undisputable danger. Absent that, the rest of the features do not really play much of a role in his moral analysis. While the child's age is acknowledged as a fact, its importance is shunted aside with the assertion that "responding to her trauma by offering a second trauma makes no sense." Here in this version of the *status quaestionis* the combination of assumptions and abstract reasoning skew the conclusion: The termination of pregnancy caused by repeated rape of a nine-year-old child (her age when she was impregnated) would automatically "exacerbate" the "original act

---

[19] Rev. Tadeuz Pacholczyk, "Is Abortion Ever Allowed for Catholics? For a 10-Year-Old Rape Victim?" *National Catholic Register* (July 15, 2022), https://www.ncregister.com/cna/is-abortion-ever-allowed-for-catholics-for-a-10-year-old-rape-victim. Though his academic training is in neuroscience, Pacholczyk practices as a bioethicist and director of education of the National Catholic Bioethics Center. See also his website at https://www.fathertad.com/.

VULNERABILITY AND FLOURISHING IN POST-DOBBS "HARD CASES" **149**

of violence." This would then cause a greater trauma than having to endure the months-long pregnancy, birth, and postpartum features.

Pacholczyk's terming the crime a "tragedy" instead of "child rape" leads him to recast the whole case. He assumes that pregnancy termination would be negatively far more impactful on the child than the alternative. How might we test the respective assumptions here? These are the questions that Fr. Pacholczyk is unwilling either to ask or seriously entertain. The deductive mode gives no real reason to do so, since the "answer" already precedes any of these questions.

The closest Fr. Pacholczyk comes to personalism briefly appears in the needs of the "young woman" (as he now describes the ten-year-old child rape victim) when he states that what this child needs is the support of family and friends, as indicated in the quote above. All people would likely agree what the child needs in the aftermath of this sort of outrageous crime (a.k.a. "tragedy") is "love, hope and compassion." However, wouldn't the contours of this practical support best be discerned by the child's caregivers who also recognize she is still a "child" and not yet a "young woman"? Might this compassionate care therefore involve terminating the physical and psychological consequences of this rape, this criminal act?

Prudence, Humility, and Ethical Restraint

Were Fr. Pacholczyk right in his conclusions, it certainly is *not* because of his methodology. A more inductive manner, which seeks both to check our assumptions and discern the morally relative features of the concrete case, likely leads to a sounder conclusion than an abstract deduction far removed from the hard case. Recall Chief Justice John Roberts's caution of the tendency to hold to "a relentless freedom from doubt" in our judgments. Moral absolutism from any part of the ideological spectrum rarely leads to better informed, sounder ethical judgments. What if we were to apply Roberts's "judicial restraint" to our ethical judgments? As Roberts reminded the Court, the decision involved only those items that absolutely required adjudication. Where "it is not necessary to decide more to dispose of a case, then it is necessary not to decide more."[20]

---

[20] Roberts, "Opinion on Thomas E. Dobbs."

An analogue to Roberts's description of "judicial restraint" would be to propose a prudent "ethical restraint" in complex cases like these. In other words, ethical restraint might suggest that the wisest thing to do may be simply to limit ourselves to an affirmation of key foundational moral values such as the sanctity of an informed conscience, commitment to the hierarchy of values implicit in human flourishing, and the common good. Here also is where the principle of subsidiarity interpreted in a preferential option for the "vulnerable" better shows the glory of God in human flourishing. Attention to vulnerability leads more effectively into the foundational component of Christian ethics that is compassion. Subsidiarity here is compassion in action, which holds that practical reason dictates concrete decisions ought to be made at the lowest possible level rather than somewhere higher up in the ethical ionosphere. This requires that those closest to, and most responsible for, the practical moral decision should be empowered, trusted, and supported, even if others may possess greater academic or religious "authority" credentials.

Pope Francis has tackled this same problematic many times and has outlined a conscience-based subsidiarity and accompaniment in *Amoris Laetitia*:

> We have long thought that simply by stressing doctrinal, bioethical and moral issues, without encouraging openness to grace, we were providing sufficient support to families, ... We also find it hard to make room for the consciences of the faithful, who very often respond as best they can to the Gospel amid their limitations, and are capable of carrying out their own discernment in complex situations. We have been called to form consciences, not to replace them.[21]

Our "homework" must be to reflect on additional perspectives needed to enlighten better our consciences, even if some of these dif-

---

[21] Pope Francis, *Amoris Laetitia* (2016), no. 37. Much of the negative pushback Pope Francis has received in initiatives, such as *Amoris Laetitia*, may be connected to this reluctance to issue moral denunciations. See James T. Bretzke, SJ, "In Good Conscience: What *Amoris Laetitia* Can Teach Us About Responsible Decision Making," *America* (April 8, 2016), https://www.americamagazine.org/issue/article/good-conscience.

VULNERABILITY AND FLOURISHING IN POST-DOBBS "HARD CASES" **151**

ferent perspectives stretch our comfort zones. Risking these encounters is necessary if we can admit that some of our own assumptions might be not only limited but also limiting our ability to see all of the morally relevant features in a complex situation.[22] Recognizing one's limitations, therefore, can be a helpful methodological starting point to overcome our moral astigmatism and better envision how the Spirit of God is endeavoring to help us remember and learn what heretofore may have been too hard for us to bear (cf. Jn 14:26 and 16:12–13). This openness to the Spirit also requires cultivation of humility—a virtue whose importance Pope Francis has underscored in providing the "base of Christian life," while at the same time serving as an antidote for "the great antagonist of the most mortal of sins, namely arrogance."[23]

Concluding Proposition:
Consider Revising Our Understanding of ERDs

Thus, considering these two "hard cases," let me add to the *status quaestionis* with a possible revision of the interpretation of the legitimate cases contained in the current Ethical and Religious Directives for Catholic Health Care Services (ERDs). Directive no. 47 asserts pregnancy terminations that "have as their direct purpose the cure of a proportionately serious pathological condition of a pregnant woman are permitted when they cannot be safely postponed until the unborn child is viable, even if they will result in the death of the unborn child."[24]

Discussion around ERD no. 47 has focused on what medically would constitute either a "direct" or "indirect" abortion, such as which procedures are allowed in difficult pregnancy cases, for example, those involving an ectopic fetus or uterine cancer. However, what if we were to broaden what might constitute the "serious pathological condition of a pregnant woman" in a more inductive manner? Then factors such as age, psychological capacity, overall health, emotional, physical, eco-

---

[22] For a contribution to this sort of discourse, see Sandra Sullivan Dunbar, "Catholic Abortion Discourse and the Erosion of Democracy," *Journal of the Society of Christian Ethics* 43, no. 1 (2023): 55–73, https://doi.org/10.5840/jsce202341776.

[23] Pope Francis, "Cycle of Catechesis. Vices and Virtues. 20. Humility," General Audience of May 22, 2024.

[24] U.S. Conference of Catholic Bishops, *Ethical and Religious Directives for Catholic Health Care Services*.

nomic support, and so on could all be considered morally legitimate. It might be even possible to say that in these particular cases, maybe the course of action that would most promote human flourishing would be to release the unborn child into God's providential care where no one is ever definitively lost and God's healing grace is extended to all.[25]

This concluding paragraph, posed as a *quaestio disputata* in our *status quaestionis*, will be contentious. But if with humility, effort, and good will, we consider that ethical restraint in our discernment, then it might be possible to respond more adequately to vulnerable individuals such as the Texan Kate Cox and the Ohio child rape victim. It would help us to focus more explicitly on what would foster their individual human flourishing such that we work more concretely for the (greater) *Gloria Dei* that only will occur through the *Vivens Homo* of the flourishing of God's creatures made most perfectly in God's own image.

---

[25] This sentiment is widely used in postabortion healing programs and is drawn from Pope John Paul II's special words to women who have suffered the loss of a child through abortion. See Pope John Paul II, *Evangelium Vitae* (1995), no. 99.

Women, Synodality, and Social Poetry

Callie Tabor

In various remarks and interviews from the early days of his pontificate to the present, Pope Francis has named a concern that the church lacks a "profound theology of women."[1] He seems to perceive what we might call a theological vulnerability left open by insufficient reflection on the role of women in the church. Speaking to the International Theological Commission (ITC) in November 2023, in unscripted remarks, Pope Francis elaborated on this concern: "The church is a woman and if we do not understand what woman is or what the theology of womanhood is, we will never understand what the church is. One of the great sins we have witnessed is 'masculinizing' the church."[2] Women are vulnerable to being treated as nonessential to the life of the church without an adequate theologizing of "womanhood," which in turn limits our understanding of the church and ability to carry out its mission. Flourishing, for both women and the church, then depends on the working out of this "theology of womanhood" according to Francis.

This chapter interrogates this framing of women's theological vulnerability and flourishing, arguing that while the Synod on Synodality seeks to form a listening church, the ability of not only Pope Francis but the institutional church more broadly to listen to women is hindered by the fact that there already exists an operative "theology of woman-

---

[1] Pope Francis first called for this "theology of women" in 2013. See "A Big Heart Open to God," *America Magazine* online, September 30, 2013.

[2] Claire Giangravé, "Pope Asks Theologians to 'Demasculinize' the Church," *Religion News Service*, November 30, 2023, www.religionnews.com.

154
CALLIE TABOR

hood" forming imaginations—one inspired by John Paul II and Hans Urs von Balthasar. In contrast to this imagined ideal womanhood, I propose to root a theology of women in women's own imaginations, one less concerned with strictly defining "womanhood" than with women realizing their full flourishing. Pope Francis himself has signaled the importance of imagination to flourishing in his discussion of "social poets"—those who "create hope where there appears to be only waste and exclusion."[3] By placing Pope Francis's discussion of the poetic into conversation with Audre Lorde's classic essay "Poetry Is Not a Luxury," I hope to illuminate the significance of women's creative efforts toward their own flourishing. Beyond the theological vulnerability Pope Francis perceives, the poetic allows women to address creatively the tangible vulnerabilities created by patriarchy within and beyond the church. As Lorde suggests, by putting their dreams into thought and then into action, women create possibilities for their lives beyond the confines of patriarchal roles.

Are They Listening?

Monsignor Piero Coda, the general secretary for the ITC, connected Francis's remarks on women's participation in the church and a "theology of womanhood" directly to the current Synod on Synodality with its emphasis on listening to the sense of the faithful, especially at the margins.[4] As the Working Document for the Continental Stage of the Synod entitled *Enlarge the Space of Your Tent* notes, "women remain the majority of those who attend liturgy and participate in activities," and yet "most decision-making and governance roles are held by men."[5] Despite being in the majority of those participating in the life of the church, women are pushed to the margins not only in decision-making roles but also in preaching, ministry, and theological reflection. It is perhaps not surprising then that the report from the Holy Land noted, "Those who were most committed to the synod process were women who seem to have realized not only that they had more to gain, but also

---

[3] Pope Francis, "Video Message of the Holy Father Francis on the Occasion of the Fourth World Meeting of Popular Movements," October 16, 2021.

[4] Giangravé, "Pope Asks Theologians to 'Demasculinize' the Church."

[5] Synod of Bishops, *Enlarge the Space of Your Tent: Working Document for the Continental Stage*, October 27, 2022, no. 61, www.synod.va.

WOMEN, SYNODALITY, AND SOCIAL POETRY

more to offer by being relegated to a prophetic edge, from which they observe what happens in the life of the Church."[6] The Korean report echoes a similar sentiment. Indeed, both the Working Document for the Continental Stage and the Synthesis Report make clear that the call for women to be valued as "baptized and equal members of the people of God" rang out on every continent.[7] Proposals for recognizing this value ranged from general urging to include more women in decision making and pastoral ministry roles to specific calls to increase women's access to theological education; to pay women just wages; and to use more inclusive language, imagery, and narratives in liturgy and prayer.[8] As in the Synod on the Family and the Synod on the Amazon, calls to ordain women to the diaconate were renewed.[9]

While it is too soon to know for certain how many of these proposals will be implemented by church leadership, Francis's discussions of the "theology of womanhood" suggest there is a blockage in the inner ear of the institutional church when it comes to women's voices. Each time Francis speaks of including more women in decision-making roles or theological reflection in order to develop the "theology of womanhood" that he perceives as lacking, he adds that the impetus for this is the need to learn from women's "feminine genius" or to live fully the "Marian" principle of the church "because there is the bride Church, the woman Church, without being masculine."[10] Through these images, he invokes, without fully elaborating, the theologies of John Paul II and Hans Urs von Balthasar. It is difficult to see why there would be a need for a "theology of women," when, by using these phrases, Francis imports a theology of gender that already assumes the role of women in the church. In both these theologies, womanhood is reduced to a romanticized vision of a limited set of traits including sensitivity, gen-

---

[6] The references to the Holy Land and South Korea are both quotations from regional/national-level reports that are included in *Enlarge the Space of Your Tent*, no. 61.

[7] *Enlarge the Space of Your Tent*, no. 61; Synod of Bishops, *Synthesis Report: A Synodal Church in Mission*, October 28, 2023, www.synod.va.

[8] *Synthesis Report: A Synodal Church in Mission*.

[9] *Enlarge the Space of Your Tent*, no. 64; Elizabeth Elliott, "Synod Puts Women Deacons on the Table," May 12, 2016, www.ncronline.org; *Final Document of the Amazon Synod*, October 26, 2019, no. 103, secretariat.synod.va.

[10] "Pope Meets Council of Cardinals to Discuss Church's Feminine Dimension," *Vatican News*, December 4, 2023, www.vaticannews.va.

156 CALLIE TABOR

erosity, maternal instinct, and receptivity that is always in "response" to the normative humanity of men.[11] Beginning with this assumed understanding of what a woman is creates a challenge for listening to women and supporting their flourishing, since their lived experiences are filtered through an imagined category of "woman" with associated roles this type of human is to play in church and society.

Flourishing and Social Poetry

One way to respond to this challenge might be to forward an alternative "theology of womanhood," one that attempts to avoid the complementarian pitfalls of John Paul II and von Balthasar. However, given the diversity of women's lives, any attempt at a definition will inevitably be incomplete and even exclusionary. Even within the field of feminist theology, whose specialty is theological reflection through the experiences and concerns of women, accounts of "women's" experiences have at times been exclusionary—most frequently when White feminists have taken their experiences as representative of the whole of "womanhood."[12] Instead, to locate this problem as one of religious imagination, I turn to women's own imagining, where acts of "social poetry" become the basis of flourishing in particularity, which can help to develop the concept of the "social poet" in Francis's vocabulary of creativity and action.

"Social poetry" is a phrase Francis first introduces in his addresses to the World Meeting of Popular Movements, an initiative begun under his papacy that gathers grassroots organizations from across the globe.[13] In 2014 he describes the work of those who take discarded materials

---

[11] Balthasar describes the reality of woman primarily as that of being man's *Antwort*, answer, and *Antlitz*, face. Faced with his aloneness, man looks around and discovers the security and delight of the face of the woman, who answers his searching gaze with her own, and therefore offers to him a new possibility of fulfillment and completeness. Hans Urs von Balthasar, *Theo-Drama III. Dramatis Personae: Persons in Christ*, trans. Graham Harrison (Ignatius Press, 1992), 284–85. John Paul II first discussed the "feminine genius" in *Mulieris Dignitatem* (1988), no. 31.

[12] An example of this critique comes from Audre Lorde to Mary Daly. See "An Open Letter to Mary Daly," in Audre Lorde, *Sister Outsider: Essays and Speeches*, reprint (Crossing Press, 2007), 66–71.

[13] Francis, "Address of the Holy Father at the Second World Meeting of Popular Movements."

WOMEN, SYNODALITY, AND SOCIAL POETRY

and repurpose them for further use as "poetry."[14] Through his next three addresses to this global meeting, he names these workers and activists "social poets" because of the millions of individual actions of change they compose, which are nevertheless connected like words in a poem.[15] In his 2021 address, he centers the idea of social poetry, explaining that "poetry means creativity, and you create hope."[16] Francis sees those participating in popular movements to be reshaping society through *poiesis*, which in this framework, as Vincenzo Rosito notes, is not creation out of nothing but creation out of that which has been "thrown away," thus critiquing our current economic system through this creativity.[17] Out of communities that appear "useless" to the gaze of the market, these poets craft practices of hope.

More recently, Francis has expanded this category to the realm of higher education, calling for the mission of Catholic universities to be the training of social poets who, "upon learning the grammar and vocabulary of humanity, have a spark, a brilliance that allows them to imagine the unknown" especially toward the creation of a more just society.[18] In his own use of the term, being a social poet is not limited to one form of life but is a way of being that is at once individual and communal, as individual poetic acts contribute to a collective change. Social poets address social structures that make themselves and others vulnerable to harm through both practical action and creativity that allows them to imagine new pathways for flourishing.

I propose to expand this idea of social poetry to the lives of women in conversation with Audre Lorde who, decades before Francis, wrote of poetry as a source of women's flourishing. This poetic imagining supports women's flourishing by allowing them to envision and enact new

---

[14] Pope Francis, "Address of Pope Francis to Participants in the World Meeting of Popular Movements," October 28, 2014.

[15] Francis, "Address of the Holy Father at the Second World Meeting of Popular Movements"; Pope Francis, "Address of His Holiness Pope Francis to Participants in the 3rd World Meeting of Popular Movements," November 5, 2016.

[16] Francis, "Video Message of the Holy Father Francis on the Occasion of the Fourth World Meeting of Popular Movements."

[17] Vincenzo Rosito, " 'Social Poets' and 'Sowers of Change': The Role of Popular Movements Within the Church and Society," *Politics and Religion Journal* 11, no. 2 (2017): 271–82.

[18] "The Mission of the University Is to Train Social Poets," *Rome Reports*, May 4, 2023, www.romereports.com.

158   *CALLIE TABOR*

ways of being in the world. Even where enactment may be constrained by systems of oppression, imagining keeps alive the possibility of flourishing. Further, by living into their own creativity and desires for their lives, women illustrate the imaginative shortcomings of the reigning complementarian theology of womanhood, exposing its inadequacy as an interpretative framework. For true synodal listening to take place, this imaginative idol of "womanhood" must be removed; otherwise, what women have to say continues to be refracted through this distorted lens. Synodality aims at bringing about conversion, as those at the center are called not merely to listen to those on the peripheries but to "journey" with them toward union with God, the fulfillment and true source of flourishing.[19] Social poetry supports this synodal conversion through the disrupting of the imaginative idol.

Not a Luxury: Women as Social Poets

Literary scholar Sheila Hassell Hughes writes that in the turn to women's literature as a resource, White feminist theologians have at times appropriated literature by women of color by decontextualizing their work in a way that supports a simple identification through the category of "woman" while erasing other forms of difference.[20] She argues that to maintain the integrity of the text, it is crucial for the White feminist scholar to resist the temptation to decontextualize imaginative literature and to read in what she names an "ex-static" posture, wherein one steps outside oneself to share the vision of the other, in order to then see and name one's own privileges, so that through the process of being "beside oneself" one is "open to transformation."[21] Though I am dealing here with an essay by Lorde rather than her poems themselves, I seek to follow Hughes's "ex-static" reading style and not to elide differences. Lorde first published her now-classic essay "Poetry Is Not a Luxury" in 1977 in *Chrysalis: A Magazine of Female Culture* while poetry editor at the magazine, using the position to "advance a theory of poetry

---

[19] International Theological Commission, "Synodality in the Life and Mission of the Church," March 2, 2018, nos. 50–55.

[20] Sheila Hassell Hughes, " 'Eye to Eye': Using Women's Literature as Lenses for Feminist Theology," *Literature and Theology: An International Journal of Religion, Theory, and Culture* 16, no. 1 (March 1, 2002): 2.

[21] Hughes, " 'Eye to Eye,' " 12.

WOMEN, SYNODALITY, AND SOCIAL POETRY 159

that was personally and socially meaningful for women."[22] In "Poetry Is Not a Luxury," Lorde chooses to privilege the category of "women," but it is important not to decontextualize this from her larger oeuvre wherein she speaks directly to differences between women of color and White women as well as lesbians and straight women of all races.

I will return to the significance of difference for Lorde momentarily, but to turn first to "Poetry Is Not a Luxury," here Lorde argues that for women, poetry is a necessity since it is through poetry that we "give name to the nameless so it can be thought"—and then lived.[23] Poetry is not an excess or a fantasy, but rather "it is the skeleton architecture of our lives" through which Lorde argues that women will free themselves from the "white fathers" who dismiss poetry as nonrational and treat women themselves as nonrational, childish, sensual—and we might add, receptive and maternal.[24] Lorde invokes both the literal writing of poetry and poetry as the creative bringing forth of ideas and actions that might allow women to flourish beyond this patriarchal vision of womanhood.

Lorde shares with Francis a critique of our current economic system, while having a deeper understanding of the ways in which patriarchy, racism, and heterosexism are intertwined with capitalism, creating hierarchies of being that can label those who deviate from the norm as "surplus."[25] Perhaps connected to this shared sense of the economic violence that "throws away" communities and cultures, Lorde highlights how poetry is not the creation of something "new" per se but a new "illumination" of what exists, understanding it differently:

> For there are no new ideas. There are only new ways of making them felt—of examining what those ideas feel like being lived on Sunday morning at 7 A.M., after brunch, during wild love, making war, giving birth, mourning our dead—while we suffer the old longings, battle the old warnings and fears of being silent and impotent and alone, while we taste new possibilities and strengths.[26]

---

[22] Roderick A. Ferguson, "Of Sensual Matters: On Audre Lorde's 'Poetry Is Not a Luxury' and 'Uses of the Erotic,'" *Women's Studies Quarterly* 40, no. 3/4 (October 1, 2012): 295.

[23] Lorde, *Sister Outsider*, 37.

[24] Lorde, *Sister Outsider*, 38.

[25] Lorde, *Sister Outsider*, 114; Pope Francis, *Laudato Sí* (2015), no. 123.

[26] Lorde, *Sister Outsider*, 39.

160   CALLIE TABOR

Lorde here rejects new ideas—what we might read as the approach of the "white fathers" she mentions earlier in the essay. Discussing "Poetry Is Not a Luxury" with Adrienne Rich, Lorde said she understood how using the figures of the "rational white man" and the "emotional dark female" in the essay might strike some as reinforcing stereotypes, but that to leave rationality to the White man "is like leaving him a piece of that road that begins nowhere and ends nowhere."[27] Logic alone is insufficient to the poetic work Lorde envisions here. While the activists and workers whom Francis names "social poets" create from what has been deemed "minor and unviable 'material,'" no longer of use to the economic system, Lorde invites women to pick up the ways of knowing left behind by severing knowledge from feeling and from the act of living.[28]

This kind of knowing aligns more with women's flourishing than the articulation of a "theology of womanhood." Lorde's rejection of "new ideas" does not displace the value of women's own theologizing, but her evocation of the events of life from the great moments of birth and death to the ordinariness of a Sunday morning invites theology to arise out of and to accompany these realities. Great experiences of childbirth and war carry with them very apparent existential vulnerabilities, but Lorde suggests that the everyday moments of quiet desperation and unrealized longing also keep women from flourishing. Recognizing that this theological language moves beyond the frameworks Lorde uses in her essay, I argue that living out the hope of new possibilities amidst the events of life as Lorde describes is one way that women live into the presence of God's love for them as equal bearers of the *imago dei*, seeking out the fullness of life. In "Uses of the Erotic," a companion piece to "Poetry Is Not a Luxury," Lorde seeks to reclaim eros from being reduced to the pornographic or even merely sexual, arguing that eros is a love that is a "lifeforce" and "creative power."[29] Through the creativity of poetry, Lorde sees women embracing eros. Though less frequently

---

[27] In this interview Lorde also explains that she sees the "Black mother" as a figure who represents the poet that can be accessed in each person, including in men, but that she sees men as less willing to reckon with this kind of power inside themselves. Lorde, *Sister Outsider*, 100.

[28] Rosito, "'Social Poets' and 'Sowers of Change,'" 276.

[29] Lorde explains that she sees "Poetry Is Not a Luxury" and "Uses of the Erotic: The Erotic as Power" as two parts of a "progression" in this interview with Adrienne Rich. Lorde, *Sister Outsider*, 55, 81.

WOMEN, SYNODALITY, AND SOCIAL POETRY

utilized than agape in the Christian tradition, eros also names the love of God and the love of humans reaching back toward the divine.[30] M. Shawn Copeland describes the love of Jesus toward those oppressed under empire, for eros not only encourages embracing the desire for creativity, knowledge, and life, but it also "validates our refusal of docility and submission in the face of oppression."[31] Through poetic acts of imagination that support alternative ways of being in the world, women might embrace this divine eros for their flourishing and name it, not as something new, but rather, as Lorde describes, as something that has been repressed by dividing knowledge from life.

This poetic knowing is at once personal and social—what Roderick A. Ferguson calls an "aesthetics of existence" crafting individual and communal transformation.[32] This poetic "aesthetics of existence" aims at flourishing in and through difference. Joan M. Martin argues that Lorde's work contributes to an understanding of difference as significant to both the methodology and epistemology of womanist thought, wherein Lorde values difference but also clearly names its distortions.[33] Too often, Lorde argues, those with power ignore differences, and in the community of women, this has been most consistently White women who fail to recognize that there are different "entrapments" within the current system of power wherein "white women face the pitfall of being seduced into joining the oppressor under the pretense of sharing power."[34] Extending this to thinking about women as "social poets," White women have at times accepted a "theology of womanhood" as premised solely on our experiences, and social poetry invites us instead to begin from the flourishing of women who have not had their poetic vision "entrapped" by this temptation.

As Martin argues, poetry is Lorde's chosen vehicle for movement from this destructive relationship to difference as threat into a vision

---

[30] Benedict XVI writes of eros as leading to the divine and toward the other, such that eros and agape are not so distinct as sometimes argued. In God eros and agape are united. Pope Benedict XVI, *Deus Caritas Est* (2015), nos. 5–7.

[31] M. Shawn Copeland, *Enfleshing Freedom: Body, Race, and Being* (Fortress Press, 2010), 64.

[32] Ferguson, "Of Sensual Matters," 296.

[33] Joan M. Martin, "The Notion of Difference for Emerging Womanist Ethics: The Writings of Audre Lorde and bell hooks," *Journal of Feminist Studies in Religion* 9, no. 1–2 (January 1, 1993): 39–40.

[34] Lorde, *Sister Outsider*, 118.

162   CALLIE TABOR

of difference as a source of "creative power."[35] In poetry, words that one might never expect to see connected are joined, and the movement of these differences together, as words fall off the tongue, becomes the basis for a different way of looking. This poetic emphasis on difference highlights the inadequacies of a single description of women's role in the church. Though space does not permit me to develop this comparison, one might argue that rather than interpreting "womanhood" as a symbol of the feminine church as Francis does, we might fruitfully reverse the direction of the metaphor and extend his image of the church as a polyhedron—unified but always maintaining difference—to the realities of women's lives and flourishing.[36] The synodal project aims at offering both a process and a theological framework for allowing difference to inspire ecclesial action without fear that this will undermine unity. However, as this article's discussion of women and the church has suggested, the synodal process may be stymied by the theological interpretation of the "woman," which offers not unity but sameness. The ideal of "woman" encourages conformity rather than unity in difference and makes it more difficult for women who do not fit this ideal to be heard.

Guided by Lorde's interpretation of women as poets, we might return to synodal listening and the "theology of womanhood," which, I have argued, restricts the ability of the institutional church to hear women. Poetry asks not for mere listening, but rather an attentiveness that is open to transformation. If one merely "listens" to the poem, one is unlikely to enter into its spirit. As Lorde suggests, replacing one logic for another will not suffice to be transformed. Rather, I would argue, the male leadership of the Catholic Church is being called to allow the poetry of women's lives to "illuminate" their understanding in a new way, in a continuing conversion process of letting go of an imagined "woman" in order to see the flourishing that women are creating for themselves in various ways, through the love of God in their lives. By doing so, leadership will address the truer vulnerability for women in Catholicism, which is not a lack of a "theology of womanhood" but a lack of recognition of the theological insights already being lived and written by women, which cannot be reduced to a single set of proposi-

---

[35] Martin, "The Notion of Difference for Emerging Womanist Ethics," 43.
[36] Pope Francis, *Evangelii Gaudium* (2013), no. 236.

tions. In the midst of harms created by patriarchy, racism, classism, heterosexism, and more, both within and beyond the church, women are writing about their vulnerabilities but also imagining, living, and writing about their desires to flourish, spurred on in this action by the God of life. It is only through deeper attentiveness to this "social poetry" that the church will be able to attend to women's vulnerabilities and truly support their flourishing.

The Annunciation

A Biblical Handmaid's Tale

Alaina Keller

"Mary said, 'Behold, I am the handmaid of the Lord'" (Lk 1:38, NABRE). Translated from the Greek *doulē*, the term "handmaid," or "female slave," has garnered much debate surrounding its usage and usefulness for cultivating a positive Mariology for women. Indeed, for several biblical studies scholars, the title and its corresponding image are problematic at best and irrecuperable at worst.[1] As "handmaid" remains the only title that the Virgin Mary claims for herself in the scriptures, its dismissal in scholarship would signify the dismissal of Mary's own words, of which precious few remain. This chapter, then,

---

[1] Judith Lieu, *The Gospel of Luke* (Epworth Press, 1997; reprinted Wipf and Stock, 2012), 7, 9; Amy-Jill Levine and Ben Witherington III, *The Gospel of Luke*, The New Cambridge Bible Commentary (Cambridge University Press, 2018), 37, 352. While Lieu underlines the problematic nature of the term "handmaid" due to its possibility for exalting passive submission to power, Levine and Witherington add how modern contexts of slavery and trafficking question the recuperation of the term, despite its positive connotation in the text. These commentaries helpfully complicate the term in biblical studies, which has historically focused on representing Mary's ideal discipleship or humility as "handmaid." For the image of handmaid as ideal disciple, see Raymond E. Brown, SJ, *The Birth of the Messiah: A Commentary on the Infancy Narratives in the Gospels of Matthew and Luke* (Doubleday, 1993); Joseph A. Fitzmyer, *The Gospel According to Luke I–IX*, The Anchor Bible (Doubleday, 1981). For a brief examination of Mary's humility, see François Bovon, *Luke 1: A Commentary on the Gospel of Luke 1:1–9:50*, Hermeneia: A Critical & Historical Commentary on the Bible, ed. Helmut Koestar, trans. Christine M. Thomas (Fortress Press, 2002).

THE ANNUNCIATION   165

proposes a constructive reading of the term "handmaid" by looking beyond Luke to the kenotic lens of Philippians. In comparing Mary's self-identification as "female slave" with the *kenosis* of Jesus Christ in Philippians 2:5–11, in which he took "the form of a slave [*doulou*]," the term "handmaid" encompasses not only willed self-emptying into vulnerability but also subsequent exaltation. "Handmaid" thus becomes a title that must be reckoned with as it stretches beyond the patriarchal interpretation of women's passive *fiat* to authority and embraces the possibility for female, and therefore human, flourishing.

Retrieval of the term "handmaid," before any comparison between a Marian and Christic *kenosis*, begins with its most prominent image in contemporary society: the Handmaid in Margaret Atwood's *The Handmaid's Tale*. In the Republic of Gilead, a theocratic dictatorship inspired by seventeenth-century Puritan communities, Atwood images the Handmaid as a woman whose capacity for childbearing grants her certain status in a society where birthrates have dramatically decreased.[2] Yet, this alleged "position of honour,"[3] which consists in being assigned to high-ranking men to bear them children, imposes a two-fold diminishment: that of will and of identity. Offred, the red-clad narrator of this tale, observes how the concept of freedom has changed in Gilead to undermine the Handmaid's agency. Rather than the "freedom to" of the past, she notes how women are now granted the "freedom from."[4] They are removed from active doing to passive enclosure within society, having knowledge of others' power but little access to their own, excluding childbearing. Though Offred grasps at power through physical theft and prohibited relationships, Gilead's society consistently rejects any claim to female agency. It also prevents any claim to identity, beginning with the Handmaids' names. Offred, whose real name is forbidden, receives this designation upon becoming the Handmaid of Commander Fredrick ("of Fred"), and other names, such as Ofwarren and Ofglen, illustrate the Handmaids' reduction of identity to property.[5] Moreso than property, they are child bearers; the Handmaid is a "worthy vessel" so completely defined by her body

---

[2] Margaret Atwood, "Margaret Atwood on What 'The Handmaid's Tale' Means in the Age of Trump," *New York Times*, March 10, 2017, http://www.nytimes.com.

[3] Margaret Atwood, *The Handmaid's Tale* (Vintage Books, 1998), 13.

[4] Atwood, *The Handmaid's Tale*, 24–25.

[5] Atwood, "Margaret Atwood."

166   *ALAINA KELLER*

that her entire worth is contained in her womb.[6] To be pregnant is to "be saved," but to be without child is, in Offred's words, to "see despair coming toward me like famine. To feel that empty, again, again."[7] Offred does disavow this bodily definition through composition, for she both "composes" herself before others in an act of agency and controls her identity through the written composition of her story, hidden for future readers.[8] Those in power, however, persist in systematically deconstructing the will and identity of this composed Handmaid, emptying her of self.

While Luke's infancy narrative paints a different picture of the "handmaid" as the recipient of sublime grace, Mary's self-designation as such similarly precipitates a diminishment, an emptying, of will and identity within an androcentric understanding. At the Annunciation, Mary questions the angel Gabriel, "How can this be," upon hearing his proclamation of her miraculous conception before she consents to his message (Lk 1:30–38). Her responses exhibit a strong sense of agency. Furthermore, her Magnificat demonstrates her knowledge of exactly who she is. She reiterates—she composes—her identity as "handmaid" and positions herself among the lowly and afflicted, who are to be "lifted up" by God (Lk 1:46–55).[9] Still, despite this song of victory, the patriarchal interpretation of the "handmaid" resists her self-possession of will and independent identity. What appears as consent in Luke's depiction is reimagined as female submissiveness, a "conformist acceptance" in which Mary receives rather than cooperates with God.[10] Humility becomes Mary's most-extolled virtue in this depiction, and as her prostration before God is, in turn, directed toward her son, the image becomes abstracted into a female prostration before the male.[11]

---

[6] Atwood, *The Handmaid's Tale*, 65.

[7] Atwood, *The Handmaid's Tale*, 26, 74.

[8] Atwood, *The Handmaid's Tale*, 66, 39–40.

[9] Elizabeth A. Johnson, *Truly Our Sister: A Theology of Mary in the Communion of Saints* (Continuum, 2005), 265. Commentaries differ as to the nature of the "lowly" with whom Mary identifies, from those suffering from material poverty to the lowly of the psalms to the *anawim*. See Lieu, *The Gospel*, 11; Levine and Witherington, *The Gospel of Luke*, 40.

[10] Ivone Gebara and Maria Clara Bingemer, *Mary: Mother of God, Mother of the Poor*, trans. Phillip Berryman (Wipf & Stock Publishers, 2004), 69; Marina Warner, *Alone of All Her Sex: The Myth and Cult of the Virgin Mary* (Vintage Books, 1983), 177.

[11] Warner, *Alone of All Her Sex*, 178, 180–83.

THE ANNUNCIATION	**167**

Her lack of identity arises from this patriarchal image of prostration, in which Mary, like Offred, is reduced from multifaceted femaleness to the singular role of child bearer. Eyes lowered, arms clasped across her chest, she is a mere "vessel" or "void" in which God's new creation comes into existence. Mary may assert her agency in composing her response to God's grace, but the patriarchal image identifies her solely with her virginal womb, open to God's overwhelming, masculine-coded power. She, the true handmaid, then points to the Father above her and to the Son within her; while full of her Son, she is empty of herself. In this androcentric reading of the Annunciation, Mary's motherhood becomes "true womanhood," an ideal that women, as sexual beings, cannot attain.[12] As subordinate handmaids, they merely point, like Mary, to the masculine power that dominates.

Thus far, the imaged handmaid of both *The Handmaid's Tale* and Luke's Annunciation, who is emptied vessel, receiver, and child bearer, precludes any possibility for female, as well as human, flourishing. A feminist theological understanding of flourishing begins with what Rosemary Radford Ruether names "the promotion of the full humanity of women," based in "neither a hierarchical model that diminishes the potential of the 'other' nor an 'equality' defined by a ruling norm drawn from the dominant group."[13] The end goal, then, is a model of mutuality, in which persons-in-relation are celebrated not only in their equivalence but also in their uniqueness.[14] Women and other persons previously on the margins of power are "filled" with value and return to the center, where *all* individuals gather. Such a model immediately opposes the patriarchal image of the will-less, identity-less handmaid. Because full humanity arises in the mutuality and interrelation of persons, the agency that enables encounter and the self-identification that enables sharing-in-encounter are essential to flourishing. Female flourishing, then, is not the emptied, subordinated existence of the handmaid, but rather the understanding of one's own dignity, not

---

[12] Elisabeth Schüssler Fiorenza, *Jesus: Miriam's Child, Sophia's Prophet: Critical Issues in Feminist Christology* (Continuum, 1994), 164–65.

[13] Rosemary Radford Ruether, *Sexism and God-Talk: Towards a Feminist Theology* (Beacon Press, 1983), 18, 20.

[14] Ruether, *Sexism and God-Talk*, 20; Elizabeth A. Johnson, *She Who Is: The Mystery of God in Feminist Theological Discourse*, tenth anniversary ed. (Crossroad Publishing, 2003), 32.

168 ALAINA KELLER

constituted in relation but in oneself as a woman who then relates, an active moral agent. The term "handmaid" needs rethinking.

In order for the "handmaid" to be compatible with female flourishing, it must undergo its own *kenosis* to rid itself of patriarchal meaning. With this emptying, or what Ruether and Elizabeth Johnson call a *kenosis of patriarchy*, dominant and privileged voices are transcended by an empowering image of "the new humanity."[15] This *kenosis*, I argue, occurs when comparing the Marian title "handmaid" (*doulē*) with that of the Christic title "slave" (*doulos*) in Philippians 2:5–11, a comparison that adopts Jane Schaberg's fifth approach in a feminist reading of the scriptures: a "focus not on individual texts but on the Bible in general, in the hope of finding a theological perspective . . . some central witness that offers a critique of patriarchy."[16] Paul's letter to the Philippians introduces the title "slave" in a short hymn that describes how Jesus emulates the humility to which Paul calls his audience. Comprising six verses, the "metaphoric myth" can be divided into two parts. The first is a downward self-emptying into the distinctly human "form" of a slave and then into his obedient death on the cross; the second is an upward exaltation and reception of the divine name.[17] Although Jesus obediently suffers as a "slave," this title does not denote the same lack of will and identity as in the patriarchal image of the "female slave." Christ's obedience, rather than being a kind of unwilled subordination, is instead a human characteristic that reveals God's radical identification with humanity in its limiting conditions.[18] As a descent into humanity, his *kenosis* can be interpreted as a descent into vulnerability, what James F. Keenan sees as one such human condition:

---

[15] Ruether, *Sexism and God-Talk*, 137; Johnson, *She Who Is*, 161.

[16] Jane Schaberg, *The Illegitimacy of Jesus: A Feminist Theological Interpretation of the Infancy Narratives*, twentieth anniversary ed. (Sheffield Phoenix Press, 2006), 27.

[17] Paul A. Holloway, *Philippians* (Hermeneia), ed. Adela Yarbro Collins (Fortress Press, 2017), 114–29. In Holloway's view, this divine name means the divine name "Yahweh," also suggested by reference to Jesus as "Lord" (*kurios*).

[18] R. P. Martin, *Carmen Christi: Philippians ii. 5–11 in Recent Interpretation and in the Setting of Early Christian Worship* (Cambridge University Press, 1967), 227; John M. G. Barclay, "Kenosis and the Drama of Salvation in Philippians 2," in *Kenosis: The Self-Emptying of Christ in Scripture and Theology*, ed. Paul T. Nimmo and Keith L. Johnson (Eerdmans Publishing, 2022), 11–12.

THE ANNUNCIATION **169**

Then I recognized that the word "vulnerable" does not mean "having been wounded" but rather "being able to be wounded." I began to see how it means being exposed, open, or responsive to the other; in this sense vulnerability is the human condition that allows me to hear, encounter, receive, or recognize the other even to the point of being injured.[19]

The human Christ, in the form of a slave, remains open to a complete interrelation with humanity and its sinfulness that not only involves his incarnation and ministry but, at the end of the first section of the hymn, results in the ultimate woundedness of his crucified body. Paul emphasizes how this vulnerability is consented to through reflexive actions: "he emptied himself . . . he humbled himself" (Phil 2:7–8).[20] Yet, even when emptied and humbled, Christ never loses his divine or "angelic" identity, for some form of irreducible divine "essence" is maintained from the state of lowly human vulnerability to Christ's exaltation.[21] And, indeed, Christ-who-was-slave is highly exalted, receiving equality with God following his obedience.[22] His return to glory illustrates God's power and preference for exalting the lowly, that obedience and openness bring a reversal of fortunes or, in other words, a shift from the margins of power to the center.[23] For the self-emptying slave in Philippians, neither the will nor identity is stripped from the person, but he instead experiences flourishing on account of his vulnerability.

This understanding of the male slave's *kenosis* begins to empty the term "female slave" of its patriarchal meaning, namely, that a handmaid *must* deny her will and identity. Still, Christ's unique identity as man

---

[19] James F. Keenan, SJ, *The Moral Life: Eight Lectures* (Georgetown University Press, 2023), 24.

[20] Holloway, *Philippians*, 120. James Keenan affirms the need for agency, or self-reflexivity in this case, alongside vulnerability to decide the manner of response; Keenan, *The Moral Life*, 33.

[21] Holloway, *Philippians*, 126. For a brief introduction on the historical debates surrounding *how* the divine self-emptied and what it emptied itself *of*, see Paul T. Nimmo and Keith L. Johnson, "Introduction: The Canvas of Kenosis," in *Kenosis: The Self-Emptying of Christ in Scripture and Theology*, ed. Paul T. Nimmo and Keith L. Johnson (Eerdmans Publishing, 2022), 1–5.

[22] Martin, *Carmen Christi*, 244.

[23] Martin, *Carmen Christi*, 247.

170   ALAINA KELLER

and God demands further investigation into relating *kenosis* to female vulnerability and flourishing: how can a being who is not God and not male empty herself without losing her identity and will? Sarah Coakley and Ruth Groenhout each answer this question as they envelop *kenosis* within a feminist framework. In "*Kenōsis* and Subversion," Coakley challenges Daphne Hampson's critique of female *kenosis* by suggesting a positive view of female *kenosis* as "power-in-vulnerability."[24] Coakley subverts notions of the "masculinist" power and "feminine" vulnerability by focusing on a "feminist reconceptualizing" of self-emptying in light of Christ's own kenotic vulnerability.[25] She favors the interpretation of *kenosis* as Christ's choice never to "snatch" or "grasp" at "certain (false and worldly) forms of power—forms sometimes wrongly construed as divine," and she suggests that this lack of grasping encourages openness and responsiveness.[26] For Keenan, this openness is directed to the other; for Coakley, one responds to the divine. To extend Christ's *kenosis* in one's own life, consistent with Christian feminism, is to engage in a regular *askēsis*, an "act of silent waiting on the divine in prayer" that empowers the individual who "make[s] space for God to be God."[27] Though this practice is risky, the action of yielding to divine power rather than worldly power brings one closer to the cross and resurrection that upends traditional female submission. Women still are vulnerable, still humble, but the object to which they direct their attention is "the subtle but enabling presence of a God who neither shouts nor forces, let alone 'obliterates.' "[28] For Coakley, self-emptying before this God is not annihilation of the will and identity but "the place of the self's transformation and expansion into God," a form of deeply antimasculinist empowerment.[29]

Groenhout follows Coakley's example in arguing for the possibility for female *kenosis*, with an emphasis on determining when *kenosis* is appropriate for women. To deny women's ability to undergo *kenosis*, or engage in self-sacrifice, is to deny women's moral agency and to restrict

---

[24] Sarah Coakley, *Powers and Submissions: Spirituality, Philosophy, and Gender* (Blackwell Publishers, 2002), 5. For Hampson's statements against female *kenosis*, see Daphne Hampson, *Theology and Feminism* (Basil Blackwell, 1990), 155.

[25] Coakley, *Powers and Submissions*, 22, 33–34.

[26] Coakley, *Powers and Submissions*, 11, 34.

[27] Coakley, *Powers and Submissions*, 34.

[28] Coakley, *Powers and Submissions*, 35–36.

[29] Coakley, *Powers and Submissions*, 36.

THE ANNUNCIATION *171*

women's experience of sacrifice to victimization.[30] In a balance between pure emptiness (nihilism) and less emptiness (risk), Groenhout identifies "proper" self-sacrifice as the emptying of a valued self for a good aim. A self that is not self-loved is not a sacrifice, and sacrifice that perpetuates unhealthy behavior devalues the act itself.[31] To answer the question—"how can a being who is not God and not male empty herself without losing her identity and will?"—Coakley and Groenhout concur that a true "emptying" consists in opening oneself, being vulnerable, to God, the best of all aims, in whose divine power women participate as free moral agents and are thereby "exalted," not subordinated.

This understanding of *kenosis*, then, remains consistent with female flourishing, which also underscores personal dignity in oneself and active moral agency. In addition, if one identifies the woman who self-empties, who is vulnerable, in such a way as a [female] slave like Christ, then the term "handmaid" can also embrace the possibility for [female] flourishing. One final question remains: Does Mary, the idealized image of handmaid, undergo this true *kenosis*?[32] Returning now to Luke's Gospel, guarded against patriarchal imagery, we find a Mary who has lost neither her will nor her identity as a "handmaid." Just as Ruether notes that, in the feminist worldview, "women name themselves as subjects of authentic and full humanity,"[33] so does Mary claim the identity of handmaid for herself.[34] Not only does she make this decision about her body and sexuality without regard for Joseph, her betrothed, but she deliberates before God, who waits for her response.[35] Her response, as question and consent, indicates independent thought and action, what Johnson calls a profound "self-determining act of personal autonomy" that carries with it the definition of her person-

---

[30] Ruth Groenhout, "Kenosis and Feminist Theory," in *Exploring Kenotic Christology: The Self-Emptying of God*, ed. C. Stephen Evans (Oxford University Press, 2006), 295.

[31] Groenhout, "Kenosis and Feminist Theory," 303, 307.

[32] Several sources do reference a Marian *kenosis*: John Paul II, *Redemptoris Mater* (2022), no. 18; Amy Peeler, *Women and the Gender of God* (Eerdmans Publishing, 2022), 79; Christopher O'Donnell, O.Carm., *Life in the Spirit and Mary* (Michael Glazier, 1981), 45.

[33] Ruether, *Sexism and God-Talk*, 19.

[34] Peeler, *Women and the Gender*, 77–81.

[35] Peeler, *Women and the Gender*, 66. On Mary's decision regarding body and sexuality, see Reuther, *Sexism*, 153; Barbara E. Reid, *Wisdom's Feast: An Invitation to Feminist Interpretation of the Scriptures* (Eerdmans Publishing, 2016), 57.

172   ALAINA KELLER

hood. More so than many other women faced with the possibility of childbearing, Mary acts as a completely free, responsible moral agent to determine her life's trajectory and accepts the inevitable sacrifices therein. Her "yes" to the angel's message, her choice to be vulnerable to the divine, is a true assent. Beyond true, Mary's "yes" becomes God's own, cosmic "yes" as God favors the humiliated, among whom Mary positions herself as the lowly mother of their savior. She says "yes" to their exaltation in the Magnificat and "no" to the sin of the mighty. As the fecund site of this revolution, she becomes an active participant in God's justice and divine outrage.[36] In emptying herself and being open to God, Mary's will is not only maintained but glorified.

Throughout Luke's narrative, Mary also preserves, even expands, her identity while being a self-emptying handmaid. Although the gospel writer notes that "the power of the Most High will overshadow you" (Lk 1:35), this "overshadowing" does not present Mary solely as the "void" or "vessel" that Offred sees as "empty again, again."[37] She may be the definitive human vessel of the Holy Spirit—the *Shekinah*, the site of Yahweh's glory—but her identity encapsulates more than her open womb.[38] She is blessed because of her hearing and doing, and in hearing and doing, she undergoes Coakley's idea of *kenosis*: She "waits upon the divine in prayer" and has "made space for God to be God."[39] Yet, unlike other women whose self-emptying "place[s] the self's transformation and expansion into God," Mary's identity is reified as hearer of the Word when God, as Word, transforms and expands into her.[40] Not only God, but other women as well, for where "God dug and opened space for himself,"[41] so can women find themselves in Mary. Here, her vulnerability and blessedness gain another definition: inclusiveness.[42] Her identity as multifaceted femaleness remains open to all beings in

---

[36] Gebara and Bingemer, *Mary*, 167–69; Johnson, *Truly Our Sister*, 271–72.

[37] Atwood, *The Handmaid's Tale*, 74.

[38] Gebara and Bingemer, *Mary*, 107.

[39] Coakley, *Powers and Submissions*, 34. Another description for "making space" for God in Mary's *fiat* is "letting be," as in Enda McDonagh, *Vulnerable to the Holy* (Columba Press, 2004), 12.

[40] Coakley, *Powers and Submissions*, 34.

[41] Gebara and Bingemer, *Mary*, 107.

[42] Tina Beattie, "The Magnificat of the Redeemed Woman," *New Blackfriars* 80, no. 944 (Oct. 1999): 448.

THE ANNUNCIATION 173

their uniqueness and desire for mutuality as a site where the female and divine have already attained mutuality.[43] Mary here cannot be further from the annihilated mother that directs attention elsewhere; rather, she directs attention to herself *as* the "handmaid of the Lord"—"Behold" (Lk 1:38)—in whom women find different ways of being virgin, mother, daughter, spouse, hearer, disciple, or prophet.

Finally, as Mary maintains her will and identity in the downward, self-emptying process, her *kenosis* as handmaid is true insofar as it follows the upward movement of Christ's exaltation. At the beginning of the Magnificat, Mary places herself at the nadir of her self-emptying process, where God has "looked upon his handmaid's lowliness" (Lk 1:48). Immediately following this line, however, Mary calls attention to the reversal of her fortunes: "Behold, from now on will all ages call me blessed" (Lk 1:48). She is not a handmaid in Offred's Gilead. In God's Kingdom, which celebrates the weak, Mary empties herself and, like Christ, is elevated in her vulnerability as one for whom the Mighty one has done "great things" (Lk 1:49). She is indeed blessed, but more than simply "looked upon" as a handmaid, Mary's exaltation reaches completion in her participation in bringing about God's Kingdom.[44] Much like Christ, who descended to humiliation to "envelop" the entirety of humanity within God's love,[45] Mary not only sings about but embraces the lowly of Israel, whose savior she bears and with whom she identifies.[46] She thereby becomes a prophet for them, announcing God's reversal of the unjust moral, social, and economic order that has *already been accomplished* on account of her faith-filled *fiat*.[47] As the handmaid who made liberation possible, including her own, Mary leads the lowly to exaltation in her song of victory as she herself is exalted.[48] Once in a state of humiliation, they are ultimately "lifted up," "filled with good things," and "helped" by their God (Lk 1:52–54).

Compare this image of the uplifted handmaid to the Handmaids in the Republic of Gilead or in the androcentric imagination. The term is

---

[43] Gebara and Bingemer, *Mary,* 107; Ruether, *Sexism and God-Talk,* 20; Johnson, *She Who Is,* 32.

[44] Gebara and Bingemer, *Mary,* 71–73.

[45] Barclay, "Kenosis," 13.

[46] Johnson, *Truly Our Sister,* 270.

[47] Schaberg, *The Illegitimacy of Jesus,* 89.

[48] Ruether, *Sexism and God-Talk,* 155.

174 ALAINA KELLER

still challenged by several questions,[49] but a comparison between the "*doulē*" in Luke and the "*doulos*" in Philippians reveals that "handmaid" *can* positively describe the individual who opens oneself to God and participates freely in his divine power. While this chapter does not fully resolve the problematic nature of the term "handmaid," for to do so would be to erase the history of female suppression, it invites serious consideration for the title that a young, vulnerable woman chose for herself before the power of God, a choice upon which humanity's redemption rested. As opposed to the Handmaids ensconced in red, Mary the handmaid declares her flourishing, "Behold!" and invites other women, other persons, to do the same.

---

[49] For example, the question of race: How does the term's racial component affect its usefulness?

Weakness as the Conduit for the Mechanics of Grace

Paul's Paradoxical Spirituality of 2 Corinthians 12:5–10

Brett McLaughlin

"Therefore, I am content with weaknesses, insults, hardships, persecutions, and constraints, for the sake of Christ; for when I am weak, then I am strong."[1] Paul the Apostle's journeys and personal struggles are well known by the Christian audience. He encounters rival proselytizers competing for converts,[2] and must carefully articulate the spirituality and ethics of a novel religion. Central to Paul's espoused theology is each Christian's identity in the crucified and resurrected Christ. God's power is manifested paradoxically in the suffering of Christ and death is impossibly overthrown. Central to this proclamation is the presence of human weakness and afflictions in the lives of Christians.[3] In the Second Letter to the Corinthians, Paul boldly declares how God's grace and power arrived in his own person at the acceptance of a thorn in the flesh.[4] This chapter argues that Paul is announcing the burden of weakness as essential to the transmission of the gospel, thus bearing a public imitation of the crucified Christ. Paul initiates an exchange of

---

[1] 2 Cor 12:10. All biblical quotations taken from the New American Bible (NAB).

[2] See 2 Cor 11:4–5 or Gal 1:6–9.

[3] I will retain the term "Christian" to describe a Gentile convert to Christ, acknowledging that Paul himself never called believers in Jesus, "Christians."

[4] 2 Cor 12:7.

176   *BRETT McLAUGHLIN*

boasting among the Corinthians[5] but evades discussion of his heavenly vision and focuses upon weakness instead. Weakness is the very manner of his ministry and format by which he delivers the Christian message. Even though he boasts of weakness, the evangelist is timid of speaking how God's power is arriving in him. Inherently Paul delivers a paradoxical revelation on the workings of divine power and grace.

The Second Letter to the Corinthians arrives within Paul's corpus of epistles circa 55 CE, but its Pauline characteristics generally rule out challenges to its authorship. The letter strikes the reader as fragmented and odd: chapters one through nine praise the Corinthians's uprightness, while chapters ten through thirteen reverse and caution them to pledge themselves to Paul and his gospel. Paul himself had introduced Christianity to Corinth, so he would have taken particular attention and responsibility for its progress amidst contending evangelizers.[6] The letter carries two primary themes, the glory of God and the reputation of Paul himself. Repeatedly Paul contrasts human wisdom and God's grace "as Paul ranges from appeal to cajoling, warning, anguish, anger, love and longing in his efforts to get across."[7] Ralph P. Martin posits that the Corinthians would have expected a boast from one of their evangelizers, but Paul repeatedly boasts of God.[8] Between his two major epistles to the Corinthian community, external agents Paul deems false apostles have undermined his authority.[9] Paul responds by legitimating his apostolic authority in weakness. It is indeed a thorough autobiographical meditation, though peculiar as Paul propounds his own vulnerability and frailty.[10] It is especially surprising since, as R. V. G. Tasker summarizes, "the general impression of Paul that the reader obtains from

---

[5] Beginning in 2 Corinthians 10:8, Paul deploys the concept of boasting from self-presentation unto the glory of God, personal foolishness as in 11:17, or weakness as in 11:30. Boasting is present from the start of the Corinthian correspondence in 1 Corinthians 1:31.

[6] Victor Paul Furnish, *II Corinthians: Translated with Introduction, Notes, and Commentary* (Doubleday, 1984), 22, 29, 30–32.

[7] Frances Young and David F. Ford, *Meaning and Truth in 2 Corinthians* (Eerdmans Publishing, 1987), 12, 15.

[8] Ralph P. Martin, *Second Corinthians*, Word Biblical Commentary (Zondervan, 2014), 602.

[9] Alexandra Brown cites 2 Corinthians 10:2, 12; 11:4, 12–13, 15. Alexandra R. Brown, "The Gospel Takes Place: Paul's Theology of Power in Weakness in 2 Corinthians," *Interpretation* 52, no. 3 (1998): 271–72.

[10] Richard Bauckham, "Weakness—Paul's and Ours," *Themelios* 7, no. 3 (1982): 4.

WEAKNESS AS THE CONDUIT FOR THE MECHANICS OF GRACE **177**

his Epistles, not least from 2 Corinthians, and from Acts is of a man with an exceptionally strong constitution and remarkable powers of human endurance."[11] Calvin J. Roetzel goes so far as to suppose Paul adopts the mantle of the fool, mocking the pretentions of his critics and adversaries. He writes, "Thus Paul parodied the pretentious and grand claims of his critics and boldly stated and simultaneously used his body as a weapon. He presented it as shamed, bloodied, imprisoned, shipwrecked, beaten, hungry, sleepless, and scarred as imitation [of?] Christ (12:10)." Paul disrupts the typical forms of "rhetorical brutality."[12]

Although Paul has recounted how fourteen years ago someone ascended to the heavens in verses 1–4 of chapter twelve, he shifts the conversation and debunks the notion that mystical experiences verify apostleship.[13] Paul employs irony in verse 5, that one might boast of such a vision, but weakness is more appropriate and his own criteria for apostleship. It is not a blunt attack on his opponents, but a roundabout manner of critique.[14] Mark A. Seifrid proposes that Paul wants his listeners only to associate what they see and hear from him, not mystical experiences.[15] In verse 6a, he even implies, if he were to narrate such a mystical experience, "I would not be foolish, for I would be telling the truth" as if his opponents falsified their stories.[16] Raving of mystical visions and ecstatic prayer are ruled out as qualifications for leadership.

Jan Lambrecht, SJ, supposes that Paul shifts attention away from boasting in merit or the flesh, in favor of boasting in the Lord. He is not rejecting boasting all together, since Paul himself spoke with pride of the growth of the church in Corinth.[17] But he draws a line between boasting according to the flesh and boasting in the Lord.[18] Elsewhere in Paul's Letter to the Romans (3:28), he underscores how all are justi-

---

[11] R. V. G. Tasker, *The Second Epistle of Paul to the Corinthians* (Eerdmans Publishing, 1958), 175.

[12] Calvin J. Roetzel, "The Language of War (2 Cor. 10:1-6) and the Language of Weakness (2 Cor. 11:21b–13:10)," *Biblical Interpretation* 17 (2009): 95.

[13] Furnish, *II Corinthians*, 546.

[14] Martin, *Second Corinthians*, 583, 586.

[15] Mark A. Seifrid, *The Second Letter to the Corinthians* (Eerdmans Publishing, 2014), 444.

[16] R. P. Hanson, *II Corinthians* (SMC Press, 1954), 86.

[17] Jan Lambrecht, *Second Corinthians* (Liturgical Press, 1999), 206.

[18] Lambrecht cites 2 Corinthians 11:17–18 and 10:17 as examples. See Lambrecht, *Second Corinthians*, 206.

178   BRETT McLAUGHLIN

fied by faith; hence, no boasting is appropriate. Lambrecht analyzes, "It would seem that Paul considers *all* boasting in a certain sense foolish and also dangerous. The fact that in [2 Corinthians] 12:9 Paul will boast most gladly of his weaknesses probably does not mean that he sees this boasting as normal and free of danger."[19] He does not engage in boasting as a first reaction or defined stance toward hardship; boasting occurs for Paul in contexts of hardship only following reflection.[20]

In the wider Jewish and Hellenistic context, accounts of one's personal sufferings may establish the true prophet and philosopher. Corinthians stereotypically expected status among leaders.[21] P. J. Gräbe notes that Greek *peristalsis* catalogues of hardship and weakness separated authentic philosophers from false ones; Paul's litany of weakness establishes his authenticity. Moreover, Paul likely has in mind the struggles of the Jewish prophets.[22] Lambrecht cites Scott B. Andrews that overcoming "catalogues of hardships" are publicized to ennoble oneself.[23] But Paul suggests his *continuing* struggles; he subverts the archetype that leaders are those who vanquish challenges.[24] He sets forth a pattern of leadership where affliction is borne.

Paul clearly designates an angel of Satan as an agent of God's purpose to inflict the thorn in verse 7. Satan has been portrayed as accomplishing God's tasks in the scriptures.[25] One should not shift the meaning to presume that Satan was behind the affliction. Martin reasons that if Paul sought to blame Satan he would not have chosen ἐδόθη ("was given") to convey that. He cites Galatians 3:21, Ephesians 3:8 and 5:19, and 1 Timothy 4:14 that "was given" usually meant God's favor.[26] Lambrecht sees the tense as a divine passive, and the aorist indicates the thorn arrives at a specific time. It symbolically reverses the effect

---

[19] Lambrecht, *Second Corinthians*, 207.

[20] Jan Lambrecht, "Strength in Weakness: A Reply to Scott B. Andrews's Exegesis of 2 Cor 11:23b–33," *New Testament Studies* 43 (1997): 289.

[21] Craig S. Keener, *1–2 Corinthians* (Cambridge University Press, 2005), 239.

[22] P. J. Gräbe, "The All-Surpassing Power of God Through the Holy Spirit in the Midst of Our Broken Earthly Existence: Perspectives on Paul's Use of Δυναμις in 2 Corinthians," *Neotestamentica* 28, no. 1 (1994): 153.

[23] See Scott B. Andrews, "Too Weak Not to Lead: The Form and Function of 2 Cor 11.23b–33," *New Testament Studies* 41, no. 2 (April 1995): 263–76.

[24] Lambrecht, "Strength in Weakness," 285–86.

[25] Furnish cites Job 2:6–7; Noach 1948:6. See Furnish, *II Corinthians*, 547.

[26] Martin, *Second Corinthians*, 606.

WEAKNESS AS THE CONDUIT FOR THE MECHANICS OF GRACE   **179**

of the heavenly transport in verse 2; this person is obviously not in a heavenly realm but quite tormented.[27] The phrase is not in the form of judgment and punishment, but (κολαφίζῃ) "to strike with the fist or buffet" Paul.[28] Satan is inflicting less than deadly abuse upon Paul, but it is clearly following God's design or initiative.

So that Paul would not remain too "elated" or become arrogant, a clearly pernicious malady was given to him. Martin identifies that the only other site for (ὑπεραίρωμαι) "become conceited" or be elated is in 2 Thessalonians 2:4, when someone puffs up himself against God.[29] The thorn forestalls any inclination Paul might have to egotism or autonomy from God.[30] Rudolf Bultmann sees it as unmistakably chronic, "an expression of the antigodly cosmos which also threatens and entices the believer."[31] The thorn should not be assumed as the common persecution of Christians; "thorn in the flesh" is an intensely personal description. In salvation history, it might be compared to Philo's rendering of an angel wrestling with Jacob in Genesis 32:25.[32] Paul's thorn in the flesh was likely well known to the Corinthians; it would not sound ambiguous to their ears.[33] Against the interpretation of an incapacitating illness, Furnish argues that Paul never could have performed so much travel, ministry, and organization if it were a withering condition.[34] In the most recent issue of *Biblical Archaeology Review*, Ben Witherington III looks to Galatians 6:11, that Paul necessitated large letters and a scribe such as in Romans 16:22. Following this, Witherington believes some sort of eye affliction regularly impeded Paul.[35] Though countless scholars have opined and search Paul's texts for a lucid indication of this plight, several contemporary scholars acknowledge we simply have no access to the precise malaise Paul was experiencing.

In verse 8, Paul thrice petitions God to remove the thorn, perhaps

---

[27] Seifrid, *The Second Letter to the Corinthians*, 446–47.

[28] Furnish, *II Corinthians*, 547.

[29] Although 2 Thessalonians is contested if authorship by Paul.

[30] Martin, *Second Corinthians*, 606.

[31] Rudolf Bultmann, *The Second Letter to the Corinthians*, trans. Roy A. Harrisville (Augsburg Publishing House, 1985), 224.

[32] Furnish, *II Corinthians*, 550.

[33] Martin, *Second Corinthians*, 584.

[34] Furnish, *II Corinthians*, 550.

[35] Ben Witherington III, "Finding Paul's Weakness," *Biblical Archaeology Review* (Summer 2024): 62–63.

180   BRETT McLAUGHLIN

resembling threefold prayers elsewhere in the tradition. Bultmann helpfully observes that Paul shuns any Stoic response to his plight; Epictetus acts quite differently to hardships.[36] Commentators over the centuries have supposed Paul follows Jewish and Greek models here, but Keener suggests Paul may have just decided to pray three times. Some think it could resemble Jesus's prayer at Gethsemane in Mark 14:32–41, in which the Father also declined to remove the looming suffering.[37] Yet Lambrecht rebuffs this notion as Paul would have unlikely written τρὶς ("three times") to refer to the Gethsemane scene. Significantly, this is the only instance in Paul's letter where he states that he prayed to *Jesus*; this is the sole moment in the entire Christian scriptures where παρεκάλεσα "to beg" is in the action of prayer.[38] Verse 8 obviously indicates Paul has fervently asked for divine relief from the thorn that has been sent.

Paul acknowledges an explicit response, "My grace is sufficient for you, for power is made perfect in weakness,"[39] that he seems content with. Jerome Murphy-O'Connor, OP, describes, "The response he received is couched in the form of a divine oracle (12:9). This does not mean that Paul was conscious of a heavenly voice speaking within his mind. The form simply emphasizes the importance to which he attaches the insight."[40] There is no pledge of relief from the Lord, but Paul receives an epiphany that God's grace operates through weakness. Christ himself is the exemplar of this, empowered as he was crucified.[41] Paul then receives such power, because he accepts the response and continues in his work with the thorn. Martin looks to the verb tenses in verse 8: the aorist for "begged" and the perfect tense for his reception of the answer. Given that the Greek perfect tense implies the continuing effects of a past action, even though Paul stops praying for relief, he grips the answer from the Lord with "vitality and vibrancy in the present."[42]

In verses 9 and 10, Paul declares he is "content" with weaknesses in

---

[36] Bultmann cites Epict Diss I, 1, 7–13; IV, 10, 14–16.

[37] Keener, *1–2 Corinthians*, 240, 241.

[38] Lambrecht, *Second Corinthians*, 202, 203.

[39] 2 Cor 12:9.

[40] Jerome Murphy-O'Connor, *The Theology of the Second Letter to the Corinthians* (Cambridge University Press, 1991), 119.

[41] Furnish cites 2 Corinthians 13:4; 1 Cor 1:17–18, 22–24. See Furnish, *II*, 550.

[42] Martin, *Second Corinthians*, 585, 613.

WEAKNESS AS THE CONDUIT FOR THE MECHANICS OF GRACE   *181*

clear alignment with the ministry and sufferings of Christ.[43] εὐδοκῶ ("well content") is a potent word in Greek, as it is end and summary of Epicurean thought, according to Philodemus of Gadara.[44] Elsewhere in Romans 8:38–39 Paul has expressed that nothing can separate a Christian from the love of Christ.[45] Bauckham depicts, "If he experienced the dying of Jesus in his frailty and sufferings (1:5; 4:10–12), he also found in every escape from death, every encouragement after anxiety and depression, every convert made in the midst of persecution, a participation in the resurrection of Christ."[46] Resurrection joys allow him to persevere through the hardship. It is Paul's very participation in the experiences and the person of Christ that is the relief itself.[47]

Paul's prayer reveals that weakness is the very mode in which his ministry is conducted. Murphy-O'Connor explains, "he sees 'weakness' as the concrete modality in which his ministry is lived out. In reality, to boast of his weaknesses is to express pride in the ministry entrusted to him, and it is his commitment to this ministry which gives him a claim to the power of Christ."[48] Paul takes the experience and the symbolism of the cross onto his own self, and proposes to his audiences that the image of Christ and his gospel should be borne through weakness.[49] This is a sociological, not a psychological weakness: Paul does not have to pretend to humble himself before God, but he must accept that he is losing capabilities for the accomplishment of his mission and prestige.[50] Importantly, this is not simply enduring adversaries and false apostles, but the manifestation of the power of God in his persisting afflictions.[51]

Significantly, Paul's argument does not overcome those Corinthi-

---

[43] "When suffering and weakness are accepted by us with our eyes turned toward God, we become more and more like him who 'in the days of his earthly life offered up prayers and petitions, with loud cries and tears, to God who was able to deliver him from the grave; and he submitted so humbly that his prayer was heard." Barnabas Ahern, "Joy in Weakness," *The Way* 11, no. 2 (1971): 127.

[44] Seifrid, *The Second Letter to the Corinthians*, 453.

[45] Martin, *Second Corinthians*, 614.

[46] Bauckham, "Weakness—Paul's and Ours," 5.

[47] Seifrid, *The Second Letter to the Corinthians*, 449.

[48] Murphy-O'Connor, *The Theology of the Second Letter to the Corinthians*, 121.

[49] Brown, "The Gospel Takes Place," 282.

[50] In other words, this weakness only lies in Paul's status and relations in the human community. It does not affect his sense of self, nor personhood before God. See Murphy-O'Connor, *The Theology of the Second Letter to the Corinthians*, 120.

[51] Furnish, *II Corinthians*, 550.

182 BRETT McLAUGHLIN

ans who still expect accomplishment or ranking among leaders, and moreover, Paul does not iterate the capacity of this power within him. Lambrecht analyzes that Paul here does not feel comfortable elaborating how Christ and God's power is galvanizing his mission.[52] In addition, whereas contemporary audiences might recognize Paul's emphases here as typical theology from Paul, his contemporaries may dismiss human weakness as a feature of divine power. Any challenger or opponent to Paul could still scorn weakness language as evasive;[53] wouldn't someone in God's favor be obviously empowered by him? Paul must strive to force through a novel paradigm.

The argument does not somehow transform weakness into strength, or equate all grace with power. The thorn or stake still remains evil; Paul never transforms the thorn in the flesh into something good.[54] Lambrecht asserts that Paul's paradox leads to reflection but does not name a hardship as salutary.[55] Paul still has to rely on the strength of an inner self.[56] One must also avoid conflating grace and power as equivalent. Paul arrives at a place of contentment, but power is never something that he owns or holds. Power is a continual gift to him that could cease. Even with his profound level of Christic imitation, he remains entirely dependent.[57]

Alongside his own explication of his style of leadership, Paul here redefines God's power for the Corinthians. Joshua Heavin names it as "power *made perfect* in weakness." 2 Corinthians 13:3–4 continues Paul's articulation of divine power: "For indeed he was crucified out of weakness, but he lives by the power of God. So also we are weak in him, but toward you we shall live with him by the power of God."[58] Citing Isaiah 57:15 and Psalms 113:4–9, Seifrid posits that Paul inverts the concept of royal temporal power, because the Most High God settles among the lowly, not palaces.[59] Paul uses the language of Israel in the wilderness, for the power of Christ to live in the midst of the encamp-

---

[52] Lambrecht, "Strength in Weakness," 290.

[53] Martin, *Second Corinthians*, 602.

[54] Martin, *Second Corinthians*, 611.

[55] Lambrecht, *Second Corinthians*, 208.

[56] Lambrecht, *Strength in Weakness*, 290.

[57] Seifrid, *The Second Letter to the Corinthians*, 49.

[58] Joshua Heavin, "Power Made Perfect in Weakness: *Theologia Crucis* in 2 Corinthians 13:3–4," *Journal of Theological Interpretation* 13, no. 2 (2019): 252, 255.

[59] Seifrid, *The Second Letter to the Corinthians*, 450.

WEAKNESS AS THE CONDUIT FOR THE MECHANICS OF GRACE 183

ment.[60] What's more, unlike earthly power, God's power does not seek increase but remains present in those situations of human weakness. Those Christians experiencing weakness sit, as Alexandra Brown puts it, in the time between the times where the crucified lie before the resurrection.[61] The paradox will only dissolve at the eschaton.[62]

Paul reshapes the conventional impressions of power and grace throughout the Second Corinthian correspondence. Despite the fact that Paul has just referred to a mystical transport through the heavens, he utilizes irony in boasting of frailty against his ostentatious rivals. This is not an unreflective retort by Paul. He wants his audiences to focus upon his preaching and actions, not reports of ecstatic states or charismatic powers. True boasting should only be according to the Lord, not the flesh and merits. Compared to other Hellenistic lists of hardship in leadership, Paul is idiosyncratic in pointing out that he carries continuing affliction that he will be unable to overcome.

The thorn in the flesh that Paul receives is most definitely injurious, quite the opposite of the heavenly vision he just recounted. Though he comes to a peace with the malady, he is certainly not espousing stoicism. In point of fact, this is the only situation in all of Paul's letters where he *begs* for relief and explicitly prays to Jesus. The divine answer matches the concentration of the prayer: Paul receives a response of tremendous importance, that he keeps present in his mind. In the Greek, he is "well content," a noteworthy posture for Hellenists.

Paul champions weakness as the method by which his ministry is undertaken, with a firm association to the experience of Christ crucified. As Michael J. Gorman stresses, God is cruciform or crosslike; Paul's discourse of power in weakness is revelatory of God. "We discover that the same Jesus who went to the cross in faith and love (Gal. 2:15–21) continues by the Spirit to create a community of crosslike faith and love."[63] Cruciformity is not mere tenacity through physical suffering, but self-gift for the wholeness of others.[64] This is not a call for humility

---

[60] Seifrid, *The Second Letter to the Corinthians*, 451.

[61] Brown, "The Gospel Takes Place: Paul's Theology of Power in Weakness in 2 Corinthians," 281.

[62] Lambrecht, *Second Corinthians*, 208.

[63] Gal 2:15-21. Michael J. Gorman, *Apostle of the Crucified Lord: A Theological Introduction to Paul and His Letters* (Eerdmans Publishing, 2004), 118–19.

[64] Gorman, *Apostle of the Crucified Lord*, 140.

or a different stance before God; it is a weakness before society and the community. The thorn or stake remains permanently evil and present. Although Paul boasts and highlights his weakness, he does not boast or illustrate the divine power coursing through him. He never constructs an airtight argument, as his opponents can always cast him aside as being inconstant. Though divine power streams through his work and ministry, it is never something Paul holds, but a gift that continues.

Relearning Vulnerability

Sifting Through Jean Vanier's Legacy of Care and Abuse

Elise Abshire

Catholic theologian Jean Vanier, born in 1928 in Geneva, Switzerland, is the founder of the original L'Arche community in Trosly-Breuil, France. L'Arche communities are spaces for persons with disabilities to live together. True to the vision of its founder, L'Arche communities are expressions of Vanier's own spirituality. Shortly after Vanier's death in May 2019, L'Arche concluded that, in the context of spiritual direction, Vanier abused at least six nondisabled women living in the communities. Vanier's spiritual mentor, Fr. Thomas Philippe, had a substantial influence on Vanier's spirituality, especially through Philippe's emphasis on a "deformed eschatology."[1] Philippe's distorted eschatology led him to emphasize vulnerability within spiritual direction, especially through the relation of a "spiritual father" and the directee. Theologian Brian Brock argues that Vanier inherited a "deformed eschatology as the fatal theological doctrine" from Philippe, also a sexual abuser who was censured by Vatican authorities.[2] Philippe formed Vanier in a spirituality that justified his sexual relations with directees. Yet, Vanier received both his distorted spirituality *and* ways to care for people with disabilities from Philippe. The harmful aspects of Vanier's spirituality then overshadowed the beautiful aspects.

---

[1] Brian Brock, "The Troubled Inheritance of Jean Vanier: Locating the Fatal Theological Mistakes," *Studies in Christian Ethics* 36, no. 3 (2023): 433.

[2] Brock, "Fatal Theological Mistakes," 433.

186 ELISE ABSHIRE

Theologians such as Brock and Natalie Wigg-Stevenson have raised questions about Vanier's pivotal role in founding L'Arche and his influence on the development of disability theology due to the revelations of abuse. It is difficult to find a disability theology book published before 2020 without encountering a discussion of Vanier's ideas or at least a mention of his name. Given Vanier's unparalleled influence on disability studies, these revelations have challenged disability theologians regarding the future directions of the field.

I had no encounter with Vanier's work until the year of his death, 2019. Most of the disability theology books I read contained many aspects of Vanier's insights given his practical work with people with disabilities and his theological reflection on that work. Thus, disability theology has been *dependent* upon Vanier's theology. His writings were even of interest to those outside academia. For example, Vanier's famous 1998 book, *Becoming Human,* won the Writers' Trust of Canada's Gordon Montador Award. Vanier himself was nominated multiple times for the Nobel Peace Prize. When the revelations emerged, I found myself trying to reconcile the beautiful aspects of Vanier's spirituality with the harmful aspects. Even if I decided not to read his books anymore, I could not get away from Vanier. He was in practically every disability and theology book, praised and heralded as a key figure in this field. Entering an academic discipline where the legacy of a key theological figure has dissolved leaves me uncertain how to navigate within the field.

In his theological works, Vanier promises spiritual flourishing if one practices vulnerability. What Vanier describes in his writings on vulnerability rings true; that is why his spiritual guidance was so compelling for both those who care for people with disabilities and for others outside of L'Arche communities. Yet, these ideas can and did become his gateways to abuse spiritual directees. In this chapter, I examine Vanier's distortion of vulnerability with the assistance of several sources, including Kelly Colwell's personal reflections from living in a L'Arche community, L'Arche's Investigation Commission Report, Brock's and Wigg-Stevenson's ideas, and the NFA (not for all) letters. Vanier destroyed many of the records of his personal correspondences. However, within those that remained, the L'Arche Investigation Commission found a set of papers disturbingly labeled NFA papers. The NFA collection included several hundred letters that were "intimate" correspondences between Vanier and Philippe as well as Vanier and female directees.[3]

While Vanier's abusive actions are egregious, his case is sadly not an isolated one. Abusive spiritual leaders are not uncommon. My own personal experience makes me especially attentive to abusive spiritual leaders. I include my own personal experience of my time in a religious community to show that Vanier's case is not infrequent. I am one voice that I hope resounds for many persons hurting from abusive spiritual leaders. Abuse does not happen in a vacuum; Vanier hurt many more people than just the women he sexually abused. People in spiritual communities and even those on the peripheries (e.g., family members and friends) experience emotional and spiritual disorientation upon realizing the person who is the spiritual locus of a community is an abuser. The founder of a religious community is the spiritual nucleus, holding the authority along with the power to deceive and hurt persons inside and outside of the community.

Unquestioning Trust
in a Charismatic Spiritual Leader

Those discerning religious life or considering living in L'Arche communities typically enter with a spiritual hunger, idealistic views, and a desire to make a deep and lifelong commitment. One allows oneself to become vulnerable by submitting in trust to the members of the community and spiritual tenets lived out there. Thus, when abuse, distortion, and betrayal are revealed, members of the community find themselves with questions, especially with questions of their own inner sense of navigation and trust.

From 2014 to 2018, I was discerning religious life with an order founded by an Argentinian priest, Carlos Buela. I was attracted to the community because of their missionary zeal, outward-appearing apostolic joy, and youthfulness. Since Buela founded the community, I also had great admiration for him. This admiration for the founder

---

[3] Bernard Granger, Nicole Jeammet, Florian Michel, Antoine Mourges, Gwennola Rimbaut, and Claire Vincent-Mory, *Control and Abuse: Investigation on Thomas Philippe, Jean Vanier and L'Arche (1950-2019)* (Frémur Publications, 2023), 26 [hereafter L'Arche Commission, *Control and Abuse*].

188   ELISE ABSHIRE

is not unlike those who entered L'Arche communities with a sense of admiration for Vanier. In 2016, the Vatican found an accusation of Buela's sexual abuse of a seminarian to be credible. To complicate matters further, former cardinal Theodore McCarrick, credibly accused of sexually abusing seminarians, had a great influence on our community's spirituality. Buela was close friends with McCarrick. The former cardinal was notoriously given higher ranks in the hierarchy of the Catholic Church while the truths of his abuse were kept secret within this ecclesial hierarchy. Our community was thus caught up within a web of abuse by Buela and McCarrick.

The L'Arche community was also in many ways unknowingly caught up in a web of abuse since Vanier continued the spiritual practice learned from Philippe. The L'Arche founder had lost all perspective on obeying the church's orders concerning Philippe. Vanier continued to secretly meet with Philippe following the 1956 "strict and direct instruction from the Vatican authorities to not be involved" with him or any successor of L'Eau Vive communities, which were the original communities for persons with disabilities started before L'Arche began.[4] Three years later, Pope John XXIII even asked Vanier to break ties with Philippe. Vanier could not bring himself to break ties because he saw Philippe "as an almost Christ-like figure," and Vanier gave Philippe "a central role in his life and in his vocation."[5]

The ongoing relationship between Vanier and Philippe is eerily similar to Buela's secret contact with my religious order when the Vatican forbade Buela to be in communication with the order. Although he lived physically isolated from the community in Spain, I remember times we would Skype with him. At that time, I still truly believed that he was innocent, as I was encouraged to believe, so these meetings did not seem odd to me. Buela also sustained contact with McCarrick, and McCarrick even sent him half a million dollars for unknown reasons. In hindsight, this pattern of grooming is much like the pattern of grooming between Vanier and Philippe.

I was not physically abused by McCarrick, yet his ideas were deeply ingrained in the spirituality of the order and, thus, ingrained in me. The relationship of a spiritual community with a trusted spiritual leader is

---

[4] Brock, "Fatal Theological Mistakes," 445.
[5] L' Arche Commission, *Control and Abuse*, 805.

RELEARNING VULNERABILITY 189

already complex, even *sans* abuse. Communities have a difficult time breaking ties with abusive spiritual leaders. The founder and leaders live in the bricks of the community, and removing these persons risks questioning the whole foundation.

Learning of McCarrick's abuse was heart-wrenching for me because the former cardinal not only celebrated the Masses of my vows, but he also came over to our Juniorate house in Washington, DC, many Saturdays for Mass and breakfast. I remember feeling that I was blessed to be the one to greet him at his car and escort him up the elevator into the chapel. During his Masses, my hand was usually scribbling down every word of his homily that I could catch, treating the words as absolute truths for the spiritual life. Hanging on his every word, I had an unquestioning trust in McCarrick. Similarly, L'Arche members had an unquestioning trust in Vanier.

McCarrick presented an extremely spiritual persona, which made it all the more shocking and hurtful when the abuse news broke in 2018. After I left religious life in 2018, I believed I had developed a warped mind by being influenced so deeply spiritually by two fathers in the church that masked themselves as spiritually and morally good persons. I see my experience with Buela and McCarrick as similar to those who lived in the L'Arche community who now had to grapple with Vanier's betrayal. Buela and McCarrick presented themselves as holy persons, and, at the same time, they were using their spiritual authority to take advantage of people's vulnerability. Buela's and McCarrick's betrayal of my trust has made me question my own judgment of who to place trust in within spiritual spheres.

Former L'Arche member Kelly Colwell and I were not the direct victims of sexual abuse, but we were both left feeling betrayed by our spiritual leaders. In Colwell's article "Counting the Costs and Beginning to Heal: The Legacy of Jean Vanier at L'Arche," she shares her personal reaction to the news of Jean Vanier's abuse. Colwell emphasizes holding the tension between "recognizing and atoning for harm done by people and communities" with accepting, even celebrating, the beautiful aspects that have helped the community to flourish. Sitting in this tension, she asks "can we also celebrate good ways we have been shaped if a community was created by a manipulative leader?"[6] This

---

[6] Kelly Colwell, "Counting the Costs and Beginning to Heal: The Legacy of Jean

190 ELISE ABSHIRE

tough question holds in tension the beautiful and the harmful. On the one hand, Colwell truly believes this community made her flourish spiritually. On the other hand, she is sickened that she was part of a community started by an abuser and questions how her vulnerability could be exploited. Both of these reactions exist within Colwell at the same time, and they resonate with me after learning of Buela's and McCarrick's abuses.

Vanier's abuses and their devastating rippling effects are unfortunately not rarities in spiritual communities. Having experienced firsthand living under the direction of abusive spiritual leaders, I can see how dangerous it is for Vanier's manipulative language to have been employed in spiritual direction. I can further understand how directees believed him, trusted him, and possibly thought that what transpired was of God. I am in no way claiming to understand the feelings or the hurt of the victims of Vanier's sexual abuse.

Manipulation of Spiritual Concepts

Hauntingly, Brian Brock points out the paradox that has been present all along in the Vanierian spirituality: "It has only recently become clear how deeply paradoxical it is that what is good was wrapped up from the very beginning with manipulative and abusive behaviors justified in theological language."[7] Therefore, Brock prompts us to critically engage with the theology that disability theologians inherit from Vanier. Within Brock's writing, there are four key concepts that I found useful in considering Vanier's spirituality: manipulation of spiritual concepts, infantilized spirituality, abuse of power dynamics, and secrecy and violation of ethical boundaries. While all four aspects are important, I focus primarily on Vanier's manipulation of spiritual concepts, especially vulnerability and spiritual fatherhood, while I briefly mention the other three aspects.

Part of Vanier's and Philippe's "deformed theology" was an emphasis on an eschatological spirituality as *opposed* to earthly concepts of spirituality. While this was a central idea to the L'Arche community, Vanier brought this into the pastoral setting of spiritual direction. The

---

Vanier at L'Arche," *Canadian Journal of Theology Mental Health and Disability* 1, no. 2 (2021): 113.

[7] Brock, "Fatal Theological Mistakes," 445.

denial of earthly morality when speaking of eschatological spirituality allowed Philippe and Vanier to propose a "higher" morality than one on this earth, which led to confusion among their directees, especially women, about normally prohibited sexual activities. Philippe writes about this in his work on the contemplative life: "Direction in this sense is situated above time, on the level of eternal life . . . Although it occurs in time, its value is outside time."[8] One of Philippe's directees confirms this use of the eschatological to eschew moral boundaries: "We thought we were confirmed in grace. We could no longer sin in the domain of purity thanks to a special choice of the Most Holy Virgin . . . With the Fr [Philippe] and among us we were already living what we shall live in the heavenly city: carnal union will be central in the heavenly city, in place of the cross."[9] Philippe formed Vanier in this concept of being "outside time," and Vanier then brought this idea into his spiritual direction. Vanier and Philippe used these eschatological concepts to make those actions normally prohibited as being licit, under the guise of pleasing God within a heavenly vision of spirituality and love.[10]

Another major red flag in Vanier's spirituality, writes Brock, is that "many Christians through the centuries have sought union with God, but Vanier and Philippe presented this union in an unorthodox manner—as an exception to rather than a transformation of the ethical boundaries protecting vulnerable human beings in a fallen eon."[11] Vanier developed his idea of spiritual nuptiality from the nuptial theology of St. John of the Cross, incorporating the Song of Songs within this spirituality.[12] Vanier also used Marian theology to talk about an erotic love between Mary and Jesus as well as Mary's "womb of love."[13] One of the victims recalled Vanier using this twisted Marian relationship to describe his sexual advances in direction: "It's not us, it's Jesus and Mary. You are chosen—it's special, secret . . . It all seemed very sexual to me, not spiritual . . . I thought the problem came from me, from my spiritual indigence which was why I couldn't understand the importance of what was going on between us."[14]

---

[8] Thomas Philippe, *The Contemplative Life* (Dominican Nuns, 2009), 84.

[9] L' Arche Commission, *Control and Abuse*, 251.

[10] Brock, "Fatal Theological Mistakes," 434.

[11] Brock, "Fatal Theological Mistakes," 434.

[12] Brock, "Fatal Theological Mistakes," 448.

[13] Brock, "Fatal Theological Mistakes," 434.

[14] L' Arche Commission, *Control and Abuse*, 714.

192 ELISE ABSHIRE

Vanier's Marian theology, which focused on the relationship of Mary with Jesus, points us toward Vanier's emphasis on an infantilized spirituality. Philippe instructed Vanier in this type of spirituality, which promoted directees to be passive, vulnerable, and receptive (to Jesus in the person of the spiritual director). Manipulation can insidiously insert into this spirituality due to the unquestioning trust of the directee. In manipulating his own directees, Vanier emphasized his own vulnerability, which can be seen in an excerpt from one of his letters: "We each have the innocent heart of a child where the grace of God resides [. . .] It takes two to be fertile. [. . .] In the Christian vision of sexuality, the man and the woman make the mystery of the Trinity present. Our God is not a solitary God. God is three people."[15]

Brock does not want us to make the "fatal error" of dismissing these manipulative theological concepts without question: "The mystical reading of traditional tropes of divine union and the nuptial mystery have now become fully literal readings, ones that transcend every traditional distinction in Christian sexual ethics and instrumentalize sacramental practice. It would be a mistake to dismiss this theology as quirky or perverse as to have had little influence."[16] I would add that it would also be a mistake to deem Vanier's emphasis on spiritual fatherhood as unimportant or just a name used by some spiritual directors.

The very beauty Vanier drew out in his spiritual instruction for L'Arche was at the same time a toxin injected into his spirituality to justify dissolution of ethical boundaries. Vanier discussed spiritual vulnerability in a seductive manner. Brock's analysis suggests that Vanier and Philippe presented eschatological union with God as an exception to ethical boundaries, implying a *secretive* relationship and exclusive understanding of spirituality. From the testimony of abused women, Vanier would even state in direction, "What goes on in spiritual guidance is both crucial and necessarily secret, even from one's parents."[17] The connection between spiritual direction and keeping secrets is especially tricky here. Regarding secrets, Ignatian spirituality uses the discernment of spirits to look for the signs of the "evil spirit."[18]

---

[15] L' Arche Commission, *Control and Abuse*, 711.

[16] Brock, "Fatal Theological Mistakes," 444.

[17] Jean Vanier, *Community and Growth* (Darton, Longman and Todd, 2007), 240.

[18] "The good angel consoles for the progress of the soul, that it may advance and rise to what is more perfect. The evil spirit consoles for purposes that are the contrary, and that afterwards he might draw the soul to his own perverse inten-

Encouraging the directee to keep secrets is not the typical advice in spiritual direction; this encouragement puts the directee in an extra vulnerable position, with no conversation partners.

Spiritual Fatherhood and Vulnerability

Another way that Ignatian spirituality is helpful here is the idea of considering the angel of darkness disguised as an angel of light.[19] Through the charismatic personalities of Vanier and Philippe, they gained the directees' and the community's trust. The community members could not believe that these leaders could commit such terrible abuse. Directees were often left with feeling as though everything these leaders said was supposed to be taken as absolute spiritual truths. How could these holy men be wrong or be promoting toxic spiritualities? After all, these two men started communities that changed vulnerable people's lives. These men founded communities that were filled with authentic friendship and genuine values.

Reid Locklin and Andrea Carandang propose that Vanier had a mask that empowered others and that also hid his destructive compulsions and desires. The coauthors suggest that theology should encourage an ordinary vulnerability that is different from Vanier's idealized form of vulnerability. Locklin and Carandang believe that Vanier carefully constructed his persona: "The Vanier who abused women was not a fallen saint, succumbing to the temptations and opportunities afforded by his rising fame. This was who he had been all along: a man exquisitely and terribly attuned to the vulnerabilities of others."[20] This emphasis relates to Brock's suggestion of how "there never was an innocent Vanier."[21]

Yet, people often regarded Vanier as a "living saint" due to his role in founding the international L'Arche communities accompanying persons with disabilities, and community members experienced him as exud-

---

tions and wickedness." Louis J. Puhl, *The Spiritual Exercises of St. Ignatius* (Loyola Press, 1951), 147.

[19] The angel of darkness at times will "assume the appearance of an angel of light . . . he will endeavor little by little to end by drawing the soul into his hidden snares and evil designs." Puhl, *The Spiritual Exercises*, 148.

[20] Reid Locklin and Andrea Carandang, "A Vulnerable Persona: Wrestling with the Legacy of Jean Vanier," in *Teaching and Learning Religion: Engaging the Work of Eugene V. Gallagher and Patricia O'Connell Killen*, ed. Davina C. Lopez and Thomas Pearson (Bloomsbury, 2023), 144.

[21] Brock, "Fatal Theological Mistakes," 452.

194 ELISE ABSHIRE

ing a charismatic and inviting holiness. One woman who worked in a L'Arche community said in an interview concerning Vanier,

> There was something deeply human. He was listened to because when he spoke, he spoke of humanity. He spoke of humanity, and of God in our humanity, so it spoke to us . . . And also he was someone who could talk easily about certain weaknesses and you could relate to them, you see, he was not a guru. [. . .] He could talk about his fears, his doubts, his anxieties [. . .] in his conferences or in his retreats, and so it spoke to people, it reached them: if Vanier can be anxious, then I can too, it's not something negative [. . .] I don't doubt the fact that he was really led by the Holy Spirit.[22]

Even though members of the community related to Vanier, Locklin and Carandang suggest Vanier carefully constructed his persona for manipulation. Constructing a persona is a complicated affair. Vanier did found communities that impacted members positively and even led some to have spiritual conversions. Undeniably there was and is goodness found within L'Arche. Vanier had a way to make people with disabilities and directees feel at ease, for them to feel comfortable being vulnerable around him.

Due to Vanier's charismatic persona, spiritual directees became vulnerable with him in spiritual direction. Within direction, Vanier encouraged spiritual fatherhood and nuptial covenants. Vanier characterizes the father's authority as the one who guides, educates, and challenges the child.[23] He used the father as a figure of authority and romanticized the view of a father–child relationship. Thus, the child becomes weak compared to the father. The child is thrown off balance, in need of guidance from the father. The power dynamic allows for the one who bears authority, Vanier in this case, to be especially attentive to the limitations of a directee—or the child.[24] The child then feels dependent on the authority figure to make any spiritual decisions.

Natalie Wigg-Stevenson firmly believes that "sexual abuse is always about power."[25] For Wigg-Stevenson, the eschatological realm of

---

[22] L'Arche Commission, *Control and Abuse*, 446.
[23] L'Arche Commission, *Control and Abuse*, 469.
[24] L'Arche Commission, *Control and Abuse*, 469.
[25] Natalie Wigg-Stevenson, "When a Trusted Spiritual Leader Turns Out to Be

Vanier's spiritual manipulation made his abuse all the more difficult to stop. Vanier had such power that he could "define the theological frame of conversation" as a spiritual director. Vanier also held authority over the directees, taking them on a theological journey "that draws them deeper into the heart of God, that's a lot of power to hold."[26]

In traditional practices/understandings of spiritual direction, the directee is encouraged to be spiritually vulnerable to the director—meaning confessing all their thoughts and feelings to the director, hoping that the director will not misuse or use that knowledge to manipulate the directee. Vanier and Philippe as well as Buela and McCarrick misused that knowledge and broke the sacred trust the directee holds within spiritual direction or between a community member with a trusted spiritual leader. Vanier's insistence on his weakness and shortcomings in the fragile space of spiritual direction becomes another reason to trust in his direction, further elevating his power in the already present imbalance of power between him as the father and director and the directee as the child. In his letters, Vanier continually insists on his poverty, his misery, and his weakness.[27] By repeatedly highlighting his brokenness, he uses it to seduce the women into developing compassion, sorrow, and even admiration for him.[28] Persons within spiritual communities should be cautious when dealing with community leaders, especially those who are quite charismatic. Whether intentionally or unintentionally crafted, Vanier had a persona that fostered trust with directees. The directees then trusted his ideas of spiritual vulnerability without question.

Spiritual Communities
and Future Flourishing

Perhaps intentionally wrestling through terms that can be beautiful and yet hold the power to produce great harm precisely because of their beauty is exactly what the 2024 College Theology Society conference theme, "Vulnerability and Flourishing," is all about. Vanier hurt people

---

a Sexual Predator," *Sojourners Magazine,* July 2020, 32, https://sojo.net/magazine/july-2020/when-trusted-spiritual-leader-turns-out-be-sexual-predator.

[26] Wigg-Stevenson, "When a Trusted Spiritual Leader Turns Out to Be a Sexual Predator," 32.

[27] L'Arche Commission, *Control and Abuse,* 233.

[28] L'Arche Commission, *Control and Abuse,* 233.

196 ELISE ABSHIRE

with the spiritual tenet of vulnerability, but vulnerability can also allow for spiritual flourishing. Wigg-Stevenson reminds us that "we also have to entertain the possibility that the two branches of his [Vanier's] life stemmed from the same root: that the sensitivity to vulnerability and communal belonging that gave birth to the undeniable beauty of L'Arche was the very thing Vanier exploited for his own sexual gratification in his private spiritual direction."[29] Vanier took the true, the good, and the beautiful in spirituality theology and used it in nefarious ways.

One of Vanier's victims even shared that after reflection on the abuse from Vanier, she felt like a "spiritual whore" whose vulnerability was exploited.[30] Vanier used spiritual fatherhood to abuse the spiritual tenet of vulnerability, while also speaking about this tenet as good and beautiful. The power of a spiritual leader is rife with temptations; with power comes the possibility to manipulate or to take advantage of those under power. Spiritual communities have a grave responsibility to consider greater accountability for leaders.

Spiritual communities cannot and will not flourish as long as spiritual leaders use vulnerability as a gateway for abuse. Vanier distorted terms that can have a beautiful meaning in religious contexts; he used them for cruel purposes. Therefore, wrestling with these terms of Vanier's spirituality is necessary to mitigate future harm and cultivate possibilities for flourishing. Wrestling with these twisted spiritual uses of vulnerability empowers us to show how messy, awful, and tragic human relationships can be within spiritual and theological communities. From this process we can consider, together, a healthier spirituality of vulnerability for the future flourishing of church communities.

---

[29] Wigg-Stevenson, "When a Trusted Spiritual Leader Turns Out to Be a Sexual Predator," 31.

[30] L'Arche Commission, *Control and Abuse*, 713.

Attunement and Safeguarding in the Parishes

Perspectives of a Diocesan Priest

Anthony V. Coloma

The sexual abuse crisis in the Catholic Church was not only about the violence by priests and the religious in the church. It was aggravated by the abuse of power by the church's leadership and by the silence of the laity toward the struggles of the victims and survivors of sexual violence in the church. These egregious failures revealed the endemic numbness of ecclesial leaders and church communities toward people who suffer from abuse. No one can deny the depth of the devastation and the tremendous horror the crisis effected on the lives of the victims–survivors and their families. It haunted, and continues to do so, the very people the church promised and committed to serve. This crisis opened the church's eyes to its own vulnerabilities as a fellowship of believing pilgrims. The church faltered in protecting the least from among its members. And in this crisis, the church was both a vulnerable victim and a predator who preyed on the vulnerable.[1] In saying so,

---

[1] For this chapter, the church is understood as the fellowship of the people of God who are genuinely seeking union and reconciliation with God. The church constitutes not just its leadership but very much involves those who identify themselves to be followers of Christ. This identity finds expression in the participation of every baptized person in the life and ministry of the church that they belong to, including safeguarding and promotion of human flourishing for all. In democratizing the work of safeguarding, this does not deflect our attention from offenders and those who

198 ANTHONY V. COLOMA

this is not an attempt to downplay the gravity of the abuses enacted by church leaders nor resort to what theologian Cristina Lledo Gomez, citing Gerard Mannion, described as a form of "strategic distancing" by church authorities.[2] That is, as Lledo Gomez observed, when church leadership instead of owning up to their failures ventures into strategies to deflect responsibility and accountability, including calling upon the whole church to repent when clearly the clergy leadership needed to show repentance. By looking at the church's failures and vulnerabilities at all levels of its fellowship, it is being challenged to take a more wholistic approach to the causes and impacts of the crisis in its life and ministry. Inherent in this invitation is the demand for all those who share in the royal priesthood of Christ to be mindful of the plight of all who were made to suffer from the church's historical failure to authentically live out its identity and mission. Clearly, there is a need for real and systemic change in the church's leadership as Lledo Gomez asserts. However, the challenge for the conversion of heart is a call for every baptized and cannot be limited to the church's authorities. For authentic ecclesial reform, particularly toward safeguarding and the flourishing of all, it must be a whole parish approach.[3] Though, in this framework of coresponsibility for the church, asymmetrical power relations and abuse of power must be interrogated and interrupted for coresponsibility to flourish.

Safeguarding ought to be a shared responsibility and a common goal for every believing community. In 1985, representations were first

---

enabled them. It demands that every baptized person commit to the protection of the vulnerable and the accompaniment of those who have been harmed. Moreover, "vulnerable people" is defined as "aged under 18 or other individuals who may be unable to take care of themselves or are unable to protect themselves against harm or exploitation." For those included in this category, see Australian Government, Vulnerable People, https://www.acnc.gov.au/tools/topic-guides/vulnerable-people.

[2] Cristina Lledo Gomez, "Grace and Disgraced: Child Sexual Abuse and the Holy Roman Catholic Australian Church," in *Theological and Hermeneutical Explorations from Australia: Horizons of Contextuality*, ed. Jione Havea (Lexington Books/ Fortress Academic, 2021), 73–74, 78, 81.

[3] Safeguarding refers to "protecting the welfare and human rights of people that are connected to the church and its work, particularly people that may be at risk of abuse, neglect or exploitation." Adapted from the Australian Government, *Governance Toolkit: Safeguarding Vulnerable People*, at https://www.acnc. gov.au/for-charities/manage-your-charity/governance-hub/governance-toolkit/ governance-toolkit-safeguarding-vulnerable-people.

ATTUNEMENT AND SAFEGUARDING IN THE PARISHES   **199**

officially submitted to the American bishops regarding clerical sexual abuses. Confidentially called "The Manual," Doyle, Sipe, and Wall submitted it to the US Conference of Catholic Bishops discussing the problem of sexual molestation by Catholic clergy. They outlined ways to address the problem comprehensively and responsibly, but the church's leadership was too protracted if not unwilling to take responsibility.[4] From the time the memorandum was submitted, there had been significant developments in the church's attempt, albeit slow-moving while marred by denial and the need to preserve the status quo, to establish robust protocols to ensure integrity and accountability in ministry particularly toward safeguarding.[5] A recent survey of the diocesan websites in the US and Australia indicated safeguarding frameworks and policies had been embedded in the church's institutions and ministries.

However, the church's overall response remained focused on legal and criminal liabilities, and on implementing safeguarding procedures that seemed to focus on protecting the church institution rather than the vulnerable. Church historian Massimo Faggioli and theologian John Sheveland both observed that the complexity of the crisis made "clear that the Catholic Church needs to develop a theological approach to the sexual abuse crisis and to move beyond a merely legal-criminological focus."[6] Sheveland added that the church's response had been limited

---

[4] Thomas P. Doyle, A. W. R. Sipe, and Patrick J. Wall, *Sex, Priests, and Secret Codes: The Catholic Church's 2,000-Year Paper Trail of Sexual Abuse* (Volt Press, 2006), 99–174.

[5] Bettina Böhm, Hans Zollner, Jörg M. Fegert, and Hubert Liebhardt, "Child Sexual Abuse in the Context of the Roman Catholic Church: A Review of Literature from 1981–2013," *Journal of Child Sexual Abuse* 23, no. 6 (2014): 638–39, https://doi.org/10.1080/10538712.2014.929607. In this article, the authors synthesize the key findings and research gaps in recent inquiries regarding child sexual abuse in the Catholic Church. They have given a summary of the findings of ten inquiry reports from Belgium, Germany, Ireland, Netherlands, and the US. See Karen J. Terry, Margaret Leland Smith, Katarina Schuth, O.S.F., et al., *The Causes and Context of Sexual Abuse of Minors by Catholic Priests in the United States, 1950–2010* (United States Conference of Catholic Bishops, 2011), https://www.usccb.org. See also Divna M. Haslam, David M. Lawrence, Ben Matthews, Daryl J. Higgins, Anna Hunt, James G. Scott, Michael P. Dunne et al., "The Australian Child Maltreatment Study (ACMS), a National Survey of the Prevalence of Child Maltreatment and Its Correlates: Methodology," in *Medical Journal of Australia* 218 (2023): S5–12.

[6] Massimo Faggioli, "The Catholic Sexual Abuse Crisis as a Theological Crisis: Emerging Issues," *Theological Studies* 80, no. 3 (2019): 573. See John N. Sheveland, "Clergy Sexual Abuse and the Work of Redemption: Gestures Toward a Theology

200 ANTHONY V. COLOMA

to the "domain of prevention and less well developed in the domains of [the] ministry of healing."[7] A theological reflection on the issues opened by the crisis, Faggioli added, would allow "all members of the church to reflect on [it] as one of the signs of our times."[8] The path toward healing and theological rethinking were synthesized by Dr. Heather Banis in her concept of attunement. For Banis, this involved the "journey of accompaniment that honors victim–survivors through attentive listening, transparency, and accountability."[9] Atonement for the church's failures requires church communities to be attuned to the anguish and hopes of those who experienced violence and were marginalized by abuse.

The question this chapter ponders is this: What do the voices of the victims–survivors of sexual abuse in the Catholic Church offer to in-form and reform the parish way of living, believing, and worshipping?[10] In attending to this question, this chapter intends to affirm consonance between the church's theology and the whole parish approach toward safeguarding and the promotion of human flourishing of the vulnerable. This could be achieved by showing that (1) the preferential option to listen to vulnerable people, particularly the victims–survivors of church abuse, is a Christian vocation; (2) contemplating and learning from their stories can lead to authentic personal and communal conversion; (3) exhibiting this conversion through the examination of and change in the parish's governance and ministry can rebuild trust and serve as a catalyst for the long journey and commitment for healing, safeguard-ing, and, ultimately, toward the flourishing of all in the community.

---

of Accompaniment," *Buddhist-Christian Studies* 41 (2021): 71.

[7] Sheveland, "Clergy Sexual Abuse and the Work of Redemption," 71.

[8] Faggioli, "The Catholic Sexual Abuse Crisis as a Theological Crisis," 572.

[9] Heather T. Banis, "Resiliency, Hope, Healing: Victims Assistance Ministry in a Trauma-Sensitive Theological Context," in *Theology in a Post-Traumatic Church*, ed. John N. Sheveland (Orbis Books, 2023), 32.

[10] The focus of this chapter is to attend to the voices of sexual abuse victims and survivors in the Catholic Church. This does not deny that there are other forms of abuses that continue to insidiously impact people's lives in and outside of the church. These include, but are not limited to, domestic violence, spiritual and psychological abuses, moral injuries, to name a few; listening to their voices remains constitutive of the invitation for attunement. For the purpose of this theological reflection, this chapter focuses on the victims–survivors of church sexual abuse, since the key material that informs this reflection is the narrative published by Australia's Royal Commission into Institutional Child Sexual Abuse.

Attentive Listening Is a Christian Vocation

Revelations of sexual violence, the abuse of power by the hierarchy, and the silence from among the laity reveal sinfulness that inheres in the church.[11] Although the Second Vatican Council did not categorically address and name the church's abuses in its documents, it does confess how the church needs purification and is being demanded to follow the path of penance, renewal, and conversion.[12] As a church that responds to the call for ongoing conversion, the church abuse crisis invites "theological rethinking."[13]

In carrying out the task of conversion and theological rethinking, the church has always had the duty of scrutinizing the signs of the times and interpreting them in the light of the gospel.[14] This rethinking is "aroused and sustained by the Spirit of truth."[15] The church's mission then is a call toward a deeper understanding of and stronger solidarity with the lived realities and the complex stories of anguish of the people of God. It is the church's task to keep the eyes and hearts of its members and leadership open to be responsive to the lived experience of the people whose lives have been seriously wounded in its own institutions and ministries.

This theological rethinking requires that the church immerses and listens to the miseries of those who have been seriously affected by this crisis. Theologian Werner Jeanrond and victims assistance coordinator Heather Banis approach the issue of abuse in the church by situating the voices of the victims and the survivors at the heart of theological reflection.[16] Jeanrond acknowledges the outstanding need for an "in-depth reflection on the place and role of victims and survivors" in the "ongoing reflections on prevention and related measures for church

---

[11] See Jeanmarie Gribaudo, *A Holy Yet Sinful Church: Three Twentieth-Century Moments in a Developing Theology* (Liturgical Press, 2015), 106–34, 141–42.

[12] See Second Vatican Council, *Unitatis Redintegratio* (1964), no. 6.

[13] Faggioli, "The Catholic Sexual Abuse Crisis as a Theological Crisis," 572.

[14] Pope Paul VI, *Gaudium et Spes* (1965), no. 1 (hereafter cited as *GS*).

[15] *Lumen Gentium* (1964), no. 12.

[16] Werner G. Jeanrond, "Abuse, Cover-Up, and the Need for a Reform of Church and Theology," in *Doing Theology and Theological Ethics in the Face of the Abuse Crisis*, ed. Daniel J. Fleming, James F. Keenan, and Hans Zollner (Pickwick Publications, 2023), 248–54; Banis, "Resiliency, Hope, Healing," 34–35.

202 ANTHONY V. COLOMA

reform."[17] Echoing Johann Baptist Metz, Jeanrond advocates that "there is no way forward for church and theology without remembering the victims and survivors of abuse, without listening to their voices and taking their experiences seriously ... without reviewing and readjusting the structure of the church through the lens of their experience."[18] Nuala Kenny, who served as advisor to the Canadian Conference of Catholic Bishops Committee for the Protection of Minors on issues of abuse of power in the church, appeals for the same path for theological rethinking. For Kenny, it "requires recognition of the harms of sexual abuse, addressing the systemic and cultural beliefs and practices that foster abuse and an understanding of vulnerability."[19]

The church ought to be a community cognizant of and sensitive to the impact of the violence on the lives of the victims and the survivors of sexual abuse. Hans Zollner, SJ, recognizes this as an intrinsic aspect of the church's mission.[20] The church that theologically rethinks deeply and that remains open to conversion is a church sensitive to the plight of the abused and is open for a heart-to-heart conversation with those in anguish. This is not about pity; it is about being in solidarity. Solidarity is demonstrated when the church dialogues with the people of today about the many problems they are confronted with and brings the "light kindled from the Gospel and puts at its disposal those saving resources which the Church herself, under the guidance of the Holy Spirit, receives from her founder. For the human person deserves to be preserved; human society deserves to be renewed."[21] Since the Second Vatican Council envisions such a church, it can be implied that this includes abuse victims and survivors, prioritizing their preservation and the use of church resources for their well-being and human flourishing. This can be reinforced by the Catholic social teaching of a preferential option for the poor applied toward the vulnerable, such

---

[17] Jeanrond, "Abuse, Cover-Up, and the Need for a Reform of Church and Theology," 249.

[18] Jeanrond, "Abuse, Cover-Up, and the Need for a Reform of Church and Theology," 249.

[19] Nuala Kenny, "Clergy Sexual Abuse, Trauma-Informed Theology, and the Promotion of Resilience," in *Doing Theology and Theological Ethics in the Face of the Abuse Crisis*, 360.

[20] Hans Zollner, "The Catholic Church's Responsibility in Creating a Safeguarding Culture," *The Person and the Challenges* 12, no. 1 (2022): 5–21.

[21] *GS*, no. 3.

ATTUNEMENT AND SAFEGUARDING IN THE PARISHES 203

that the preferential option to listen to vulnerable persons becomes a Christian vocation and responsibility. In this Christian call to listen, what are the victims and survivors themselves saying?

Contemplating the Witness of Victims and Survivors

In 2013, the Australian Commonwealth formed the Royal Commission into Institutional Responses to Child Sexual Abuse. After almost four years of investigations, the Commission released the final report in 2017. In the report, over eight thousand survivors or people directly impacted by institutional child sexual abuse attended private sessions at the Royal Commission and shared their experiences and recommendations with the Commissioners.[22] Many gave consent for their accounts to be published as short narratives. The purpose of the narratives is to give a voice to survivors, inform the community, and ultimately help make institutions safer for children.[23] Real names have been changed except the names of public figures mentioned in a public context.

Reading through these narratives and prayerfully contemplating their stories proved to be gut wrenching as a Catholic diocesan priest. The stories were overwhelming. I was confronted with emotional turmoil and psychological angst. That the church has contributed to this horror made the experience of listening to their stories more harrowing. Yet if I was to take seriously my argument for the Christian call to contemplate and reflect on the joys and the hopes, the griefs and anxieties of those whose lives have been permanently damaged and injured, then I had to also listen to the harrowing stories of church abuse.

The narratives reveal how the abuse harms a person's capacity to perceive their self-worth. One person, Willis, not his real name, stood out for me. Willis described how he always saw himself as a "piece of garbage."[24] For some time, "Willis determined that he'd 'work things out' for himself. He had a beautiful wife and son, he said, and he loved his job. Nevertheless, he slept in the garage rather than the house, a

---

[22] Commonwealth of Australia, *Royal Commission into Institutional Responses to Child Sexual Abuse*, https://www.childabuseroyalcommission.gov.au/.

[23] Commonwealth of Australia, *Royal Commission into Institutional Responses to Child Sexual Abuse*.

[24] "Willis's story," *Royal Commission into Institutional Responses to Child Sexual Abuse*, https://www.childabuseroyalcommission.gov.au/narrative/williss-story.

legacy he attributed to the abuse. 'I sleep downstairs and a lot of that is hangover from when you were a child because you see yourself as worthless. You're a piece of garbage. And so I see myself as, the garage is good enough for me. I'm not worth much more. So you've still got that hangover from the days.' "[25]

Others who caught my attention were those who had lost their affection for the church they once cherished and loved, the same church that I cherish and love. Romana shared that as a young person she liked Mass "cause it was in Latin and I liked the feel of Mass at that time . . . In Lent I went every day and really liked getting up at six o'clock in the morning and going and being in that environment."[26] However, at a young age, she was sexually and physically abused by her father. Her father died of suicide. But her father's death led her to another abuse by a priest. She shared how that "experience probably was connected with me stopping my spiritual connection . . . I think something got on top of the abuse from my father and then having a priest, another male, and a nun take you there. Why would a nun take a child to wash up? Surely, they must know."[27]

Those who also affected me deeply were those who lost their sense of trust and felt angst and despair. The church is meant to be a beacon of hope and a place of trust and solidarity with the people who are suffering, but we have clearly failed this vision by failing them. One such person is Alastair who did not make an official report about his abuse in the church. "To this day," Alastair shared, "I always thought that no one would believe me. The church was God, after all. I did not even consider trying to report the matter myself, to the church or the Christian Brothers. I had been beaten up and abused enough by them. I didn't consider the police either as I did not want to get into trouble from them either. There was no avenue to complain to about anything. So," Alastair confessed, "I just lived with it."[28]

---

[25] "Willis's story," *Royal Commission into Institutional Responses to Child Sexual Abuse*.

[26] "Romana's story," *Royal Commission into Institutional Responses to Child Sexual Abuse*, https://www.childabuseroyalcommission.gov.au/narrative/romanas-story.

[27] "Romana's story," *Royal Commission into Institutional Responses to Child Sexual Abuse*.

[28] "Alastair Gregory's story," *Royal Commission into Institutional Responses to Child Sexual Abuse*, https://www.childabuseroyalcommission.gov.au/narrative/alastair-gregorys-story.

ATTUNEMENT AND SAFEGUARDING IN THE PARISHES 205

Further, there were those trapped in a life of despondency and sadness because of the church leadership's ignorance and abuse of asymmetrical power dynamics. Marty was sexually violated by a priest when he was in primary school and by a Marist brother when he was in high school.[29] Yet, it did not deter him from his childhood dream of joining a religious order. In the seminary, Marty recounted sexual advances by a priest, who happens to be one of the founders of the order. Marty shared that the "activity" with the priest "became more intimate, involved pornography, and lasted for a number of years. Marty got by with the help of alcohol until, one day, 'the alarm went off.' "[30] Marty further shared that "I'll never forget this." The priest "was all vested up, and he starts mass and it's, 'Lord be with you,' and I just went, 'I can't cope with this!' "[31] When asked about the impact of the abuse, Marty fell silent, and let his mother speak for him. "Very, very depressed very often," Judith said. "There were times that I was fearful for his life."[32]

These few examples illustrate the serious and life-altering impact on the lives of the women and men who were violated in the Catholic Church, informing the church how it got things so wrong and how it can do so much better. The abuse left survivors with permanent emotional and psychosocial injuries that we cannot even imagine. It is in this sacred space that the church is missioned to find the saving power of Christ by walking with survivors and allowing their stories to inform and shape theological reflection. If they need to "speak out, to vent, to cry, to express their anger and their wishes for the future," then we must give them the space for this. If "they want the institution that has caused them so much pain to admit it and do everything humanly possible to remedy it," then the church community must take these important steps of public acknowledgment, repentance, and ac-

---

[29] "Marty and Judith's story," *Royal Commission into Institutional Responses to Child Sexual Abuse,* https://www.childabuseroyalcommission.gov.au/narrative/marty-and-judiths-story.

[30] "Marty and Judith's story," *Royal Commission into Institutional Responses to Child Sexual Abuse.*

[31] "Marty and Judith's story," *Royal Commission into Institutional Responses to Child Sexual Abuse.*

[32] "Marty and Judith's story," *Royal Commission into Institutional Responses to Child Sexual Abuse.*

206 ANTHONY V. COLOMA

tions toward remedying its failures.[33] The task of listening ought not be limited to the promoters of safeguarding nor the pastoral council of the parish. The disposition of attunement ought to be a fundamental mandate for those who identify themselves as a follower of Christ.

Conclusion: A Parish Community That Listens

The church's atonement for its failures toward the victims and survivors of church abuse manifests itself in the parish's capacity to be attuned to their plight. This conversion in the parish's way of life marked by attunement rather than self-preservation can serve as a catalyst for genuine reform and human flourishing. A parish that becomes aware of the impact of the ongoing suffering of abuse victims is on the path of attunement and conversion. Mediating this experience of conversion remains the clarion call for those who identify themselves as a parish in communion with the Triune God. This involves solidarity with the victims and survivors of abuse. This approach helps the church to avoid such failures like abuses of power, secrecy, and betrayal within the institutional environment. If the church fails to learn from the past, it is in danger of retraumatizing survivors and perpetuating a culture of abuse. A parish community that patterns their lives and ministries in the spirit of attunement promotes an environment that prioritizes safety for all. The church can learn from institutions applying the foundational principles of being a trauma-informed organization. The principles are trustworthiness, transparency, accountability, collaboration, shared responsibility, and mutuality, and applying them to the church's life and ministries.[34] It begins when every member of the parish opens their

---

[33] Zollner, "The Catholic Church's Responsibility in Creating a Safeguarding Culture," 11.

[34] There are organizations that provide trauma-awareness training for institutions and communities. The Australian Catholic Safeguarding Ltd. (ACSL) offers courses and webinars on safeguarding and trauma awareness. They audit dioceses and religious communities regarding their safeguarding practices that other church organizations can benchmark. Queensland University of Technology Associate Professor Judith Howard developed, in 2017, a biennial conference on trauma education. She has been offering webinars on trauma-awareness approaches through ACSL. The US-based Awake Community makes available resources for communities that focus on building greater awareness on the issue and impact of sexual abuse through their blogs and their Courageous Conversation series. The Institute of

hearts and attentively listens to the stories the victims reveal and then commits themselves to taking positive and compassionate action. The parish becomes authentic to the church's mission and identity when it finds itself in the margins, like Christ, tending and speaking out for those in the margins and the powerless.

Anthropology at the Pontifical Gregorian University initiated academic programs for church leaders to promote human dignity and care for vulnerable people as a practical commitment of the Catholic Church.

La Fiesta de La Virgen de la Puerta

Vulnerability and Flourishing
Concretely Exemplified

Caitlin Cipolla-McCulloch

Otuzco, Peru, "Capital de la Fe," is an Andean town in the Sierra Liberteña, the northern region of Peru, and is home to an image of Mary, the Mother of God. La Virgen de la Puerta is an image of Mary who is in relationship with her faithful.[1] She rests above the door of the church in the center of town, behind a clear glass window on both sides, and is visible throughout the year. La Virgen de la Puerta is an image made vulnerable by the natural elements of the mountain town where she resides. She is celebrated lavishly each December with prayer, pilgrimage, food, drink, song, dance, and even fireworks. The community who forms around her, her fieles, themselves are vulnerable and offer to her their variety of needs, the fabric of their lives. La gente Otuzcana, in their vulnerability, ask her intercession for their daily tasks and also sometimes simply consult her about the best possible solution for situations they face in the day-to-day. A good harvest, healthy rains, and success in the marketplace are all ways in which the people of Otuzco plead to La Virgen for assistance. She promotes their flourishing by interceding on their behalf. For Otuzcanos, their

---

[1] I do not italicize Spanish. I do not differentiate Spanish as a foreign or unknown language. Spanish was the first language used for publication in the Americas. Utilization of the original texts which describe La Virgen de la Puerta, except for a single source, all occur in Spanish and I utilize the original texts, when possible, to convey the story of La Virgen and the community which surrounds her.

LA FIESTA DE LA VIRGEN DE LA PUERTA   209

relationship with La Virgen is not merely one of intercession; it is also a relationship of accompaniment, inviting her to walk with them in their everyday lives.[2] They share their vulnerability with her and invite her to walk alongside them. She is there with them, in close proximity throughout the year. They also celebrate with joyful abundance and participate in festival activities that promote human flourishing. This proximity is of key theological significance. The actions of the fiesta are a Mariological performance within and through bodily and communal practices. This is not a mediation, priestly or otherwise. This is because there is not a sense in which Mary is somewhere else. She is right there with the people. There is an immediacy to her presence and the celebration of the fiesta. The performative practices of the fiesta are simply the sharing in the flourishing she brings.

This chapter examines how the fiesta de La Virgen de la Puerta illuminates the relationship of this image of Mary with the Otuzcano community through the elements of fiesta, with a specific emphasis on food and drink. While it is possible to consider the reciprocal ways in which both the Marian image and the Otuzcano community are vulnerable, I emphasize how the vulnerability and flourishing of the Otuzcanos concretely manifest in their festive celebrations. Until now, the only published academic description of the fiesta written in English is in Robert Smith's *The Art of Festival* (1975), an anthropological ethnography. Smith's text focused primarily on what was happening from a human behavior perspective. He did not immediately analyze any theological importance upon the behaviors the community exhibited in connection to La Virgen. In my experience of the fiesta, however, it was not only the overt religious ritual that held theological significance, it was also the practices surrounding the ritual, the feeding of pilgrims, which evidence the accompaniment of La Virgen at the fiesta.

In *Mujerista Theology*, Ada María Isasi-Díaz describes the experience of the festival procession during her work in Peru in the 1960s.[3] The faith of the people in the poor neighborhoods, she explains, was a faith of vulnerability. During the procession of the fiesta patronal, the people present themselves before God and each other, exposing

---

[2] For more information, see Ada María Isasi-Díaz, "Lo Cotidiano: A Key Element of Mujerista Theology," *Journal of Hispanic / Latino Theology* 10, no. 1 (August 2002): 5–17.

[3] Ada María Isasi-Díaz, *Mujerista Theology* (Orbis, 1996).

their vulnerability at the hands of oppressive regimes that trapped them in poverty. Isasi-Díaz writes, "the faith of the poor and the oppressed that maintains them, that is their sustenance in the most trying of situations."[4] The same faith allows for lavish celebrations and abundance. Isasi-Díaz recognizes that the procession itself is part of a theological conversation that takes place in the movement, action, and exchanges, not just in texts. She writes, "theology is not a disembodied discourse but one that arises from situated subjects."[5]

Isasi-Díaz's insight that theological discourse is embodied—arising from "situated subjects"—informs my methodological approach.[6] I look to the embodied practices of the community that surrounds La Virgen de la Puerta as windows into the theological significance of the fiesta. Indeed, being embodied is the condition for being vulnerable, the condition in which many pilgrims arrive at the fiesta. It is also the condition for the experience of abundance and flourishing that is celebrated in the fiesta. As Isasi-Díaz says, the "subject" is situated historically, within systems of oppression, and within communities with distinctive practices of knowledge and human relationship. The history of La Virgen de la Puerta and her presence among la gente Otuzcana informs how she is celebrated in the fiesta today. Moreover, the festival practices of creating, consuming, and sharing food and drink are significant features of the way in which people gather for the festival, are in relationship with each other, and how they understand La Virgen's accompaniment in their lives.

Below I situate the fiesta patronal of La Virgen de la Puerta within the history of this image of Mary, contextualizing the importance of La Virgen to the local community with particular attention to the ways this history reveals human vulnerability. I then turn to the contemporary celebration of the fiesta patronal, highlighting food and drink as central features of the fiesta. Finally, this chapter argues that food and drink are concrete signifiers of the relationship between La Virgen and the community that gathers to celebrate her annually in Otuzco. La Virgen de la Puerta has accompanied the community of Otuzco in their vulnerability for over three centuries and continues to contribute to their flourishing. The vivid experience of her accompaniment is a

---

[4] Isasi-Díaz, *Mujerista Theology*, 30.
[5] Isasi-Díaz, *Mujerista Theology*, 3.
[6] Isasi-Díaz, *Mujerista Theology*, 3.

LA FIESTA DE LA VIRGEN DE LA PUERTA   **211**

reason why the celebration of La Virgen de la Puerta remains a thriving popular devotion today.

Brief History of the Image

There are some disputed details of the story of La Virgen de la Puerta; however, this is an accepted narrative embraced by the people. Though inhabited long before colonial times, in 1560, Otuzco was founded by the Augustinian Fathers who named the town "Pueblo de la Inmaculada Concepción de Nuestra Señora de Copocabana de Otusco."[7] The history, *Reseña Histórico-Biográfica del Culto a la Inmaculada Virgen de la Puerta de Otuzco: Patrona del Norte del Perú y Reyna de la Paz Mundial,* recounts that Otuzco acquired an image of the Immaculate Conception, most probably an image from Spain, and selected as the central date for its local celebration the Feast of the Immaculate Conception on December 8. However, since 1664, the fiesta has been celebrated on the Octave of the Immaculate Conception on December 15.

Due to the many riches that the Peruvian Viceroyalty had, bands of pirates from other European countries frequently tried to invade the seas of the Americas. Though Otuzco was not a port city, in the seventeenth century, its proximity to the port of Huanchaco in Trujillo meant piracy was a concern. This concern left Otuzcanos feeling vulnerable, and in 1670, pirates advanced into the sea in Trujillo. Word of their arrival spread quickly to the nearby town of Otuzco. After three days of waiting, the pirates never arrived. In order to commemorate the grace that the people of Otuzco received and to remain always protected by Mary, the Otuzcanos placed an image of Mary above the door of the church. From that moment on, they called the image "Nuestra Señora de la Puerta."[8]

This history helps one to understand how and why popular devotion to La Virgen de la Puerta came into being and why there is a festive celebration of her companionship of the Otuzcanos. The fiesta de La Virgen de la Puerta is made up of several key elements: pilgrimage, food, drink, the ritual of la bajada, procession, devotional activities

---

[7] Francisco Rodríguez Torres, *La Mamita de Otuzco* (Editorial Rayo Verde S.A.C., 2016), 22.

[8] *Reseña Histórico-Biográfica del Culto a la Inmaculada Virgen de la Puerta de Otuzco: Patrona del Norte del Perú y Reyna de la Paz Mundial* (Imprenta Marañon, 1959), 17–23.

requiring objects such as candles or ex-votos, Mass, music, and dance. This chapter will explore the central elements of the Fiesta Patronal or Fiesta Principal de La Virgen de la Puerta: food and drink.

Food and Drink as Central Elements of Fiesta

Before engaging with the food and drink elements of the fiesta to La Virgen, I want to provide a brief note about fiesta. Fiesta Patronal or Fiesta Principal is an annual celebration, which may take place over one or multiple days, to honor important holy images in a particular community. These holy images often depict saints who serve as patrons of specific locations, although devotion to particular images may extend much further than a local area. The events of a Fiesta Patronal or Fiesta Principal include elements of prayer such as Mass as well as other devotional activities and festive song, dance, food, music, and other elements of a large communal party (in the case of La Virgen de la Puerta, there are fireworks). It is truly a time of abundance and flourishing.

The activities of pilgrims who journey to the shrine church require corporeal sustenance, and thus the fiesta de La Virgen de la Puerta's strong emphasis on food and drink attends to this need. As the anthropological ethnographer Robert J. Smith writes, "Feasting is one of the great elements of the festival."[9] The feasting in Otuzco is both great and small. In the streets of Otuzco, there are myriad booths of food available to the pilgrims. There is also ample food in restaurants all around the plaza principal. This is a public festival that takes place in the streets. The largest feast is organized by the mayordomías of the caseríos[10] who sponsor the festival. It is typically held in a large room, often for the musicians, bands, and other large donors, on the principal day of the festival.[11] However, celebration also occurs privately on a smaller scale with family and friends in homes. Regarding the human activity of the celebration, Smith writes, "The feast of the Central Day, then,

---

[9] Robert J. Smith, *The Art of the Festival* (University of Kansas, 1975), 110.

[10] The mayordomías of the caseríos in this case are the stewards of the festival. Often they are a married couple. They sponsor the festival, helping underwrite a large part (sometimes all) of the cost. They can hold a special role, sometimes leadership in the local community, and their leadership and wealth help allow the fiesta to occur annually.

[11] Smith, *The Art of the Festival*, 110–11.

is the primary ceremony of the joyful aspect of the festival, bringing people together to share abundance and good-tasting food symbolic of the occasion."[12] Feasting in honor of La Virgen brings people together in a way distinct from other times during the year. The feasting is a concrete manifestation of human flourishing.[13]

Feasting provides an opportunity for locals to interact amongst themselves and also to interact with a broader pilgrim community. The mission of the people of Otuzco during the fiesta is to embrace hospitality. They offer their own homes as a place to stay, as well as food, for the thousands of pilgrims who visit during the fiesta. They also install improvised little kiosks that serve typical food of the region.[14] This offering of self in the form of life's basic necessities is part of how Otuzcanos enter into fiesta; it is also how they nourish the vulnerable humanity who descend upon their town, which facilitates their human flourishing.

The gente del pueblo (people of the town) accompany the pilgrims who come to honor La Virgen each year. The pueblo provides the festive foods for the celebration, which are often sweet treats, but it also provides substantive meals, platos típicos, from the local area as well. Otuzcanos work the land to provide for themselves during the rest of the calendar year, a true embrace of simplicity and vulnerability, but they work the land and provide in a special way for the many visitors who have made promises to La Virgen during the fiesta. In this way, they provide in abundance in order to outwardly promote the notion of human flourishing during the celebration. La Virgen de la Puerta provided for them in the midst of their vulnerability during the calendar year; to honor her, they provide for others.

In addition to eating, drinking is a unifying activity during the whole of the festival. Smith again provides an anthropological account of this: "Lasting as it does from beginning to the end of the celebration, it ties together the various activities that are limited in time to one, two or

---

[12] Smith, *The Art of the Festival*, 111.

[13] Psalms 65:12–13 provides a helpful language which supports what I mean by flourishing. "You adorn the year with your bounty; your paths drip with fruitful rain. The meadows of the wilderness also drip; the hills are robed with joy."

[14] "Durante los días de la fiesta, los pobladores de Otuzco se dedican a ofrecer alojamiento y comida a los miles de visitantes que llegan en estas fechas. También instalan puestos improvisados donde venden platos de la zona como el tradicional caldo de cabeza." Torres, *La Mamita de Otuzco*, 83.

214   *CAITLIN CIPOLLA-McCULLOCH*

three hours. The festival is a time of intense social interaction."[15] The manner of drinking is also important: one does not drink alone. It is a communal experience and one that evokes a certain kind of hospitality. The way this communal drinking occurs typically takes on one of two forms: the round and the toast. This chapter will explore the form of the round first. Either chicha or beer is used when drinking a round.[16]

Beer is typically consumed from a small clear glass. "The men stand or sit around in a circle and pass it from hand to hand."[17] With either beverage, "The gourd or glass is filled, the one drinking it raises it, says 'Salud' and drinks all that is in the cup. He gives the cup a shake, emptying the dregs onto the floor, refills it and passes it to the person on his right. The cup goes around counter-clockwise."[18] The toast is when people have separate glasses or gourds. "When the various drinkers each have a glass, they only drink together. When one person desires to drink he raises his glass, says 'Salud' to everyone else, raises his glass, replies 'Salud,' and then they all drink at once."[19] Whether from one common cup or from separate glasses, in both cases, drinking is a communal fiesta activity. Drinking is done in community, and it accompanies the celebration. Smith recounts, "The drinking continues from the time of the bajada until two, three, or four o'clock in the morning; for many it continues all night long."[20] The communal drinking that occurs exposes the community in a vulnerable way. The consumption of alcohol can, at times, emphasize personal vulnerability, but it also occurs in such a way that encourages the capacity for human flourishing, perhaps by having less anxiety or preoccupation in the midst of the popular

---

[15] Smith, *The Art of the Festival*, 114.

[16] In this case, we are mostly referring to chicha de jora, which is a fermented corn drink that has varying alcohol percentages and has been consumed by Andean peoples since the days of the Incan empire. There is also a chicha morada, which is made from purple corn and is not fermented. Chicha morada can also be experienced during the fiesta, but that is more typically served at restaurants that have a "menú" option for lunch. Importantly also, the fact that chicha is made from corn holds special significance for the People of the Triple Alliance who revered gods/goddesses of agriculture fertility. Of special mention in this group is Cinteotl, the maize god or goddess. See Joseph Kroger and Patrizia Granziera, *Aztec Goddesses and Christian Madonnas: Images of the Divine Feminine in Mexico* (Ashgate Publishing, 2012), 22.

[17] Smith, *The Art of the Festival*, 113.

[18] Smith, *The Art of the Festival*, 113.

[19] Smith, *The Art of the Festival*, 113.

[20] Smith, *The Art of the Festival*, 113.

LA FIESTA DE LA VIRGEN DE LA PUERTA 215

religious practice. Though the celebration has a punctuated calendar of events, people often complement the events with communal drinking and sometimes connect the many events together into one fluid or liminal time by partaking in alcohol. The opportunity for deep corporeal celebrations, where individuals bring all of who they are to celebratory activities, including drinking, illuminates the capacity for human flourishing encouraged by these sorts of cultic popular practices.

The fiesta de La Virgen de la Puerta is a corporeal celebration engaged through consumption of festive food and drink. The streets of Otuzco offer Otuzcanos and pilgrims who gather for the fiesta myriad options for sweet treats, and substantive meals throughout the celebration. Sweet treats and other festive offerings abound as the fiesta is a celebration meant to signify joy and abundance. The treats themselves manifest an excess, often characteristic of abundance and flourishing. In speaking about the celebration of a different image, one of *Cristo Aparecido* in Mexico, Jennifer Scheper Hughes, a historian of religion, offers, "Though foreigners may find the resulting experience [of fiesta] overwhelming, the intended effect on local people is to create a baroque sense of abundance and joyful exuberance that fills every space with color and sound."[21] The joyful abundance and exuberance physically manifest through the wide variety of food offerings that surround the church and fill the markets and the streets of Otuzco during the multiday celebration can be overwhelming, even as the festive offerings are a hallmark of the flourishing faith of the people of Otuzco and an offering to the many pilgrims who flock to the site. Otuzcanos engage in hospitality, nurturing the bodily needs and vulnerabilities of the thousands of pilgrims who fill their town once a year during the three-day fiesta to accompany La Virgen de la Puerta. The consumption of alcohol throughout the fiesta offers an opportunity for building community through sharing in a common toast or cup. Food and drink are an integral part of this time set aside from the ordinary, which fieles of La Virgen engage in each year.

The Mariology surrounding La Virgen de la Puerta was initially steeped in a Spanish understanding of Señora whereby Mary received the "highest and most excellent privilege" as Lady (Señora) and Queen to "be at the same throne as the divine Persons and to have a place in it,

---

[21] Jennifer Scheper Hughes, *Biography of a Mexican Crucifix* (Oxford University Press, 2010), 219.

as Empress, when all the rest" of humankind are servants of the supreme King (God).[22] What I have sought to express in terms of the theological significance of this particular fiesta is how the people of Otuzco have adapted the Spanish Mariology in a new time and space and with fidelity to their embraced vocations. Examination of the fiesta activities of the Otuzcanos illuminates a different theological reality than the Spanish Mariology of Mary as a distant queen. In the contemporary moment, for the people of Otuzco, Mary is in their midst and present alongside them. A concrete manifestation of who La Virgen de la Puerta is for the people of Otuzco is evident in the consideration of food and drink practices. Food and drink are essential corporeal features of daily life. La Virgen de la Puerta nurtures vulnerable humanity in daily life. She is proximal, not some distant reina. In celebration of her fiesta, she invites humankind to promote the flourishing of pilgrims who journey to the celebration. They, too, are in proximity with other pilgrims, offering food and drink, which, while simple, also connotes an intimacy when understood more broadly within the Christian tradition. While a comprehensive treatment of all elements of the fiesta is beyond the scope of this chapter, the focus on the corporeal practices surrounding food and drink has particularly exemplified the vulnerability and flourishing of humanity that are part of participating in fiesta.

Conclusion

The fiesta patronal of La Virgen de la Puerta is a celebration that highlights the vulnerability and flourishing of humanity, as seen in the festive celebrations of La Virgen with the pueblo Otuzcano in Northern Peru. The food and drink and the customs associated with these elements of the fiesta demonstrate the significance of how vulnerable humanity is nurtured by La Virgen and the people of Otuzco during the fiesta patronal. The presence of La Virgen de la Puerta with the vulnerable throng who gathers to honor her permits the expression of the flourishing popular devotion that has marked her celebration for over three centuries.

The fiesta de La Virgen de la Puerta itself is an activity of human

---

[22] María Jesús de Ágreda, *Vida de La Virgen María Según La Venerable Sor María Jesús de Ágreda* (Montaner y Simón, 1899), 364–65. Translated from Spanish by the author.

flourishing. It is an abundant celebration with festive food and drink. Both sweet treats and substantive meals permeate the community during the celebration. Streets are filled with temporary kitchens, which provide nourishment for the thousands of pilgrims who descend on Otuzco during the celebration. Otuzcanos are provided the opportunity to engage in hospitality, attending to the needs of the many pilgrims who bring their human vulnerabilities and fill the town of Otuzco once a year to accompany La Virgen de la Puerta.

The fiesta is an opportunity to visualize concretely the role La Virgen plays in the lives of her people. The festive food and drink, which are part of the celebration, provide corporeal sustenance to vulnerable participants in the fiesta as well as provide an opportunity for the community of Otuzco to engage in hospitality and celebrate abundance. The people are in close proximity with each other and La Virgen herself throughout the celebration. It is a time of intimacy. This three-day fiesta filled with popular devotion and with a manifestation of flourishing is an activity that is corporeal for both the people who celebrate as well as the image of Mary herself who is festively dressed and processed throughout Otuzco during the celebration.

One final note merits consideration in exploration of La Virgen de la Puerta and the themes of vulnerability and flourishing. While this chapter has primarily focused on her festival and how she tends to the needs of pilgrims, and pilgrims tend to her needs and the needs of others, it is important to recognize her ability to accompany and support those outside the celebration. The presence of La Virgen de la Puerta extends beyond the festival-goers and could offer implications for inclusion in the church. The celebration of La Virgen de la Puerta illuminates the specific relationship between La Virgen and her people. Beyond the festival, she cares for people who are excluded by society and the church, the vulnerable, promoting their flourishing.[23] Congruent with an understanding of the image of God's abundance, characterized in Psalm 65 as bounty dripping with fruitful rain, we see how, both in and beyond the fiesta, La Virgen de la Puerta embodies abundance. Though beyond the scope of my argument in this chapter, this broader impact is a relevant pastoral concern for further exploration.

---

[23] Torres states that outside the fiesta, La Virgen de la Puerta more broadly accompanies different groups. She engages the particularly vulnerable, those on the margins, including the sick, people who are queer or trans, migrants, and farmers. Torres, *La Mamita de Otuzco,* 195.

Paradoxical Flourishing

Theology as Embraced Vulnerability

Richard Lennan

In his 1937 book *Le Saulchoir: A School of Theology*, Marie-Dominique Chenu details the methodology and guiding spirit of the faculty that exiled French Dominicans established in Belgium in 1904. Far more than a biography of an institution, Chenu's text is a dissertation on the relationship between history and theology, an inquiry into how the former influences the latter, and a review of possible theological responses to the ebb and flow of history. Chenu sketches two historical milieux, one stable and one volatile, whose contrasting social and intellectual conditions provide the seedbed for contrasting forms of theology.

Situations marked more by constancy than flux enable theologians to pursue calmly what Chenu terms "the homogeneous elaboration and constructive evaluation of powerful original perceptions."[1] When faith is uncontested and existing hermeneutical frameworks are able to absorb new questions, theologians can be sure-footed and composed, proceeding confidently to articulate insights consistent with time-honored expressions of faith and religious practice. Theologians in these settings tend also to work together harmoniously, often encouraged and supported by the unifying commitments of an identifiable "school." While the absence of theological turbulence has a certain

---

[1] Marie-Dominique Chenu, *A School of Theology: Le Saulchoir*, trans. Joseph Komonchak and Mary Kate Holman (ATF Press, 2023), 19.

PARADOXICAL FLOURISHING

appeal, Chenu recognizes that the circumstances conducive to tranquility are never permanent. Accordingly, when "new cultural, literary, aesthetic, intellectual, and religious movements" transform "the climate and techniques of a milieu," much that had seemed to be certain and clear begins to lose its aura of invulnerability.[2]

The shift from solidity to fluidity disrupts theology no less than other disciplines. If theologians in this new situation are to do justice to what Chenu names the "human and Christian 'presence' which, in the light of faith, gives the work of the mind the freshness of continuous creation," they must exercise their craft with imagination and creativity, offering more than cosmetic adjustments to prevailing methods for expounding and communicating faith.[3] Amplifying the magnitude of this task is the fact that social change can cause ruptures among the community of theologians. This happens when conflicting perspectives lead theologians to cluster in rival "camps," rather than in diverse yet complementary schools.

As his model for creative theologizing in periods of social and ecclesial disruption, Chenu showcases the response of Thomas Aquinas to the ferment of the twelfth and thirteenth centuries. Thomas's constructive synthesis of Aristotelian thought and Christian theology demonstrated that historical change and unfamiliar ways of thinking are not invariably hostile to inherited faith. By presenting new vistas onto the expansive capacity of faith, Thomas showed that established theologies had not exhausted the adaptive capacity of Christian life, nor of the God who is its inspiration.

A measure of Thomas's creative genius, at least by way of contrast, is that more than a few of his contemporaries reacted to the tectonic shifts convulsing their religious world by pursuing what Chenu categorizes as forms of theology that "cease to be open to new sets of problems and to the progress of methods."[4] Chenu's contention is that a theology that closes itself to emerging questions loses its vigor and becomes defensive. When this occurs, he maintains, theology as a discipline "rests on its acquired conclusions and fails to return to its principles whose purity

---

[2] Chenu, *A School of Theology*, 9.
[3] Chenu, *A School of Theology*, 9.
[4] Chenu, *A School of Theology*, 9.

220   *RICHARD LENNAN*

might enable it to remain 'contemporary.'"[5] In such a setting, the desire for invulnerability triumphs over grace-endowed creativity.

Beyond its option for timidity over creativity, defensiveness leaches theology of its capacity to offer support and guidance to members of the community of faith as they seek to navigate the uncertainty affecting their society and church. Exponents of a more defensive theology might enjoy endorsements from within the church and academy, as was true for Thomas's critics, yet Chenu leaves little doubt that defensiveness among theologians is a disservice to the future of faith. Nonetheless, the fact that some of Thomas's colleagues at the University of Paris, his Dominican superiors, and officeholders in the wider church rejected his theological synthesis is indicative of the tension that can exist between defensiveness and creativity in theology, between the former's desire for a refuge from change and the openness of the latter to questions that presage the possibility of change.

Since myriad cultural shifts and multiple centuries separate today's theology from the contested contemporary reception of Thomas Aquinas, we might hope that the intervening period has nurtured attitudes more congenial to theological creativity. Could it be that ecclesial DNA has evolved in recent centuries to accept that the constructive practice of theology in changing times must necessarily exceed tweaks to existing paradigms of thought and action? Could it also be that later creative approaches to the ongoing reception of tradition in circumstances more fluid than fixed, approaches like that of Le Saulchoir itself, have received scholarly and ecclesial support, however measured and nuanced, rather than condemnation?

Alas, the fate of Chenu's little book tempers this hope: in 1942, Chenu's *Le Saulchoir* was placed on the Catholic Church's *Index of Forbidden Books.*[6] Nor, of course, was Chenu the last theologian to face ecclesial censure, loss of employment, or, to update the variety of constraints that theologians might experience, trolling on social media.

The negative reception of Thomas, of Chenu, and of so many other theologians throughout the church's history indicates that creative theology is vulnerable to more than the vicissitudes of history. This

---

[5] Chenu, *A School of Theology*, 9.

[6] For the narrative surrounding the reception of Chenu's work, see Joseph Komonchak's introduction to Chenu, *A School of Theology*, xxxv–xlvi.

PARADOXICAL FLOURISHING 221

vulnerability inevitably owes much to the murky cocktail that blends narrow perspectives on God's action in history with envy, lack of understanding, and fear. The nontheological factors underscore that neither the production of theology nor its reception ever takes place in an atmosphere of unalloyed intellectual virtue and ecclesial holiness. This truth notwithstanding, the thesis of this chapter is that *vulnerability is the intimate companion of theology*. Moreover, the text will contend that theology's relationship to vulnerability would exist even if all denizens of the academy and church were saintly figures motivated exclusively by unimpeachable integrity and boundless fidelity to the gospel of Jesus Christ and the grace of the Holy Spirit.

To make the case for its thesis, this chapter will first argue that the incompleteness of history expresses, even perhaps is sacramental of, creation's eschatological orientation. In other words, since the transcendent God is the ultimate subject of theology, no theology, of whatever political or ecclesial stripe, will ever pronounce the definitive word about God, illuminate without remainder the dynamics of God's presence to creation, or fashion an exhaustive accounting of faith in God. This incompleteness similarly denies to theologians the right to claim that today's theology will certainly answer tomorrow's questions. Engagement with God, therefore, locates vulnerability not at the margins of theology but at its center.

Second, and related, there is the vulnerability that arises from the communal dimension of Christianity, specifically from the fact that the church is not, and will never be, an artifact of our own design. This consideration negates the legitimacy of any theological claim to a new and improved Christian faith or to a church reinvented *ex nihilo*. Less dramatically, the existence of the ecclesial community across times and cultures invalidates any equation of the church with the preferences of a single "party," worldview, or context. God's transcendence, which renders God ungraspable while also being the source of the church, likewise disrupts every claim to finality for ecclesial structures, and even for theologies seeking to reform those structures.

Since encounter with the ungraspable God is constitutive of theology, it could appear that frustration, rather than thriving, is likely to be the category most applicable to theologians. In response to this perception, this chapter will claim that vulnerability and thriving exist in a paradoxical relationship. Beyond implying that vulnerability and

222   *RICHARD LENNAN*

thriving are not directly opposed, the invocation of "paradox" alludes to the possibility that vulnerability might be integral to the thriving of theologians.

This paradox intimates that theology and theologians could thrive even in circumstances that seem, at first blush, to be more demanding than comforting, more testing than affirming. For this to be so, "thriving" must convey something other than a care-free life. Equally, if thriving in relation to doing theology is to resonate with everyday understandings of well-being, then the thriving of theology and theologians must refer to something other than heroic endurance in the face of unrelenting misery. In order that the concept of theological thriving might not remain a chimera, an aspiration of this chapter is to illuminate something of the possible dimensions and contours of such thriving, doing so without eliminating the vulnerability intrinsic to theology.

A final prefatory note: I write as a systematic theologian not a clinician. Consequently, the treatment of both vulnerability and thriving in this text prescinds from factors proper to medical, psychological, or explicitly pastoral analyses. While neither oblivious nor indifferent to the painful realities of human suffering that "vulnerability" conveys, especially when suffering results from injustice and violence, my presentation employs the term in a specific way. Here, "vulnerability" functions as a window onto the incompleteness intrinsic to humanity's relationship with the incomprehensible God.

For theologians *qua* theologians, this incompleteness affects every effort to articulate an understanding of God, of faith in God, and of the dynamics of the ecclesial community, including its participation in the world. Consequently, no theology, as creative, well-crafted, and insightful as it might be, will eliminate every present-day question. Nor, even more certainly, will any theological formulations ensure that there will be no future questions that require research, reflection, and imagination.

The focus on God and the church gives a specifically theological framing to the discussion of vulnerability. It connects vulnerability to the fact that human beings, and so theologians, are indeed human rather than divine. This fact might well carry the potential to inflict a degree of woundedness, at least on the unbridled ego, but my conviction is that this type of woundedness can be a path to thriving. And so,

PARADOXICAL FLOURISHING

to the first form of vulnerability: theology as talking about God within an unfinished history.

The Vulnerability of Historicity

The tenth chapter of the Acts of the Apostles introduces Cornelius, a Roman centurion. Inspired by a vision, Cornelius seeks an encounter with Simon Peter; through this encounter, Cornelius receives the Holy Spirit and is baptized (Acts 10:1–48 NRSV). This event would appear to be good news for the fledgling Christian community, a manifestation of the power of the Spirit to form disciples of Christ among those who were outside the law. In fact, as we know, the baptism of Cornelius provokes an existential crisis for the church. The crisis arises from a fear that the inclusion of Gentile converts would rupture the continuity of such an expanded community with the long history of faith in the God of the covenants that was particular to the people of Israel.

Whether we regard it as shocking that such a crisis convulsed the Christian community after only nine chapters of Acts or remarkable that no similar crisis occurred before the end of chapter nine, the baptism of Cornelius records the church's initial experience of the challenge posed by questions arising from unanticipated events. The capacity of this challenge to roil the church remains undiminished. Confirmation for this assertion is abundantly evident in present-day controversies over liturgical forms and access to ordination, processes of decision-making in the church, and proposals for the fuller inclusion of groups underrepresented in various facets of the church's life because of race, gender, or sexual orientation. In all these instances, the ecclesial community lacks a way of proceeding that smoothly aligns new questions with existing answers or enables turmoil-free adjustment of beliefs and practices when appropriate.

Disruption resulting from new questions reverberates in the theological community as in the wider church, often challenging the comfort of all practitioners. To embrace the questions requires acceptance of the vulnerability attendant on the willingness to dwell in the uncertainty the questions foster. This vulnerability expands when disputed questions are politically charged, as is true today. In partisan times, openness to questions arouses suspicion that theology has succumbed to the blandishments of contemporary thought over received truth. This

224   *RICHARD LENNAN*

suspicion metastasizes if theological reflection results in proposals for reconsideration of any elements of the church's life regarded as having been settled by divine ordinance.

Political differences usually absorb a disproportionate amount of oxygen, in the church as in civil society. It is crucial, therefore, that theologians maintain their focus on the theological import of the questions, engaging with the possible shape of authentic responses to God rather than solely with the narrowly political implications of disputed questions. Theology matters as new questions, while disruptive, can be portals of grace. Questions can help to expand our understanding of God and spark more generous responses to other people, in whom grace is also at work. In these ways, the questions can facilitate thriving. Since grace, like the wind, "blows where it will" (Jn 3:8), it invites rather than commands. Thus, attentiveness to what Karl Rahner terms "the perhaps possible possibility of a revelation" will always require more than a cursory assessment of new questions.[7]

When theologians ignore new questions or dismiss them without a genuine hearing, they render theology irrelevant to the life and mission of the contemporary church. They are also in danger of ignoring the *sensus fidelium*, which is so often the seedbed for new questions. Conversely, proceeding too quickly to propose changes can carry the presumption that grace will always confirm our own worldview, rather than being a stimulus for its expansion. The willingness to wrestle with the questions can be a profession of faith in the God who exceeds our grasp, and so too our best ideas. This act of faith can also be an agent of vulnerability, especially when it is far from immediately clear what responses to the questions might be reconcilable with the living tradition of faith or further its creative rereception.

Anticipating a theme from this chapter's next section, it is important to underscore that a corollary of faith in the ungraspable God is that theologians are not free, either individually or collectively, to devise the faith of the church as if it did not precede them. Since the church does not begin anew in every year, century, or millennium, each generation of the ecclesial community is always the receiver of all that preceded it—the good, the bad, and the indifferent. While inherited faith means

---

[7] Karl Rahner, "The Ignatian Mysticism of Joy in the World," in *Theological Investigations*, vol. 3, trans. K.-H. & B. Kruger (Crossroad, 1982), 284.

that creativity in theology can never be an unbounded absolute, the eschatological dimension of that faith always renders faith open to fuller realization.[8]

The impetus for this development is the fact that each generation of the ecclesial community lives with questions unique to its experience. Engaging this uniqueness will rarely produce a perfect echo of the ways in which previous generations expressed and lived their faith, even though it is the same faith. What must be paramount, then, is a commitment to discern what "the Spirit of truth" (Jn 16:13) might be enabling in the here-and-now as an authentic reception of the faith that none of us initiates. Living and working within this space qualifies as acceptance of vulnerability, but theology and theologians cannot thrive without doing so.

While Catholic theology is no stranger to the tension between the past and the present, it thrives when theologians seek, as the British scholar Clare Watkins expresses it, "to speak *truthfully* about concrete realities and *faithfully* about the historical and present promise of the work of the Spirit, enlivening what we understand to be 'the body of Christ', the church."[9] Watkins's contemporary description of the task of theology in relation to the past and the present resonates with what Rahner wrote seventy years ago: "No real achievement is ever lost to the Church. But theologians are never spared the task of prompt renewal. Anything which is merely conserved, or which is merely handed down without a fresh, personal exertion, beginning at the very sources of Revelation, rots as the manna did."[10]

Theologians are not repositories of easy answers to difficult questions. Even so, theologians can model for the wider ecclesial community the conviction that a life-giving faith need not fear entry into uncharted territory. This faith aims not to eliminate God's mystery or to suppress its ripples in an ever-changing world but to respond as creatively as possible to its summons in history, doing so in dialogue with the ecclesial

---

[8] On the "bounded openness" of the tradition of faith, see Serene Jones, *Feminist Theory and Christian Theology: Cartographies of Grace* (Fortress, 2000), 170.

[9] Clare Watkins et al., "Practical Ecclesiology: What Counts as Theology in Studying the Church?," in *Perspectives on Ecclesiology and Ethnography*, ed. Pete Ward (Eerdmans Publishing, 2012), 168; original emphasis.

[10] Karl Rahner, "The Prospects for Dogmatic Theology," in *Theological Investigations*, vol. 1, trans. C. Ernst (Crossroad, 1982), 10.

226 *RICHARD LENNAN*

community's living tradition, the needs of the present, and the faith of the whole church, including its mediation through official teaching. This way of proceeding disrupts a quiet life, but it does reflect what it means to participate in a Spirit-formed community that is both a body composed of "varieties of gifts" (1 Cor 12:4) and is a pilgrim to the fullness of God.

Many disputes in the life of the church cast the past against the present, settled truths against emerging insights. Both stances are inadequate to the extent that they leave the future out of consideration, and so neglect the fact that God's fulfilled reign is "already ... but not yet." Well over a century ago, Maurice Blondel proposed a formula by which the church, and so theologians, might be faithful to the movement of grace while also doing justice to the complexity of history: "With the help of the past," he wrote, "[the church] liberates the future from the unconscious limitations and illusions of the present."[11] To the degree that theologians employ this formula, the inescapable specter of vulnerability notwithstanding, they aid not only their own thriving but that of the ecclesial community, the topic for this chapter's second half.

The Vulnerability of Ecclesial Theology

Vulnerability to the mystery of God gives a certain nobility to theology amidst the incompleteness of history. The banning of Chenu's *Le Saulchoir*, on the other hand, might typify for many Catholics, especially in the academy, a more jarring facet of the profile of theology and theologians in the church. The censure of Chenu, which continued the repressive stance adopted by Catholic authorities during the Modernist crisis, represents something of a long-standing default response toward theologians exploring the terrain that new questions open. As noted earlier, such defensiveness, along with the suspicion and restrictive policing it breeds, can be inimical to acknowledgment of the creative fidelity of theologians.

It could appear, then, that the work of theologians would be freer and more appealing if those exercising power in the church abandoned restrictive practices. While a more constructive relationship between bishops and theologians is surely desirable, it would be injudicious to

---

[11] Maurice Blondel, "History and Dogma," in *The Letter on Apologetics and History and Dogma*, trans. A. Dru and I. Trethowan (Holt, Rinehart and Winston, 1964), 281–82.

PARADOXICAL FLOURISHING 227

assume that this or any other single reform would either usher in the millennium of freedom and thriving for theologians or ensure that no theological formulation would ever again need refinement, let alone fail to be compatible with the faith of the church. Accordingly, my contention in this section of the chapter is that the primary restraint on theologians within the ecclesial community issues not from the church's authorities, but from the particularity of the church as a community of faith. This particularity, the product of the interplay between God's transcendence and God self-revelation in history, identifies the church as a specific body, as *this* community, one in which we all participate but do not initiate. The argument here is that the church's specificity can be a gift to theology, albeit one with its own complexity and challenges.

The church's grounding in God's revelation mediated through a community in history endows theology with the potential to thrive through ever-deeper exploration of God and the implications of faith for life in the world. This grounding is also, simultaneously and paradoxically, the seat of vulnerability for all theology's practitioners. As Rahner acknowledges—in the key of paradox—communal faith is "humbling" because it refuses my claim to be the sole authoritative source for the interpretation and practice of faith, but it is nonetheless "liberating" as it opens my understanding and practice to resources inaccessible within the limits of my single lifetime.[12]

As a community of faith, the church is particular among all associations of people as it has its origin and draws its ongoing sustenance from God's self-revelation in Jesus and the Holy Spirit. Since the church is other than an exclusively human endeavor, it can never be simply "my" church, or even "our" church but only ever "God's church." Through God's intention, the church is unique. Vatican II's *Lumen Gentium* encapsulates this uniqueness in its opening statement: the church is "like a sacrament (*veluti sacramentum*)—a sign and instrument, that is, of communion with God and of the unity of the entire human race."[13] Sacramentality is the epitome of particularity; it differentiates the ecclesial community from a human project whose every element is fungible.

Since the self-giving of God that brings about the church is not a dis-

---

[12] Karl Rahner, "Dogmatic Notes on 'Ecclesiological Piety,'" in *Theological Investigations*, vol. 5, trans. K.-H. Kruger (Crossroad, 1983), 347.

[13] Pope Paul VI, *Lumen Gentium* (1964), no. 1. Quotations from the council's texts come from Austin Flannery, ed., *Vatican Council II: Constitutions, Decrees, Declarations; The Basic Sixteen Documents* (Liturgical Press, 2014).

crete event of the past, grace is the lifeblood of the church in every age. This claim differs from any suggestion that grace provides a blueprint for the church's frictionless movement through history or, as argued earlier, that grace abrogates any need for the ecclesial community and its theologians to confront difficult questions whose specifications exceed existing answers. Even more crucially, grace furnishes members of the church with no immunity to sin, complacency, or apathy. Rather than a magical force, the abiding gift of the Spirit prompts and supports the Christian community's pilgrimage, beckoning the church, through history's variability, to discerned faithfulness in the life of discipleship. Theologians, steeped in the living memory of the tradition, attentive to the density of the present, and alert to the Spirit's call from the future, can aid the community's discernment of authentic responses to grace.

While the authenticity of the church depends on conformity to the gospel, the likelihood that it will be the gospel that shapes the life of the church in any time or place is not guaranteed. Thus, a positive response to the Spirit implies openness to conversion, the need for which is an indelible aspect of the pilgrim community's unfinished reality. Conversion as an imperative further showcases the paradox of ecclesial thriving: conversion can be freeing but is always decentering, calling into question every sense of superiority and invulnerability. The fact is that all members of the church, irrespective of position or circumstance, are addressees of the summons to conversion, which can be a catalyst for connecting "us" and "them." Only a church whose every member values the struggle for unity over the comfort of division can hope to be transparent to grace and so truly sacramental. This is surely a crucial ingredient for a synodal community.

Theologians, of course, share in the call to conversion and so share in this aspect of the vulnerability proper to the whole church. In reflecting on the forms of conversion applicable to the guild of theologians, Sarah Coakley suggests that it is humility, which she defines as the practice of providing "patient, rational, and nonaggressive accounts of one's own theological position," while also "engaging others' varying, and vying, accounts of [truth]," that can best exhibit theologians' openness to God and acceptance of their own limitations.[14]

---

[14] Sarah Coakley, "Theological Scholarship as Religious Vocation," *Christian Higher Education* 5 (2006): 66.

The second aspect of ecclesial particularity relevant to the work of theology is that God's church is never less than a community of diverse people. This community differs from a random association of otherwise unrelated individuals, yet it is also dissimilar to a gated enclave of the like-minded, one consisting only of those who endorse unreservedly the biases of gatekeepers. As a result, theological visions for well-ordered ecclesial life miss the mark, if they mistake seamless sameness for the preferences of the God who "makes the sun rise on the evil and on the good" (Mt 5:45).

God's radical inclusivity, manifested in unrestricted access to baptism, fosters a church whose defining feature will be a messy liveliness, not a bland neatness. This complexity, reflective of the pluriformity that grace engenders, signals ecclesiologists to be alert to the danger of presuming that a community of clones could ever be a fruitful model of the church. Since defense of diversity differs from endorsing division, theology pursued in and through the ecclesial community, theology that aims at the creatively faithful reception of the living tradition in the emerging circumstances of the present, will almost certainly carry the potential for arousing both support and opposition, as discussed earlier. This potential illuminates the vulnerability of theology, but what of its thriving? A broader and deeper commitment to the synodal experience of the Catholic Church may open a path to this thriving, but it is a path that will need to be built as it is walked rather than one that is already exhaustively surveyed, well-maintained, and fully illuminated.

Synodality offers an epochal opportunity for the church to make decisions about the characteristics of faithfulness in this moment of history. These decisions will have implications for all facets of the ecclesial community's life, including the practice of theology. The processes of synodality have their source in attention to the Spirit. For this reason, Pope Francis stresses that "a synodal Church is a Church that listens; listening is a reciprocal listening in which everyone—faithful people, episcopal college, Bishop of Rome—has something to learn, each one listening to the others, and all listening to the Holy Spirit."[15] Synodality, accordingly, privileges the Spirit-formed equality and unity of the baptized above any prerogatives of rank or office. It seeks, too,

---

[15] Pope Francis, "Address on the Fiftieth Anniversary of the Synod of Bishops" (2015).

230 *RICHARD LENNAN*

to build a church better reflective of the grace proper to the "already . . . but not yet" of God's Reign. This outcome requires the conscious appropriation of the church's catholicity, its existence as other than a community of sameness.

The synodal vision, especially as Pope Francis has progressively articulated it in the last several years, is compelling. It remains to be seen, of course, whether there will be a thoroughgoing appropriation of synodality across the church and how such an appropriation might change the Catholic Church, might further and enhance the thriving of the church's mission and members. Rather than speculate on these issues, I would like to raise a subsidiary topic, one that currently has only a low profile in synodal discussions: What is the role of theology and theologians in a synodal church? The Synthesis Report from the synod session in October 2023 nominates "theological formation" as a building block for a properly synodal church, and Pope Francis in 2023 provided an opening for a broad discussion of the theological vocation in his *Motu Proprio* on theology.[16] These are positive steps, but the synod document offers no details on what theological formation might involve and how it could take place, while Pope Francis's text is still not available in English.

Theologians have always been part of the ecclesial landscape, but their place in portraits of that landscape has often been either blurred or marginal. It is noteworthy that while there has been widespread discussion of how synodality can accommodate the particularity of gender, sexual orientation, and popular piety, there has been scant attention paid to theology as a distinct facet of the church's life, and even less discussion of the ways in which theology and theologians might contribute to enhancing synodality. This observation is not a plea for a takeover of synodality by professional theologians but a recognition that the place of theology in a synodal church remains unclear. This lacuna exists even though synodality, if it is to be other than a parliamentary process, will thrive through theological articulations of the identity and mission of the ecclesial community as a body of baptized disciples.[17]

---

[16] *A Synodal Church in Mission: Synthesis Report* (2023), pt. 3, art. 14e; https://www.synod.va/en/synodal-process/the-universal-phase/documents.html. Pope Francis's *Motu Proprio, Ad Theologiam Promovendam* (2023).

[17] For the contribution and reception of theology within Australia's Plenary

PARADOXICAL FLOURISHING **231**

My claim here is that "the church," interpreted broadly, does not have a shared understanding of the role of theology. This absence is as detrimental to the thriving of the ecclesial community as it is to the thriving of theologians. Asking how theologians might share their gifts in the wider church is a worthwhile question at every moment of the church's life, but it is one that the synodal moment makes urgent. The twenty-first century is not the patristic age, not the period of monastic theologians, and not even the era of the still-spectacular contributions of theologians at Vatican II, so it is crucial to inquire how contemporary theology might be of service to today's ecclesial community. Without a shared commitment to this inquiry, the broad gap presently existing between the theological academy and various facets of ecclesial life, including everyday piety and episcopal authority in the church, will remain.[18]

Advocating for reliable bridges between theologians and the wider church does not gloss over the gloomy history of institutional responses to theology. It does not ignore the fact that officials in the church, and even members across the church, have often disregarded and suspected theologians, rather than welcomed and encouraged them. The direction of this negativity tends toward women theologians, lay theologians as a cohort, theologians doing their work attentive to a variety of minority voices, and every theologian open to questions that affect the reception of tradition. Although grace and the spirit of synodality do not require that theologians discount this history, they do invite the theological guild to ask what a more constructive relationship to the ecclesial community, even to its episcopal authorities, might require of us, not merely of everyone else. Doing so can be an acknowledgment of both our own need for conversion and the gift that is participation in the community of faith.

A synod on the role of theology in the life of the church could be the best way to address comprehensively the myriad issues that this topic raises. Such a synod would be possible and effective only through shared vulnerability, but it could also facilitate shared thriving. The

---

Council (2018–22), see Richard Lennan, "The Plenary Council as a Practice of Theology," *Australasian Catholic Record* 100 (2023): 3–24.

[18] For the tension that can exist between theology as ecclesial and as part of the academy, see Coakley, "Theological Scholarship as Religious Vocation," 55–68, and Alister McGrath, *The Future of Christianity* (Wiley-Blackwell, 2002), 120–54.

notion of a synod on theology might sound decidedly quixotic, or one whose realization is unimaginable this side of the eschaton. Whatever the prospects of such a proposal, there is a present need for renewed exploration of what it means to be a theologian in the ecclesial community. Without a shared understanding of this vocation, and a shared process for considering it, it may be that theologians will become less ecclesial and the church less formed and informed by theology. Neither outcome is conducive to the thriving of the church's mission or of theologians.

This chapter has maintained that theology's grounding in the mystery of God represents for all practitioners the ultimate source for both theology's vulnerability and its thriving. Fruitful engagement with the mystery of God is inseparable from attentiveness to the various ways that grace has already nurtured the life of the ecclesial community. In addition, it requires sensitivity to the present-day movement of grace as the pilgrimage of faith unfolds in unanticipated forms. Theologians participate in this pilgrimage while also offering resources for it. These resources, which derive from sharing in the life of the church, no less than from research and writing, are at the service of the church. This ecclesial mission speaks to the need for a continuous retrieval of the ecclesial dimension of theology, for reconciliation between the church's authorities and theologians, and for a renewed appreciation of theology as a gift to the church.

The crisis sparked by the baptism of Cornelius dissipated when sound theological reasoning, communal discernment, and creative leadership all converged. To affirm authoritatively the outcomes of that convergence, the apostle James used a phrase that even today is nothing less than stunning: "it has seemed good to the Holy Spirit and to us" (Acts 15:28). That is the voice of a thriving community, one unafraid of vulnerability. It remains a conviction that can encourage, challenge, and inspire us even as we, like our ancestors in faith, experience the paradoxes inseparable from the pilgrimage of faith.

Contributors

Elise Abshire is a PhD student in theology at the University of Dayton. Her master's thesis research was on Teresa of Avila and disability. Elise has published in *Church Life Journal*, and while her focus of research is usually in theological disability studies, her other areas of interest include examining different spaces of vocation within the church, hagiographical writing styles, as well as Mardi Gras and the liturgical life.

James T. Bretzke, SJ, is professor of moral theology at John Carroll University. Prior to coming to John Carroll in 2019 he taught for a quarter century in Jesuit graduate theology centers in Berkeley, Boston, Manila, and Rome, as well as other Jesuit schools in Korea and the US. He is the author of numerous scholarly articles, reviews, and books, and, most recently in 2025, *Moral Debates in Contemporary Catholic Thought: Paradigms, Principles, and Prudence.*

Cynthia L. Cameron is the Patrick and Barbara Keenan Chair of Religious Education and associate professor of religious education at the University of St. Michael's College at the University of Toronto. Her research focuses on adolescence, developmental psychology, and practices of Catholic religious education. Among her recent work is *Nobody's Perfect: Redefining Sin and Mistakes in Adolescent Christian Education,* coedited with Lakisha Lockhart-Rusch and Emily Peck, forthcoming from Fortress Press in 2025.

Caitlin Cipolla-McCulloch is a doctoral candidate at the University of Dayton. She holds two bachelor's degrees from the University of Dayton and a master's degree from Mt. St. Mary's Seminary and School of Theology. Her research areas engage intersections of Latin American studies and theology, Mariology, and the Marianist Charism. Caitlin's dissertation is tentatively titled "Mary as Nurturer: A New Model for

234 CONTRIBUTORS

Contemporary Times." She works at the North American Center for Marianist Studies (NACMS).

Anthony V. Coloma is a Catholic priest from the Diocese of Maitland-Newcastle in Australia. He is chaplain of San Clemente High School (Mayfield) and Catherine McAuley Catholic College (Medowie). He also serves as associate priest for the City Pastoral Region in Newcastle. He received his Master of Theology from the Sydney College of Divinity and concurrently earned his STL from the Catholic Institute of Sydney. He is currently doing research studies at the University of Notre Dame Australia.

Cristofer Fernández, OFM Conv., is a Conventual Franciscan of Our Lady of the Angels (East Coast) Province. He is a religious brother with a background in conservation science and field ecology, and is a contingent scholar interested in ecotheology, decoloniality, and peace and justice studies. Brother Cristofer works with the poor houseless and migrants of Syracuse, NY, at Franciscan Northside Ministries. He also serves as cochair of his province's JPIC commission.

Alaina Keller is a doctoral student in the Department of Theology and Religious Studies at Georgetown University. Based in the field of comparative theology, she studies points of encounter between Catholicism and Buddhism, and she is writing her dissertation on Catholic and Buddhist approaches to the Virgin Mary as "handmaid."

Barbara Anne Kozee is a PhD student in theological ethics at Boston College. Barb completed her M.Div. at Jesuit School of Theology of Santa Clara University with a certificate in women's studies in religion. Her research focuses on issues of gender, sexuality, culture, and politics with an emphasis on interdisciplinary and qualitative methods.

Richard Lennan is a priest of the diocese of Maitland-Newcastle (Australia). He is a professor of systematic theology in the Clough School of Theology and Ministry at Boston College, where he also chairs the Ecclesiastical Faculty. He holds a Master of Philosophy from the University of Oxford and a doctorate in theology from the University of Innsbruck (Austria); his dissertation was on Karl Rahner's ecclesiology. Richard's most recent book is *Tilling the Church: Theology for an*

Unfinished Project (Liturgical Press, 2022). His forthcoming publication *Karl Rahner's Spiritual Theology*, Classics in Western Spirituality series, is coedited with Peter Fritz (Paulist Press).

Cristina Lledo Gomez is Senior Lecturer in Theology and Presentation Sisters Chair at BBI–The Australian Institute of Theological Education. She is also research fellow for the Australian Centre for Christianity and Culture, Charles Sturt University. Cristina is the author of *The Church as Woman and Mother: Historical and Theological Foundations* (2018), coeditor of *500 Years of Christianity in the Philippines: Postcolonial Perspectives* with Agnes Brazal and Ma. Marilou Ibita (2024), and *Divine Interruptions: Maternal Theologies and Experiences* with Julia Brumbaugh (2025).

Susan McElcheran is a doctoral candidate in theology at Regis St. Michael's College, University of Toronto, and holds doctoral fellowships from the Louisville Institute and the Social Science and Humanities Research Council of Canada. Her research focuses on the intersection of intellectual disability studies and the Christian mystical tradition. Her work has been published in the *Toronto Journal of Theology* and is forthcoming in *Contagion: Journal of Violence, Mimesis, and Culture.*

Brett McLaughlin, SJ, is a doctoral candidate in systematic theology at Boston College. His doctoral dissertation project, "Reign over Envy: The Kingdom of God's Subversion of Conflictual Desire" is an expansion of his 2020 STL dissertation on René Girard and Raymund Schwager's hypothesis of desire, envy, conflict, and the Christ-event.

Stephen Okey is an associate professor of theology at Saint Leo University in Saint Leo, Florida. He earned his master's degree in theology from the University of Chicago Divinity School and his PhD in systematic theology from Boston College. He is the author of *A Theology of Conversation: An Introduction to David Tracy*, published in 2018 with Liturgical Press Academic. His research interests are in public theology, Catholic social teaching, and technology.

Alfred Kah Meng Pang has a PhD in theology and education from Boston College. Born and residing in Singapore, he is currently an adjunct lecturer and independent researcher. He researches and writes on spirituality and ethics in Catholic education, with a focus on Lasallian spirituality and pedagogy. He is also engaged in the Archdiocese of Singapore as a consultant and trainer at workshops forming parish leaders to do adult faith formation, as well as teachers and school leaders for the mission of Catholic education. Alongside this passion for faith formation is his commitment toward LGBTQ inclusion in churches and schools. He is the coordinator of the LGBTQ-Allies Working Group in the Religious Education Association. He is also currently involved in a Catholic ministry to LGBTQ Christians in Singapore

John N. Sheveland is a Catholic theologian with a range of interests including interreligious dialogue, safeguarding, and synodality. He is a professor of religious studies at Gonzaga University in Spokane, WA. John holds a PhD in Systematic and Comparative Theology from Boston College. He is editor of *Theology in a Post-Traumatic Church* (Orbis, 2023). He has served on the USCCB National Review Board since 2019 and on the boards of the College Theology Society and Society for Buddhist-Christian Studies. He is a book review editor for *Horizons: Journal of the College Theology Society.* His articles have appeared in a variety of journals and books. John is also the author of *Piety and Responsibility* (Ashgate, 2011; Routledge, 2017).

Jason Steidl Jack is a gay Catholic theologian and assistant teaching professor of religious studies at St. Joseph's University New York. His research and advocacy focus on the history of LGBTQ Catholic ministry in the US Catholic Church. His first book, *LGBTQ Catholic Ministry: Past and Present*, was published by Paulist Press in 2023.

Callie Tabor is assistant professor of Catholic studies at Sacred Heart University (Fairfield, CT). She earned an MA (Hons) from the University of St. Andrews, an MA from Durham University, and a PhD in theological studies from Emory University. Her research interests include theological aesthetics and feminist theology. Previously she worked as associate director of the Aquinas Center of Theology at Emory University.

Katherine Tarrant is a PhD candidate in the University of Virginia's Department of Religious Studies. Her research interests emerge at the intersection between ecological ethics and the Catholic Social Teaching tradition, where she explores contemporary ecotheologies, traditional constructions of humanity vs. animality, and moral theologies of inter-species relationality. Her thesis work traces the historical and theological roots of contemporary eco-ethical debate in the Catholic Church.

Christopher Welch is assistant professor of religious studies at Rivier University, where he teaches a broad range of courses. He is the coauthor with Cynthia L. Cameron of *Life Abundant: God and the Created Order in Catholic Social Perspective*. His teaching and research interests include the relationship among faith, work, leisure, and consumption. He is a faculty fellow of the Network for Vocation in Undergraduate Education.

C. Vanessa White, OFS, is a professed Secular Franciscan and a tenured associate professor of spirituality and ministry at Catholic Theological Union in Chicago where she is director of the Certificate in Black Theology and Ministry. She is also associate director of the ThM Program at Xavier University of Louisiana's Summer Institute for Black Catholic Studies.

Tobias Winright is a Roman Catholic moral theologian with a wide range of teaching and research interests. He is currently a professor of moral theology at St. Patrick's Pontifical University, Maynooth, Co. Kildare, Ireland. Formerly a law enforcement officer (initially corrections, then policing, and as a police academy ethics instructor) and a lay ecclesial minister (in campus, parish, and youth ministry), he wrote his dissertation on "The Challenge of Policing: An Analysis in Christian Social Ethics." His most recent publications are the *T&T Clark Handbook of Christian Ethics* (Bloomsbury, 2021) and *Serve and Protect: Selected Essays on Just Policing* (Cascade, 2021).